Rediscovering the Joy *of* Predestination *and the* Comfort of Election

Rediscovering the Joy *of* Predestination *and the* Comfort of Election

A Reappraisal of Romans 8–11 and Ephesians 1 in Their First-Century Context

M.C. WARREN

WIPF *&* STOCK · Eugene, Oregon

REDISCOVERING THE JOY OF PREDESTINATION AND THE COMFORT OF ELECTION
A Reappraisal of Romans 8–11 and Ephesians 1 in Their First-Century Context

Copyright © 2025 M.C. Warren. All rights reserved. Except for brief quotations in critical publications or reviews, no part of this book may be reproduced in any manner without prior written permission from the publisher. Write: Permissions, Wipf and Stock Publishers, 199 W. 8th Ave., Suite 3, Eugene, OR 97401.

Wipf & Stock
An Imprint of Wipf and Stock Publishers
199 W. 8th Ave., Suite 3
Eugene, OR 97401

www.wipfandstock.com

PAPERBACK ISBN: 979-8-3852-5193-3
HARDCOVER ISBN: 979-8-3852-5194-0
EBOOK ISBN: 979-8-3852-5195-7

07/15/25

All biblical text is from *The Greek New Testament*, fifth revised edition, Stuttgart: Deutsche Bibelgesellschaft, 2014, all rights reserved.

All translations are the author's own.

Abbreviations are as per the second edition of *The SBL Handbook of Style* (Atlanta: SBL Press, 2014).

Contents

Abbreviations   vii
Introduction   ix

PART 1 | HOW DID WE GET HERE?   1

1. Developments in the Doctrines Through Christian History   3
2. Augustine: The Catholic Champion   11
3. Aquinas: The Careful Systematizer   21
4. John Calvin: The Reluctant Defender   28
5. Karl Barth: The Attempted Save   34
6. The Need for Reappraisal   41

PART 2 | EPHESIANS 1:3–14   45

7. Methodology and Background   47
8. Exegesis of Ephesians 1:3–14   64
9. Synthesis   87

PART 3 | ROMANS 8:18–9:29   89

10. Methodology and Background   91
11. Exegesis of Romans 8:18–39   108
12. Exegesis of Romans 9:1–29   129
13. Synthesis   161

PART 4 | OPPORTUNITIES AND RAMIFICATIONS   167

Bibliography   171

Abbreviations

Abbreviations are as per the second edition of The *SBL Handbook of Style* (Atlanta: SBL Press, 2014). Selected abbreviations are presented here for convenience.

ABD	Anchor Bible Dictionary
ABR	Australian Biblical Review
ANF	The Ante-Nicene Fathers
BDAG	Greek-English Lexicon of the New Testament and Other Early Christian Literature
Bib	Biblica
BJRL	Bulletin of the John Rylands University Library of Manchester
BSac	Bibliotheca Sacra
CBQ	Catholic Biblical Quarterly
CTJ	Calvin Theological Journal
CurBS	Currents in Research: Biblical Studies..
EKL	Evangelisches Kirchenlexikon
EncJud	Encyclopedia Judaica
ERE	Encyclopedia of Religion and Ethics
ExpTim	Expository Times
ISBE	International Standard Bible Encyclopedia
JBL	Journal of Biblical Literature
JSNT	Journal for the Study of the New Testament
NBf	New Blackfrairs

NCE	*New Catholic Encyclopedia*
NIDNTT	*New International Dictionary of New Testament Theology*
NovT	*Novum Testamentum*
*NPNF*¹	*The Nicene and Post-Nicene Fathers, Series 1*
*NPNF*²	*The Nicene and Post-Nicene Fathers, Series 2*
NTS	*New Testament Studies*
RevExp	*Review and Expositor*
RPP	*Religion Past and Present: Encyclopedia of Theology and Religion*
ST	*Studia Theologica*
TDNT	*Theological Dictionary of the New Testament*
*UBS*⁵	*The Greek New Testament, United Bible Societies, 5th ed.*

Introduction

The New Testament authors regard predestination and election as reasons for great joy and comfort, but sadly, as doctrines, they have become the cause of bitter arguments and despair. Did the New Testament authors not appreciate the full implications of what they were writing, or have readers of the New Testament misunderstood the texts? In my view, it is very much the latter. My aim in writing this book is to remove the depressing fog surrounding the doctrines of predestination and election and to introduce you to the exciting insights of the NT authors. In that vein, this introduction not only lays out the flow of the argument of this book but also presents my conclusions so that the benefit of this reappraisal can be appreciated from the start.

PART 1 of this book begins by surveying the development of Christian thought regarding predestination, election, and human freedom through the centuries. Predestination and election were not high on the list of concerns of the early church, leading to not much being written about them. The earliest explanation of predestination does not come until late in the second century, and it does not come as a consequence of theological exploration. Instead, it appears to be an attempt to explain how predestination could be consistent with human freedom. Respecting Greco-Roman society's emphasis on human freedom was important to apologetic writers in the second century, and this may have been an influence. Predestination was described as God deciding in advance who would be saved based on God foreseeing each person's voluntary faith. That explanation appears to have become common across the church by the time of Augustine without any evidence of it receiving careful exegetical scrutiny.

Part 1 then turns to what happened during Augustine's dispute with Pelagius. Pelagius reasoned that God could only hold people accountable for their sin if it was possible for people not to sin. Augustine saw this lack of appreciation of the doctrine of original sin as a threat to the gospel of grace, so he wrote a series of polemical works in response. It was during this argument that Augustine gradually came to present predestination not as dependent on foreseen voluntary faith, but as solely at God's discretion independent of any knowledge of the future believer. Like the church's preceding explanation of predestination, this perspective was not the result of careful exegesis but emerged from the theological argument Augustine was making. It was potentially a mistake built on a mistake.

Augustine's doctrine of predestination was not universally welcomed. It was largely ignored in the Greek-speaking part of the church and disputed strongly in the West for around a hundred years, being debated in two major church councils. Such was Augustine's influence, however, that his view eventually prevailed in the West. From that point forward, alternate views of the doctrine were not independent interpretations of the relevant texts because commentators had to interact with Augustine's thoughts on the matter.

In time, leading Christian writers tried to give the doctrine of predestination an exegetical foundation. Their efforts are also documented in part 1, with a particular focus on Thomas Aquinas, John Calvin, and Karl Barth. What becomes apparent is that each of these authors conducted his exegesis with Augustine's perspective in mind. They overlook details of the key texts and miss potential interpretations that are unrelated to Augustine's explanation. When they attempt to explain how the doctrine is compatible with other texts and teachings, at times their explanations are barely plausible. While Barth deviates from Augustine significantly, it is obvious that even Barth's study is conducted in Augustine's shadow. Part 1 concludes that what is needed is a thorough and careful exegesis of the key texts in their first-century context without the spectres of Greek apologetics or Pelagianism hanging over the exegetical task. It is necessary to know how the New Testament authors understood predestination and election before ascertaining how that might be best applied apologetically or in theological debates.

PARTS 2 AND 3 contain that fresh exegesis of two major texts relied upon by Augustine, Aquinas, Calvin, and Barth. Part 2 addresses Eph 1:3–14 and part 3 addresses Rom 8:18–9:29. These are not the only texts upon which earlier authors relied, with Calvin in particular appealing to a smorgasbord of biblical references across both testaments. Nevertheless, over the centuries Eph 1:3–14 and Rom 8:18–9:29 have been the reason why there is a debate, so these are the texts that need careful reappraisal.

While Paul's epistle to the Romans most likely precedes Ephesians, I have chosen to place the exegesis of Eph 1:3–14 first because some commentators rely on it in their interpretation of Rom 8:18–9:29. By first showing how Eph 1:3–14 can be better understood as not referring to individual predestination, the text of Romans can be explored without that distraction.

What the detailed exegesis finds is that the biblical authors did not write that God decides in advance who would be Christian, whether on the basis of foreseen faith or not. What the Father decided in advance is that his Son, Jesus Christ, is the one through whom people would be drawn into God's family. Jesus Christ was predestined, not you. Contemporary attempts to explain predestination as corporate rather than individual reflect this in part but continue to err in making predestination human-focused rather than Christ-focused.

Election of people into God's family is distinct from predestination and the two doctrines should not be confused with each other or defined together, as is sometimes the case. Predestination and election were first joined together by Augustine. By being subsumed within predestination, the doctrine of election lost the distinctive pastoral applications found in the pages of the New Testament. The reason predestination and election became confused is that the word "election" can be used to describe the doctrine of predestination, because making a predetermined decision (i.e., predestination) is to make a choice. That does not mean, however, that the New Testament does not contain a distinct doctrine of election of individuals to salvation. One must appreciate the concepts being discussed without being put off by the words an author uses.

Once this distinction between word use and an expression of a concept is appreciated, a doctrine of election to salvation can be separated out relatively easily. What my exegetical work demonstrates is that election to salvation occurs within human history, principally at the time a person enters God's family. The mystery of God's involvement in one's journey to faith remains, but it is clearly one in which each person is involved and accountable. Nevertheless, salvation is necessarily by grace alone because no one can force or earn a way into the kingdom or otherwise claim it as an entitlement. There is nothing anyone can point to about oneself that would require God to show mercy. One can only enter the kingdom because God elects to show mercy that is undeserved.

A way of understanding the distinction between the two doctrines of predestination and election is that predestination determines the means by which one may enter the family of God, whereas election to salvation is God granting entry to a person. Predestination is individually focused on Christ, albeit with corporate consequences for all of God's family. Election of people into God's family is individually focused on each Christian, although the term can be used as a collective noun to encompass all the elect.

PART 4 sums up the argument and applies this new understanding of these distinct doctrines of predestination and election to a sample of biblical texts and teachings. This section of the book is not intended to be comprehensive, but aims to illustrate the opportunities that this fresh understanding provides.

I have been working on this subject over the course of ten years. I began investigating predestination because a friend confided in me that he was annoyed with how the doctrine of predestination was taught. I set out to express the doctrine as helpfully as I could, but in doing so I noticed the inconsistencies and oddities discussed above. Wycliffe Hall, Oxford UK, allowed me to do extensive private reading over the summer of 2016, from which I concluded that something had indeed gone awry. I subsequently read for a Master of Theology by Research at Charles Sturt University in Australia, and the outcome of that research is the basis of this book. If the teaching of predestination troubles you, I hope you find sense in my work. But even more so, I hope you rediscover the comfort, humility, and joy that the biblical authors found in the predestination of Jesus Christ for believers and in the divine election of the saints.

PART 1

How did we get here?
A critical evaluation of the historical development of the doctrines of predestination and election

So much ink has been spilt on the subjects of predestination and election that it is difficult to approach biblical texts without being influenced by the major schools of thought on these doctrines, whether consciously or subconsciously. If the perspective of the NT authors is to be examined afresh, it will be helpful in the first instance to examine how major Christian authors came to develop their interpretations, and to consider how they might still be affecting reading of the relevant passages today. To that end, part one of this book begins by examining the post-apostolic references to predestination and election to understand how the doctrines came to be understood and taught. The key proponents of the doctrines over the centuries are then identified and their work is critiqued to assess the strength of their arguments, and to analyze the exegetical grounding of the doctrines in Scripture. This will allow identification of the key biblical texts that require examination in detail and will shed light on particular aspects of those texts that might need more careful scrutiny.

1

Developments in the Doctrines Through Christian History

Post-apostolic writers use the term "election" without any sense of predetermination and discuss predestination rarely and separately.[1] The letter of Clement of Rome to the church in Corinth (written ca. AD 95) is concerned with calling the readers to choose the right path. In this context, Clement refers to the Corinthian Christians as the "elect"[2] to draw attention to their obligation to be godly and to God's special commitment to them. Clement does not imply any sense of God determining their fate in advance. Other early Christian writers such as Polycarp and Ignatius also use "elect" is this vein.

Subsequently authors become more concerned with protecting the belief in human freedom. The apologist Justin Martyr only uses the language of election with respect to Israel and Jesus Christ. When it comes to the people of God, Justin emphasizes the choices people must make. In his two apologies, written ca. AD 155 and 160, Justin argues that it is Christians who choose God "by means of the rational faculties He has Himself endowed us with,"[3] and it is each Christian's righteous deeds that is the basis for eternal acceptance by God.[4] Clement of Alexandria (late

---

1. Link, "Predestination," *RPP* 10:326; Palladino, "Predestination (in Catholic Theology)," *NCE* 11:715; Rohls and Kolb, "Predestination," *EKL* 4:340; Bromiley, "Predestination," *ISBE* 3:946; Martin, "Predestination," *ERE* 10:231.
2. Clement of Rome, *1 Clement* (ANF 1:15, 16, 18, 34).
3. Justin, *First Apology* (ANF 1:306–7).
4. Justin, *First Apology* (ANF 1:307).

second century AD) also emphasizes human agency, although not to the extremes of Justin. In *Miscellanies*, the earliest extant extrabiblical reflection on predestination, Clement explains that God's decision to predestine an individual to salvation is informed by God's foreknowledge of an individual's will and disposition.[5]

Both Tertullian and Origen also retain the emphasis on human freedom.[6] In his *Apology*, Tertullian writes that God's revelation is for "everyone whose heart is set on seeking Him."[7] Tertullian uses the word "elect" sparingly to imply God's commitment to his people, often contrasted with those who are not elect, who are labelled as outcasts,[8] the wicked,[9] and the reprobate,[10] but Tertullian makes clear that the state of the non-elect is their own choosing.[11] Origin describes people as "rational creatures" who were "endowed with the power for free-will" to imitate God or fail through negligence.[12] In addressing the Marcion heresy, both Tertullian and Origen defend God's judgments in the OT as appropriate responses to human behavior, whether good or bad.[13] To explain God's election of Jacob over Esau (Rom 9:11–12), Origen goes beyond Scripture to appeal to the deserts of a person's soul prior to being born.[14]

Bromiley argues that a shift begins in Athanasius's work, *On the Incarnation* (AD 319).[15] If there is a shift, it is miniscule. Throughout the work, Athanasius consistently presents both God and humans as acting with free will. Bromiley identifies one possible instance in chapter 12, where Athanasius briefly opines that God's knowledge of human weakness led to God providing the works of creation as a witness to the Maker.[16] Bromiley interprets this as some form of supralapsarianism on the

---

5. Clement of Alexandria, *Miscellanies* 6.9, 7.17 (ANF 2:1041, 1170).

6. Bromiley, "Predestination," *ISBE* 3:946. See also Martin, "Election," *ERE* 5:260; Allison, *Historical Theology*, 455.

7. Tertullian, *Apology* (ANF 3:58).

8. Tertullian, *Apology* (ANF 3:93).

9. Tertullian, *To Scapula* (ANF 3:201).

10. Tertullian, *Prescription Against Heretics* (ANF 3:492).

11. Tertullian, *Prescription Against Heretics* (ANF 3:492).

12. Origen, *First Principles* (ANF 3:605).

13. E.g., Tertullian, *Against Marcion* (ANF 3:591).

14. Origen, *First Principles* (ANF 3:606).

15. Bromiley, "Predestination," *ISBE* 3:946. Link also refers to this possible subtle shift by Athanasius in the understanding of election but does not cite any particular work. Link, "Predestination," *RPP* 10:326.

16. Athanasius, *On the Incarnation Against Apollinaris* (NPNF² 4:290).

basis that God's decision to provide such a witness anticipated the fall. Even if Bromiley's interpretation is correct, all Athanasius's words suggest is that God anticipated the possibility of the fall. Everywhere else in *On the Incarnation*, Athanasius emphasizes the need for a free human response to God's persuasion.[17] Similarly, in *Against the pagans* Athanasius urges pagans to respond to God of their own accord and to find faith within themselves.[18]

What is apparent is that during the second, third, and much of the fourth century, while Christians were occasionally referred to as "elect," there was no attempt to develop a theology of election. The word "elect" simply implied God's commitment to his people and reminded them of their obligation to God. Predestination was considered separately and rarely, with it being based on God's foreknowledge of the individual's choices. The emphasis in these early centuries was on human freedom, and Scripture was interpreted to suit that bias.

Even late into the fourth century, Ambrose of Milan mostly used election terminology to refer to the faithful when their preciousness to God was to be emphasized.[19] On the rare occasions he discussed the predestination of individuals, it was on the basis of divinely foreknown merits.[20] Interestingly, Ambrose also referred to the predestination of Jesus Christ,[21] although he did not develop that idea. The focus of Ambrose's ministry was on combating Arianism, and that concern dominated his writings.[22] Nevertheless, Ambrose's teachings are significant because they became the subject of debate between Pelagius and Augustine early in the fifth century.

Augustine was well placed to respond to the use of Ambrose's teachings by Pelagius. Ambrose had been instrumental in Augustine's coming to faith, with Augustine benefiting both from Ambrose's preaching and his private counsel.[23] Augustine was even baptized by Ambrose. So, when Pelagius quoted Ambrose to support his belief that all people have the ability to live a sinless life in their own strength, Augustine was able to show that Pelagius was selectively quoting from Ambrose, and that

---

17. Athanasius, *On the Incarnation Against Apollinaris* (NPNF² 4:299).
18. Athanasius, *Against the Pagans* (NPNF² 4:246).
19. Ambrose, *Holy Spirit* (NPNF² 10:260).
20. Ambrose, *On Faith* (NPNF² 10:696).
21. Ambrose, *Holy Spirit* (NPNF² 10:260, 326).
22. Ramsey, "Ambrose," 232.
23. Augustine, *Confessions* (NPNF¹ 1:1168–70); Ramsey, "Ambrose," 230, 232.

Ambrose had taught that human nature was polluted and could not achieve holiness of its own accord.[24] God's grace is essential for godly living. Augustine even went on to acknowledge that he, too, had struggled with these concepts early in his ministry, and he included words to that effect in his *Retractions*.[25]

In his anti-Pelagian writings, however, Augustine insists not only that a person could not live a sinless life without the grace of God, but also that any effort by the individual toward God is God's direct work. To this end, Augustine uses the language of predestination and election from very early on,[26] and it continues to be peppered throughout his anti-Pelagian writings, often incidentally and without biblical reference. Given the positive attitude toward human free will in the early church, it is not surprising that Augustine faced considerable opposition to this aspect of his argument. In response to that opposition, Augustine crafted two further works, *The Predestination of the Saints* and *The Gift of Perseverance*. In these, Augustine lays out in considerable detail his doctrine of predestination, and in so doing relies heavily on Paul's teaching on election in Rom 9. Thus, for the first time, the two concepts of predestination and election are intertwined and become expressions of one doctrine. For this reason, Augustine will be the first of the major voices to be explored in detail below.

Both Bromiley and Link characterize the debate following Augustine as seeking to find a better balance between human will and divine predestination/election of the individual.[27] The Council of Arles in AD 473 favored John Cassian's argument that predestination was on the basis of divine foreknowledge of human initiative toward God, so it was wrong for Christians to rest solely on predestination for salvation.[28] The subsequent Council of Orange in AD 529 leaned more in the Augustinian direction by describing God as using human freedom to carry out

---

24. Augustine, *Grace and Free Will* (NPNF[1] 5:439).

25. Augustine, *Gift of Perseverance* (NPNF[1] 5:1216–17); Augustine, *Retractations*, 119.

26. Augustine, *Guilt and Remission of Sins* (NPNF[1] 5:172).

27. Bromiley, "Predestination," *ISBE* 3:947–48; Link, "Predestination," *RPP* 10:327.

28. Bromiley, "Predestination," *ISBE* 3:947; Rohls and Kolb, "Predestination," *EKL* 4:341.

his preordained will.[29] The initiative for faith was placed with God.[30] The Council of Orange, however, agreed with the Council of Arles in rejecting predestination of the non-elect. What was not debated was whether God predestines individuals or whether predestination was related to election. In these respects, Augustine had set the agenda, and it was now only a question of how his understanding of predestination and election affected and was affected by other doctrines.

This consensus remained relatively stable throughout the Middle Ages. There were isolated explorations of double predestination (election and reprobation), but they were consistently rejected.[31] Thomas Aquinas provides a useful summary of the debate up to the thirteenth century in his *Summa Theologiæ*.[32] In his dialectical style, Aquinas explores the matter in eight articles, wrestling with issues such as reprobation, perseverance, merits, and the role of prayer. For Aquinas, Rom 8:29 is the key to understanding predestination and he often bases his reasoning on this verse. Aquinas tends to agree with Augustine, including treating predestination and election together.[33] Aquinas also separately discusses the predestination of Jesus Christ and considers how this informs individual predestination.[34] Given the systematic treatment of the doctrine by Aquinas and his eminence in the history of Christian theology, his will be the second major voice to be explored in detail.

Through the latter part of the Middle Ages there continued to be varying views on the degree to which individuals were able to affect their eternal outcome, with John Duns Scotus, a contemporary of Aquinas, putting a greater emphasis on human will,[35] and in the fourteenth century William of Ockham verged on Pelagianism.[36] This set the scene for some strong reactions during the sixteenth century European reformations.

---

29. Bromiley, "Predestination," *ISBE* 3:947; Shogren, "Election: New Testament," *ABD* 2:443; Link, "Predestination," *RPP* 10:327.

30. Palladino, "Predestination (in Catholic Theology)," *NCE* 11:719.

31. Link, "Predestination," *RPP* 10:327; Palladino, "Predestination (in Catholic Theology)," *NCE* 11:716.

32. Aquinas, Question 23 "Predestination" in *Summa Theologiæ* 1a.

33. Aquinas, *Summa Theologiæ* 1a.23, 4.

34. Aquinas, *Summa Theologiæ* 3a.24.

35. Bromiley, "Predestination," *ISBE* 3:948.

36. Packer and Johnston, introduction to *Bondage of the Will*, 20; Link, "Predestination," *RPP* 10:327.

Martin Luther addressed predestination most strongly in his commentary on Romans and in his doctrinal work *The Bondage of the Will*,[37] with the latter written as a sharply worded rebuttal of his contemporary, the humanist Erasmus. Up to this point, the older Erasmus had been viewed as a fellow Reformer, as he had written his own scathing critiques of the behavior of church officials, and he had held them accountable to the standards of the New Testament. Erasmus, however, regarded it as wrong to split off from the Catholic Church, so he tried to stay neutral in the doctrinal disputes initiated by Luther. Eventually Erasmus succumbed to the pressure to show he was distinct from Luther, and Erasmus chose the subject of free will to do so. In *Discussion, or Collation, concerning Free Will*, which was addressed to Luther, Erasmus reasons that people do retain some sense of free will to do "those things that lead to eternal salvation, or to turn away from the same."[38] In *The Bondage of the Will*, Luther responds by arguing forcefully from Rom 1–3 that people are incapable of doing good, which is why justification by faith is necessary. While Luther's focus was on the necessity of God's help for good works, Luther extended this to God initiating saving faith, which naturally led to individual predestination.[39] Like Augustine, Luther used predestination and election interchangeably, including using passages on election such as Rom 9 to argue for predestination. This did not settle the debate, as the Lutheran Church softened under Luther's successor, Melanchthon, who remained a close friend of Erasmus.[40] In Lutheran theology, predestination came to be understood as the will of God that all who believe would be saved, thus restoring a role for human will.

John Calvin also drew inspiration from Augustinian predestination and pushed it further, clearly stating that "God has predestined some to salvation, others to destruction."[41] Calvin's main treatment of predestination and election appears in book 3 of his *Institutes of the Christian Religion*.[42] Like Augustine, Calvin considered predestination in the context

---

37. Palladino, "Predestination (in Non-Catholic Theology)," *NCE* 11:719.

38. As quoted by Martin Luther, *Bondage of the Will*, 137; Erasmus and Luther, *Battle over Free Will*, 6.

39. Luther, *Bondage of the Will*, 99, 214, 310.

40. Palladino, "Predestination (in Non-Catholic Theology)," *NCE* 11:720.

41. Calvin, *Institutes* 3.21. That Calvin went beyond Augustine in his strong statement of double predestination is supported by Shogren, "Election: New Testament," *ABD* 2:444; Rohls and Kolb, "Predestination," *EKL* 4:342; Palladino, "Predestination (in Non-Catholic Theology)," *NCE* 11:720.

42. Calvin, *Institutes* 3.21–23.

of the reception of the grace of Christ and alongside the doctrine of faith. Also like Augustine, Calvin regarded predestination and election as alternate expressions of the one doctrine, using the words interchangeably in his opening paragraph on the topic.[43] While Calvin's perspective was similar to Luther's, Calvin was more measured in his tone and systematic in his approach, and for that reason his will be the major voice from the Reformation that will be studied further below.

Jacobus Arminius rejected Calvin's double predestination, preferring to understand reprobation as a universal condemnation of unbelievers.[44] He also opened up the possibility that God's grace may not be applied sufficiently in all cases to bring about a saving faith, with the fault for that being found in the sinful recipient.[45] After Arminius's death, these ideas were further developed but ultimately condemned at the Synod of Dort (AD 1618–19). Nevertheless, Arminianism was popularized by John Wesley and Methodism in the eighteenth century, and in modern times some Arminians have adopted a view of human will more akin to the pre-Augustinian Christian writers.[46]

In the nineteenth century, Schleiermacher rejected this Arminian turn as "a semblance of Pelagianism,"[47] asserting that divine foreknowledge could only be understood in the sense of God's action to bring about faith, not something initiated by the individual. The rationale of God's decision must be found not only in "a divine foreknowledge" but also in "a divine good pleasure."[48] Schleiermacher keeps predestination and election connected and focused on the individual, although he accepts only single predestination, as God "passes over" those not included rather than positively discriminating against them.[49]

Karl Barth is often identified as the most prominent voice of the twentieth century on the theology of election and predestination.[50] Barth's theology is in the line of Calvin, except that with respect to predestination

---

43. Calvin, *Institutes* 3.21:1.
44. Arminius, "Disputation XL" (*Works of James Arminius* 2:393).
45. Arminius, "Disputation XLI" (*Works of James Arminius* 2:395).
46. Palladino, "Predestination (in Non-Catholic Theology)," *NCE* 11:720.
47. Schleiermacher, *Christian Faith*, 557.
48. Schleiermacher, *Christian Faith*, 552.
49. Schleiermacher, *Christian Faith*, 548–49.
50. Shogren, "Election: New Testament," *ABD* 2:444; Bromiley, "Predestination," *ISBE* 3:950; Link, "Election," *RPP* 4:396–97; Rohls and Kolb, "Predestination," *EKL* 4:343.

he is noted for stepping back from Calvin's extremes. He did this by locating both election and rejection first and foremost in Christ. Thus "God's election of man is a predestination not merely of man but of Himself."[51] Within this framework, election is focused first on Jesus Christ, then corporately on Israel and the church, and lastly on the individual. The individual is elect by being joined with Christ, and it is the rejection of what is on offer in Christ that marks out the non-elect.[52] Barth provides both a break from conventional thinking and also an illustration of how convoluted things can become within Augustine's construct of predestination. Nevertheless, since he has laid out his complete argument more systematically than what is available from the extant works of Arminius, and since he references Scripture more than Schleiermacher, his will be the fourth and last major voice that will be surveyed in detail below.

Many others have contributed to the debate, but Augustine, Aquinas, Calvin, and Barth have most clearly articulated the understanding of predestination and election that is in question. Their arguments will now be reviewed in detail, with particular attention to the biblical texts they used and their exegetical methods.

---

51. Barth, *Church Dogmatics*, 2.2:3.
52. Barth, *Church Dogmatics*, 2:2:229, 345–346.

2

Augustine: The Catholic Champion

Prior to the Pelagian crisis, neither election nor predestination was a prominent theme in Augustine's writings. While Augustine used these words more than previous writers, that was coming off a low base and the terms were not developed concepts in common use in his works. This had changed significantly by the end of Augustine's ministry, by which time predestination and election had become the subject of dedicated works. Augustine's thinking prior to the Pelagian dispute can be illustrated through a review of two of Augustine's major works, *Confessions* and *The City of God*. From that base, Augustine's anti-Pelagian writings in *The Nicene and Post-Nicene Fathers*[1] can be explored in sequence to see how his understanding of predestination and election developed and how Scripture was used in the process.

In *Confessions* (ca. AD 400), Augustine begins by questioning whether one could call on God without first believing, concluding that God must be the source of his faith.[2] Augustine sees some good in his pre-Christian life, but he credits that to God as well.[3] Nevertheless, there is no sense that his life was predetermined, only that God continued to be interested and involved. Augustine acknowledges that God's decision-making is influenced by a person's character, for God favors the humble and lowly.[4] Augustine consistently sees a dual, cooperative role for both

---

1. Augustine, *NPNF*[1] 5.
2. Augustine, *Confessions* (*NPNF*[1] 1:78–79).
3. Augustine, *Confessions* (*NPNF*[1] 1:98, 107).
4. Augustine, *Confessions* (*NPNF*[1] 1:148).

the divine and human will. He credits the inner eye of his soul for finding true light and he credits God for treating the symptoms of sin and stirring up his faith.[5] At the point of coming to true faith, it comes about both by God pressing on him to expose his fear and shame, and by Augustine submitting to the call to "take up and read."[6]

The City of God is contemporaneous with Augustine's anti-Pelagian writings but has its own separate focus and interests. Following the sacking of Rome in AD 410 by the Visigoths, Augustine wrote to defend Christianity from blame and to show the superiority of the Christian vision for life. Augustine argues that, unlike astrology, Christianity supports human free will because God's prescience is informed by foreknowledge of each person's free choices.[7] Quoting regularly from Rom 8:29, Augustine argues that it is this awareness that leads to the predestination of the faithful.[8] *The City of God* occasionally refers to election alongside predestination, but in the sense that all things are predestined, and election happens to be one of those things.[9] All of this stands in marked contrast with where Augustine would end up in his anti-Pelagian writings.

Ironically, the impetus for the writing of *The City of God* also led to the teaching of Pelagius coming into Augustine's orbit. Pelagius and his disciples had fled from the Visigoth invasion of Rome to North Africa where Augustine was ministering. Although Pelagius continued on to Palestine, one of his disciples, Coelestius, established a ministry in Carthage, and it was through him that Augustine became aware of Pelagius. Augustine discerned three major points of contention between Pelagianism and Catholic theology:

1. Pelagianism denied the doctrine of original sin;
2. it claimed grace was merited rather than unmerited and free; and
3. it claimed that a person could live so righteously that forgiveness was not required.[10]

---

5. Augustine, *Confessions* (NPNF[1] 1:197, 200).

6. Augustine, *Confessions* (NPNF[1] 1:227–229).

7. Augustine, *City of God* (NPNF[1] 2:212–4). Augustine also taught this in his commentary on Romans; see Mathijs Lamberigts, "Predestination," 678.

8. Augustine, *City of God* (NPNF[1] 2:562).

9. Augustine, *City of God* (NPNF[1] 2:743, 913).

10. Augustine, *Against the Two Letters of the Pelagians* (NPNF[1] 5:1036).

It is against the second of these errors that Augustine gradually employed a developing theology of predestination and election because, for Augustine, predestination definitively establishes that grace must be unmerited.

Initially predestination and election are no more prominent in Augustine's anti-Pelagian works than in his earlier writings. Augustine's initial focus was instead on defending the doctrine of original sin and explaining how it is compatible with free will.[11] In Augustine's first anti-Pelagian work, *Guilt and Remission of Sins* (AD 412), predestination eventually comes up toward the end of the second book,[12] with Augustine stating the following:

> Now this same Lord of ours has never yet refused, at any period of the human race, nor to the last judgment will He ever refuse, this His healing to those whom, in His most sure foreknowledge and future loving-kindness, He has predestinated to reign with Himself to life eternal.[13]

Augustine's goal in this section is to assure his readers that, although they are all afflicted with the sinful nature and continue to struggle with it, their salvation is not endangered because that salvation is achieved by Christ. To that end, Augustine initially sees predestination as having the following characteristics:

- God's decision to grant spiritual healing is based on foreknowledge;
- the timing of God's decision is not of interest; and
- predestination is focused on what the Lord is doing and the opportunity for the redeemed to join him in reigning, rather than on predetermining the fate of the individuals.

Augustine does not reference what Scripture, if any, lay behind his thoughts.

This casual inclusion of predestination into his argument is typical of Augustine up until this point. John Rist excuses Augustine's casual rhetoric by proposing that Augustine was still precise in his thoughts.[14] Rist's conclusion, however, does not seem to be supported by the way

---

11. Augustine, *Guilt and Remission of Sins* (NPNF¹ 5:211–2).
12. Augustine, *Guilt and Remission of Sins* (NPNF¹ 5:236).
13. Augustine, *Guilt and Remission of Sins* (NPNF¹ 5:255).
14. Rist, *Augustine*, 269.

Augustine's expression of the doctrine develops in the course of his writings. The suggestion by Erik de Boer that the doctrine was present in Augustine's earlier writings, even if the elements weren't developed, also appears to be overstated.[15] The evidence points to the young Augustine holding to the understanding of predestination of those before him, that predestination was based on God's foreknowledge of those who would believe and follow his calling. It was only late in the fourth century when the new Bishop of Milan, Simplicianus, requested Augustine's assistance in understanding Rom 9 that Augustine began questioning the received wisdom. In *On various Questions to Simplicianus* (AD 396/397), Augustine goes through Rom 9 and tries to maintain his original position on predestination, but reluctantly concedes that God must initiate faith, uninfluenced by any foreknowledge of a person's will or works.[16] Augustine, however, confesses that he finds the matter "exceedingly obscure"[17] and that ultimately it is not possible for beings within the creation to comprehend completely how both human and divine wills could be compatible.[18] The slightly later *Confessions* delves into these concepts, but in that work Augustine still retains a role for human initiative and does not consider how divine and human actions might relate to election or predestination. Even as late as *The City of God*, Augustine continues to justify the validity of predestination on the basis of divine foreknowledge of human merits. This suggests that early on Augustine held to the common understanding of predestination at the time, and that it was not particularly significant to him or thoroughly thought through. While his engagement with Simplicianus had challenged his understanding, at the beginning of Augustine's debate with Pelagianism, the doctrine of predestination remained undeveloped and on the periphery of Augustine's thoughts.

Augustine's second anti-Pelagian work, *The Spirit and the Letter* (AD 412) introduces election into the argument. Appealing to Rom 8:29 and 9–11, Augustine argues that election proves that the holy life is the gift of God, and that reward is by unmerited grace.[19] This line of reasoning also appears in the following work, *Nature and Grace* (AD 415), although here Augustine reintroduces the caveat that God's grace is enabled by

---

15. de Boer, "Augustine on Election," 70.

16. Augustine, *To Simplicianus* 1.2.8. This is identified by Lamberigts, "Predestination," 678.

17. Augustine, *To Simplicianus* 1.2.1.

18. Augustine, *To Simplicianus* 1.2.22.

19. Augustine, *Spirit and the Letter* (NPNF[1] 5:301, 333).

the person's willful cooperation. Augustine tries to avoid this becoming Pelagian merited grace by contending that the individual's cooperation is humble by necessity.[20] In this, Augustine shows that he is struggling to let go of the role for human will that he had taught in his earlier works, such as *Free Will*.[21] The Pelagian debate was testing that reasoning, and *Nature and Grace* would prove to be the last occasion that Augustine maintained a place for human cooperation in salvation. In his next works on the subject, *Perfection in Human Righteousness* (AD 415)[22] and *Proceedings of Pelagius* (AD 417), Augustine restates the same argument of election proving unmerited grace but without the caveat of the need for personal choice. In the latter work, Augustine's evolving understanding of election also leads him to introduce the idea of the perseverance of the saints.[23]

Augustine develops his ideas further in *Against Two Letters of the Pelagians* (AD 420). Drawing from Rom 8:28–29, Rom 9:1–21, and Eph 1:4, Augustine now joins predestination and election into the same argument, moving seamlessly from one to the other as if they are two sides of the same coin. Augustine firmly places predestination and election before the foundation of the world, and it is no longer influenced by divine foreknowledge of some characteristic of the individual.[24] Clark briefly acknowledges this shift, and yet she maintains that Augustine retains a place for human cooperation in salvation.[25] De Boer better appreciates the radical development of Augustine's thoughts, noting that Augustine was aware that he had been trying to retain the idea of free choice, but in the end had to yield to divine grace.[26] As Augustine argues from Rom 9, God is free to make some people as sheep and others not.[27] Augustine does not conduct a careful exegesis of the text because he appears to believe it obviously supports his argument. He shows no appreciation for Paul's concern for his stubborn fellow Israelites. To fend off those who might want to dispute his interpretation, Augustine simply cites Paul's reference in Rom 11:33–36 to God's unsearchable judgments.

---

20. Augustine, *Nature and Grace* (NPNF[1] 5:395–96).
21. Clark, *Augustine*, 51.
22. Augustine, *Perfection in Human Righteousness* (NPNF[1] 5:485, 494).
23. Augustine, *Proceedings of Pelagius* (NPNF[1] 5:547, 511).
24. Augustine, *Against the Two Letters of the Pelagians* (NPNF[1] 5:1007).
25. Clark, *Augustine*, 52.
26. de Boer, "Augustine on Election," 70.
27. Augustine, *Against the Two Letters of the Pelagians* (NPNF[1] 5:1059).

Grace and Free Will (AD 426/427) only has scattered references to election and none to predestination, but *Admonition and Grace* (AD 426/427) is a dress rehearsal for Augustine's major works on these matters. Once again using Rom 8:28–29, 9:11–12, 11:6, and Eph 1:4, Augustine argues that grace is unambiguously not merited. Augustine places God's election of individuals firmly before the foundation of the world[28] and not after the fall, as suggested by Lamberigts.[29] Jesus's words from the Gospel of John, such as John 6:37, are employed to further bolster the argument that God alone elects individuals to eternal life.[30] The theological implications are also starting to be worked out, with:

- the elect inevitably persevering,[31]
- the number of the elect being certain and defined,[32] and
- those not predestined/the non-elect rightly condemned.[33]

Election and predestination continue to be used interchangeably. Predestination does not, however, bring assurance, for one does not know if one will persevere.[34]

As Augustine pushed the logic of his theology of predestination to its limits, monastic leaders became concerned that Augustine had himself stepped beyond the bounds of the traditional understanding of the life of faith.[35] In response, Augustine did not take a step back but sought to persuade them in his next work, *The Predestination of the Saints* (AD 428/429). Given that purpose, it is somewhat surprising that Augustine does not reference a biblical verse containing the word "predestination" until over three quarters of the way through, and he never exegetes such a verse in detail. The reader is left with the impression that Augustine's argument is logical, not exegetical. The following examples from *The Predestination of the Saints* illustrate this:

---

28. Augustine, *Admonition and Grace* (*NPNF*[1] 5:1167).
29. Lamberigts, "Predestination," 678.
30. Augustine, *Admonition and Grace* (*NPNF*[1] 5:1169, 1175–6).
31. Augustine, *Admonition and Grace* (*NPNF*[1] 5:1168).
32. Augustine, *Admonition and Grace* (*NPNF*[1] 5:1194).
33. Augustine, *Admonition and Grace* (*NPNF*[1] 5:1169, 1197).
34. Augustine, *Admonition and Grace* (*NPNF*[1] 5:1195).
35. Wetzel, "Predestination, Pelagianism, and Foreknowledge," 51.

1. Augustine deduces that if God decides someone is to have faith, then God must be solely responsible for that faith.[36] Having made this logical deduction, Augustine illustrates his conclusion by a series of biblical verses.[37] The texts do describe God's critical involvement in bringing someone to faith, however they do not state that there is no contribution by the believer. Augustine logically establishes the doctrine and then he uses the Bible to illustrate it to some degree.

2. Why does God elect some and not others?[38] To answer this, Augustine turns to select verses from Rom 9–11 to declare that this is God's business and not ours. Augustine reads straight from the text into his current context and ignores those parts of the text that appear to present a different perspective.[39] Augustine brings his concept of election to the text rather than seeking to understand what it meant to the apostle.

Eventually Augustine arrives at his oft-quoted definition: "Predestination is the preparation for grace, while grace is the donation itself."[40] To substantiate this conviction, Augustine refers to Eph 2:8–10. While the word "predestination" does not appear in these verses, for Augustine predestination is anything that God plans in advance, and Eph 2:8–10 is an illustration of that. In this vein, Augustine goes on to refer to the predestination of Jesus Christ in Rom 1:1–4 and of the events surrounding Jesus Christ in Acts 4:24–30.[41] Augustine finally introduces the well-known passages on predestination, Eph 1:3–14 and Rom 8:28–29,[42] but he spends scant space on their exegesis. Augustine acts as if the logic of the argument makes exegesis unnecessary. This introduces a high risk of eisegesis.

Augustine responds to further objections to the doctrine in his last anti-Pelagian work, *The Gift of Perseverance* (AD 428/429). Perseverance is the necessary corollary of predestination because if God has decided that a person is to be redeemed for eternity, then logically God must not only bring someone to faith in Jesus Christ but must maintain that person's faith

---

36. Augustine, *Predestination of the Saints* (NPNF[1] 5:1210).
37. Rom 11:35–36; Phil 1:29; 2 Cor 3:5.
38. Augustine, *Predestination of the Saints* (NPNF[1] 5:1221).
39. Rom 11:28.
40. Augustine, *Predestination of the Saints* (NPNF[1] 5:1230).
41. Augustine, *Predestination of the Saints* (NPNF[1] 5:1242–4).
42. Augustine, *Predestination of the Saints* (NPNF[1] 5:1247).

until the end.⁴³ Having so argued, Augustine has to deal with the issue of those who don't endure. Augustine's response is to exhort the predestined not to question but to pray, and he goes to some length to show how the Lord's Prayer can be used as a prayer for perseverance.⁴⁴ Augustine puts considerable effort into the exegesis of Matt 6:9–13, carefully explaining the syntax and integrating it with comparable verses in Scripture. He also takes on insights from other Christian teachers and carefully explores the possibilities. The modern commentator may wince at times at Augustine's allegorization or peculiar conclusions, but Augustine produces an exegesis worthy of study. He then follows that up by quoting Eph 1:4–11 in full and states that it speaks for itself, who can argue?⁴⁵ On one of the core texts at issue, Augustine puts in no exegetical effort.

Augustine then returns to the unanswered question: what about those who don't endure? The logical conclusion is that such people were not predestined to endure. To defend this, Augustine refers to the parable of the workers in the vineyard in Matt 10:1–16, where those workers who dispute the landowner's payments are told by the landowner, "Is it not lawful for me to do what I will?"⁴⁶ Augustine overlooks the many aspects of the parable that include human agency, such as the workers volunteering to enter into their labor contracts and the landowner paying all of them the agreed wages. On top of that is the oddity that Augustine refers to a parable in which all are rewarded to explain why some people are condemned not to be rewarded. Once again, Augustine does not come to grips with all the nuances of a text, so runs the risk of simply raising more questions.

Augustine's logical problems are not over because if a person perseveres for any length of time, that is a good thing and it must have come from God, and therefore if a person ceases to persevere, it must be because God withdrew the gift, which would mean God never intended that they would make it.⁴⁷ Although Augustine did not generally teach double predestination,⁴⁸ this part of *The Gift of Perseverance* points in that

---

43. Augustine, *Gift of Perseverance* (NPNF¹ 5:1263).

44. Augustine, *Gift of Perseverance* (NPNF¹ 5:1266–70).

45. Augustine, *Gift of Perseverance* (NPNF¹ 5:1275).

46. Augustine, *Gift of Perseverance* (NPNF¹ 5:1275).

47. Augustine, *Gift of Perseverance* (NPNF¹ 5:1277).

48. Wetzel, "Predestination, Pelagianism, and foreknowledge," 50; Link, "Predestination", *RPP* 10:327.

direction.[49] To support this teaching, Augustine refers to 1 John 2:19. This is another odd choice because that verse only refers to the decisions of humans and not the decisions of God. Furthermore, Augustine's explanation raises another question. Why would God do such a callous thing? Augustine, referring to 1 Cor 10:12, explains that it is a warning against becoming high-minded. Why do people who will inevitably persevere need a warning? They don't need it. It is simply in the nature of God to display his character as a judge, whose righteousness is seen in both his condemnation of some and gracious mercy to others.[50] At this point Augustine is not engaging in exegesis but taking sentences from Scripture to fit into his floundering argument.

Augustine has further logical problems to untangle. In Luke 10:13–15, Jesus declares that Tyre and Sidon would have repented if they had been blessed with his ministry, suggesting that human outcomes are conditional.[51] Augustine responds that Jesus's words are hypothetical and that people are judged in accordance with what did happen and not what might have happened. Augustine effectively forces his understanding of predestination onto the text rather than engaging with the breadth of thought in the Bible. Similarly, the cooperative biblical injunction to "work out our own salvation with fear and trembling; for it is God that worketh in us both to will and to do for His good pleasure"[52] becomes a declaration about what God will do both externally and internally within a believer.[53] Augustine also continues to quote Scripture out of context, such as using 2 Cor 3:5, a passage on the importance of not relying on self-promotion, to dissuade Christians from seeing anything of value within themselves. Augustine appears to realize that his logic doesn't hold in the end, and retreats into tropes such as God's judgments being unsearchable (Rom 11:33)[54] and the need for God's wisdom (James 1:5).[55]

At the end of *The Gift of Perseverance*, Augustine acknowledges that he has effectively conflated various terms such as "predestination," "foreknowledge," and "election" into one concept.[56] And yet, he also concludes

---

49. Augustine, *Gift of Perseverance* (NPNF[1] 5:1279).
50. Augustine, *Gift of Perseverance* (NPNF[1] 5:1274).
51. Augustine, *Gift of Perseverance* (NPNF[1] 5:1281).
52. Phil 2:12–13, as quoted in Augustine, *Gift of Perseverance* (NPNF[1] 5:1293).
53. Augustine, *Gift of Perseverance* (NPNF[1] 5:1293).
54. Augustine, *Gift of Perseverance* (NPNF[1] 5:1284, 1291).
55. Augustine, *Gift of Perseverance* (NPNF[1] 5:1305).
56. Augustine, *Gift of Perseverance* (NPNF[1] 5:1308).

that predestination does not only apply to the individual, but also to Jesus Christ and the body of his believers. This underlines the greatness of predestination because God "predestinated both Him and us, because both in Him that He might be our head, and in us that we should be His body."[57] Typical of Augustine, he bases this triumphant conclusion not on Scripture but on theological reasoning concerning the Trinity, although Augustine may have had passages such as Rom 1:1–6 in the back of his mind. It is an extraordinary conclusion to Augustine's anti-Pelagian writings, and one is left wondering if this might not have been a better starting point.

From Augustine's anti-Pelagian works, it is apparent that Augustine establishes his new doctrine of predestination and election logically rather than exegetically. He applies the least exegetical effort to the most significant passages, suggesting that Augustine's rhetorical training was more of an influence in his development of the doctrine than his exegetical ability. Neo-Platonic influences may have also led him to adopt an abstract reading of Jewish texts that were typically more concrete.[58] Augustine reads his concept of election into texts without ever standing back and observing how election is used throughout Scripture, and what might have been meant in the text he is quoting.[59] Augustine shows greater awareness of the broad use of predestination in Scripture, including the predestination of Jesus Christ, but he still interprets Rom 8:29 and Eph 1:4–11 as concerning an individual's predetermined salvation and does not engage with the Christological aspects of those texts.[60] Ultimately Augustine's understanding of predestination is strongly affected by him fusing it with his concept of election, something he never justified. It is easy to be sympathetic toward Augustine because he was in a difficult pastoral crisis and worked tirelessly to care for his flock. Nevertheless, he delivered a superficially established doctrine that agitated the Western Church at the time and has continued to be controversial.

---

57. Augustine, *Gift of Perseverance* (NPNF¹ 5:1327).

58. Coenen, "ἐκλέγομαι," *NIDNTT* 1:537. Augustine acknowledges this influence in *Christian Instruction* (NPNF¹ 2:1169).

59. Coenen and Quell lay out the broad semantic usage of election, within which individual salvation is only a small subset. Coenen, "ἐκλέγομαι," *NIDNTT* 1:536–43; Quell, "Election in the Old Testament," *TDNT* 4:145–68.

60. Jacobs and Krienke, "Foreknowledge, Providence, Predestination," *NIDNTT* 1:695; Schmidt, "Ὁρίζω, Ἀφορίζω, Ἀποδιορίζω, Προορίζω," *TDNT* 5:456.

3

Aquinas: The Careful Systematizer

Thomas Aquinas is the leading Catholic scholar from the medieval period and his legacy remains pervasive in Western theology. Aquinas did not come across Augustine's anti-Pelagian works until the end of his life when he was a scholar in Rome (AD 1265–74), but having done so, Aquinas consciously followed the path set by Augustine when he composed the relevant section of his *Summa Theologiæ*[1] albeit with subtle developments. Aquinas is much more methodical and consistent than Augustine, which is not surprising given Aquinas is writing after the doctrine had been addressed by several church councils and had mostly stabilized. Aquinas also appears to be driven by systematic rather than pastoral concerns because his discourse on predestination and election in *Summa Theologiæ* is associated with his understanding of God's will and providence,[2] and is remote from discussions of free will, grace, and merit, from where the doctrine of predestination had originated for Augustine. For Aquinas, predestination is now a subject of theological speculation in its own right, not merely a supporting argument for unmerited grace.[3] In Question 23 of volume 1a of *Summa Theologiæ* using his characteristic Aristotelian dialectical style, Aquinas explores the doctrine of predestination in eight articles. The following detailed review of these articles

---

1. James, "Confluence and Influence," 182.
2. Davies, *Thought of Thomas Aquinas*, 168.
3. James, "Confluence and Influence," 168.

is helpfully supplemented by comparisons with pertinent sections of his commentaries and other parts of *Summa Theologiæ*.[4]

Aquinas's opening article in *Summa Theologiæ* is "whether it is fitting to think of God as predestinating?"[5] He allows John of Damascus from the eighth century to put the negative case, which rests on the early church's understanding of God foreknowing people's choices, not predetermining them. Aquinas calls on the apostle Paul to lead the affirmative case in what would appear to be a rhetorical device to compel the reader to fall in behind. Aquinas, however, only quotes part of Rom 8:30, "Whom he did predestinate, them also he called," and then proceeds to expound his own doctrine of providence rather than engage in exegesis.[6] Aquinas does not address why predestination alone was so extensively qualified in the preceding verse, a qualification which takes the focus off individual Christians and moves it on to Jesus Christ and his preeminence in God's family. The rhetorical effect of Rom 8:29–30 would have been so much more powerful without the qualification of predestination in 8:29, so Paul must have had a good reason to apply this caveat. Aquinas considers the predestination of Jesus Christ in volume 3 of *Summa Theologiæ*[7] but by being a separate and subsequent rumination, that does not influence Aquinas's consideration of predestination's relevance to the individual as much as Rom 8:29–30 might suggest it should.

In his commentary on Romans, Aquinas does consider the caveat regarding predestination in Rom 8:29, but only with respect to whether elements of the qualification referred to foreknowledge and so could be used to support an interpretation of a person's merits leading to predestination.[8] Aquinas dismisses this and then looks no further into why predestination was so qualified. This lack of curiosity is evident in his introduction to that section of his commentary which ignores the qualification altogether (as he often does), describing God as having "first of all, predestined believers from all eternity; second, calls them in time; third, sanctifies them."[9] Rather than wrestling with how the immediate

---

4. For an alternate but similar summary of Aquinas's eight articles on predestination, see Davies, *Thomas Aquinas's* Summa Theologiæ 88–90.

5. Aquinas, *Summa Theologiæ* 1a.23.

6. Aquinas, *Summa Theologiæ* 1a.23, 1.

7. Aquinas, *Summa Theologiæ* 3a.24. Davies, *Thought of Thomas Aquinas*, 169.

8. Aquinas, *Romans*, 234.

9. Aquinas, *Romans*, 233.

text might inform the interpretation, Aquinas relies on his exegesis of Eph 1:4 and 11 to determine the meaning of the Romans text.

In his commentary on Ephesians Aquinas is much more thorough and meticulous. His introduction to Eph 1:5 bears quoting in full:

> Six characteristics of predestination are sketched here. First, it is an eternal act, having predestinated; secondly, it has a temporal object, us; thirdly, it offers a present privilege, the adoption of children through Jesus Christ; fourthly, the result is future, unto himself; fifthly, its manner [of being realized] is gratuitous, according to the purpose of his will; sixthly, it has a fitting effect, unto the praise of the glory of his grace.[10]

Aquinas then draws out each of these points in detail over several pages. Aquinas shows himself to be an exceptional biblical scholar, who has thought long and hard on texts that sit behind his doctrine of predestination presented in *Summa Theologiæ*. Nevertheless, his exegesis is clearly affected by Augustine's definitions of election and predestination, and there are sections where his argumentation is weaker. Aquinas rightly recognizes that Eph 1:3 concerns what God has done for us, but when Aquinas considers Eph 1:4, Aquinas subtly changes his language to what God has done to us, and Aquinas appears unaware of the implications of this shift on his exegesis. Aquinas is also at times quick to refer to other biblical books to drive his understanding of a particular text, leaving the reader wondering if there is not more to be gleaned from the text in its own context.

In the second article in *Summa Theologiæ* Aquinas wrestles with Origen and Augustine over whether predestination somehow puts something into the individual that would then lead to the moment of being called. Aquinas in the end prefers to understand predestination as occurring in the mind of God alone. In this section there is another brief reference to Rom 8:30a, and this includes some exegetical work to justify his conclusion that the verb "predestined" is intransitive (reflecting that it only occurs in the mind of God), whereas the verb "called" is transitive.

The third article on reprobation is more a theological than biblical concern, so Aquinas turns primarily to the biblical wisdom literature to support his argument. Aquinas also appeals to God's rejection of Esau referred to in Mal 1:2–3, however his reasoning here is questionable. In context the name "Esau" is a reference to his descendants in the nation

---

10. Aquinas, *Galatians and Ephesians*, 184.

of Edom, and God's judgment of Edom is a reaction to the Edomites' wickedness. It is not a predetermined condemnation. Aquinas ends up accepting reprobation but, reflecting the lack of biblical support, Aquinas is careful not to equate reprobation with election. Instead, Aquinas expresses it as God's deliberate decision not to undo "the free decision of the one who abandons grace."[11] Davies's view that Aquinas did not teach reprobation may reflect this nuance.[12]

In article 4 of *Summa Theologiæ* Aquinas goes to the trouble of considering what relationship predestination has with election. Here he quotes Dionysius,[13] who separates the two by making predestination a general will for the salvation of people, whereas election is the choosing of individuals to participate in that salvation. Aquinas responds with the text of Eph 1:4a, "He chose us in himself before the foundation of the world."[14] Aquinas offers no exegesis at this point, presuming that the meaning is clear and that it supports his thesis. Aquinas builds on this with a logical argument similar to that used by Augustine, concluding, "By its very meaning predestination presupposes election." The detailed exegesis on this matter is provided in his commentary on Ephesians.[15] Aquinas works through each phrase and subordinate clause to argue that election is "not through our merits but from the grace of Christ," that it occurred "before we came into being," and that it was "not because we were holy—we had not yet come into existence—but that we should be holy." By identifying that election logically precedes any consideration of a person's merit, he firmly makes it equivalent to predestination.

Aquinas looks further into the role of divine foreknowledge in predestination in the fifth article of *Summa Theologiæ*. The affirmative case is provided by Ambrose, supported by citations from Rom 8:29 and 9:15.[16] In response, Aquinas shows from Titus 3:5 that God shows mercy because works cannot merit grace. For Aquinas, "No one has been so mad as to hold that our merits were the cause of God's predestining." Nevertheless, he asks whether there is something in a person that is of

---

11. Aquinas, *Summa Theologiæ* 1a.23, 3.

12. Davies, *Thought of Thomas Aquinas*, 167.

13. Now understood to be a fifth century forgery ascribed to an Athenian convert of the apostle Paul, so usually referred to as Pseudo-Dionysius. See Corrigan and Harrington, "Pseudo-Donysius."

14. Aquinas, *Summa Theologiæ* 1a.23, 4.

15. Aquinas, *Galatians and Ephesians*, 184.

16. Aquinas, *Summa Theologiæ* 1a.23, 5.

interest to God and leads to predestination. In the end, like Augustine, Aquinas considers that anything good must have come from God, so it must be through grace alone that a person is saved. If merits are involved, it is a case that "God pre-ordains that he will give glory because of merit and also pre-ordains that he will give grace to a person in order to merit glory." Merit is the effect, not the cause of predestination.[17] Aquinas seems to backtrack from this in his consideration of the doctrine of grace at the end of *Summa Theologiæ*. There Aquinas argues that each person retains a "natural light,"[18] which they can use in a preliminary search for the divine and that each person can naturally do some good because human nature is not altogether corrupted by sin.[19] Aquinas, too, appears to struggle to align his doctrine of predestination with other biblical doctrines.

Perseverance is the subject of the next article and Aquinas again begins with Rom 8:29. Aquinas concludes that "predestination most certainly and unfailingly takes effect, though without compulsion of the effect following of necessity."[20] Aquinas does not show how his conclusion is derived from the text. Instead, he makes it clear that his argument is informed by his doctrine of providence. Within God's providence, events can be necessary, that is directly caused by God, or contingent, that is a result of free choice, however contingent events are not independent of God's providence because God is the ultimate cause of every act of free choice.[21] For Aquinas, perseverance is certain, but it happens within the messy context of the choices an individual makes through life, rather than within the lifeless world of mechanical cause and effect. The seventh and penultimate article explores whether the number of the predestined is fixed. Aquinas employs some incidental biblical citations, but, as with the previous article, he resorts to reasoning based on how he has defined the theological ground up until this point to reach his conclusion that the number is indeed fixed.

The eighth and final article on predestination in *Summa Theologiæ* introduces a line of inquiry beyond what had already been covered by Augustine: "Can predestination be helped by the prayers of the saints?"[22]

---

17. James, "Confluence and Influence," 174.
18. Aquinas, *Summa Theologiæ* 2.109, 1.
19. Aquinas, *Summa Theologiæ* 2.109, 2.
20. Aquinas, *Summa Theologiæ* 1a.23, 6.
21. Davies, *Thomas Aquinas's* Summa Theologiae, 90. Addressed by Aquinas in detail in *Summa Theologiæ* 1a.22, 3–4.
22. Aquinas, *Summa Theologiæ* 1a.23, 8.

Aquinas argues that the answer is both affirmative and negative. The prayers of the saints cannot help because they cannot influence what God has already decided, yet those prayers do help because they are part of the secondary causes of providence brought about by God's grace. At this point, Aquinas's argument is purely theological and not based on exegesis.

The key contribution of Aquinas to the doctrine of predestination and election is organization. Augustine's writings were occasional and crisis-driven, so it is unsurprising that his arguments developed over time and were a little inconsistent. In contrast, Aquinas was writing after the dust had settled, providing perspective and allowing him time to work methodically through the issues. Aquinas did not reappraise Augustine's argument. Instead, he organizes the core of Augustine's thoughts and removes the clutter. Aquinas moves the doctrine of predestination/election out of its supporting role for unmerited grace to its own place alongside providence, even though he continues to acknowledge that predestination implies a relationship to grace,[23] and election presupposes love for the unworthy.[24] Aquinas did at least ask whether predestination and election are related, but he concludes, like Augustine, that both words describe the same doctrine, and therefore each idea can be read into any passage that included the other. Aquinas considers the predestination of Jesus Christ separately and subsequently, but it did not apparently affect Aquinas's interpretation of individual predestination, even though he did make some connections.[25]

Aquinas does not include much exegesis in *Summa Theologiæ*, however his commentaries show that there is considerable exegetical work behind his reasoning. The method Aquinas uses in his commentaries is impressive and stands up well even today. He describes the broad divisions of a biblical book, showing how it flows as a whole before breaking those divisions down into bite-sized sections of a handful of verses. He commences the exegesis of each section with an overview of the context and then addresses each clause in turn, allowing the context and other biblical references to inform his thinking, at times comparing competing interpretations before presenting his conclusions.

---

23. Aquinas, *Summa Theologiæ* 1a.23, 2.
24. Aquinas, *Summa Theologiæ* 1a.23, 4.
25. James, "Confluence and Influence," 172.

Aquinas is a careful thinker, but there is room for further questioning and exploration. When addressing Rom 8:28–30, Aquinas exhibits no curiosity about why predestination alone needs to be so extensively qualified. With respect to Eph 1, Aquinas notes that Eph 1:3 concerns what God does for us, but without explanation Aquinas changes his language to God doing something to us when commenting on Eph 1:4–5. Furthermore, Aquinas does not critically evaluate how the concepts of predestination and election are used throughout Scripture. Instead, he focuses on only a few passages that can be interpreted as referring to predestination of the individual and does not consider alternate meanings, which a broader appreciation of Scripture may have suggested. Aquinas is a thoughtful theologian and so any challenge to his understanding will be difficult, but there is space for further consideration of the subject.

4

John Calvin: The Reluctant Defender

Predestination is probably the doctrine that John Calvin is most known for, yet it is not as important in Calvin's theological system as is commonly believed.[1] It is referred to only incidentally in the first edition of the *Institutes of the Christian Religion*, and when predestination received dedicated treatment in subsequent editions, the doctrine was relegated to the end of book 3. Calvin's discussion of the doctrine was quite lengthy by the final edition of the *Institutes*, but this was driven by the need to address objections to predestination and was not because it had risen in significance. Understanding how Calvin's expression of the doctrine of predestination and election developed is useful for appreciating why it is expressed as it is in the final edition of the *Institutes* and in his commentaries on the key passages.

There were five editions of the *Institutes of the Christian Religion* published from 1536 to 1559. In the first edition, Calvin touches briefly on election during his exposition of the reference to the holy catholic church in the *Apostle's Creed*.[2] At this time, Calvin's expression was more akin to that of the early church writers pre-Augustine, focusing on the blessings of election rather than predetermined outcomes for individuals. Even when Calvin goes on to refer to the condemnation of the reprobate by God's eternal plan, it is focused on God's judgment rather than on a predetermined outcome. It was not until the significantly reorganized and expanded second edition (1539) that a chapter was dedicated to the

---

1. Niesel, *Theology of Calvin*, 159.
2. McGeown, "Calvin's Institutes."

doctrine of predestination/election, with Calvin following Augustine in using the terms interchangeably to refer to the same concept. This more explicit expression led to bitter public debates,[3] so Calvin's treatment was significantly expanded in the third (1543) and fourth (1550) editions to include his rebuttals of those objections.[4] The fifth and final edition (1559) reflects this fragmented and troubled development, with varying tones, repeated treatments of topics, and greater reference to Scripture in later editions in response to biblically based counterpoints.

Calvin's placement of the doctrine of predestination in *The Institutes* and his pastoral guidance concerning the doctrine suggests that it is not central to his thinking. Calvin did not follow Aquinas by including his discussion of predestination and election in the opening book of the *Institutes* on the nature of God. Instead, he placed it at the end of book 3 concerning the reception of God's grace.[5] The Geneva Catechism of 1537 likewise placed consideration of predestination after other fundamental doctrines.[6] For Calvin, the doctrine of predestination does not lead the way, but it is something to be reflected on toward the end. Perhaps taking his cue from Augustine, Calvin even places it after an exposition of the Lord's Prayer.[7] Although Calvin defends his understanding of predestination vigorously in later editions of the *Institutes*,[8] and encourages its preaching,[9] he counsels against extrabiblical speculation,[10] or making it a focus for assurance.[11] Instead, it is simply something the biblically minded believer should humbly receive.

In keeping with this relatively low profile, the 1539 edition did not introduce predestination by connecting it to a significant doctrine or key Scripture. Instead, Calvin uses it to explain a missional phenomenon. Why is it that "the covenant of life is not preached equally among all men," and why is it that "among those to whom it is preached, it does not

---

3. Each of the following explores different occurrences or aspects of these debates. de Greef, "Calvin's Writings," 46; Ganoczy, "Calvin's Life," 17; Naphy, "Calvin's Geneva," 32–33; Gamble, "Calvin's Controversies," 198–99.

4. Hesselink, "Calvin's Theology," 76.

5. Calvin, *Institutes* 3.21–24.

6. Niesel, *Theology of Calvin*, 165.

7. Calvin, *Institutes* 3.20.

8. Hesselink, "Calvin's Theology," 76. See also Calvin, *Institutes* 3.22–24.

9. Calvin, *Institutes* 3.21:1, 3.

10. Calvin, *Institutes* 3.21:1, 2.

11. Calvin, *Institutes* 3.24:6.

gain the same acceptance?"[12] Predestination serves as an apologetic argument for the lack of the universal success of the evangelical mission, and Niesel believes that this is the prime reason for Calvin including predestination in his systematic presentation of Christian doctrine.[13] That may be the case, since Calvin comes back to this rationale a number of times,[14] but by the final edition the introduction has been significantly expanded and ends up following Augustine in making the defense of unmerited grace the primary goal of the argument.

In the 1559 edition of the *Institutes*, Calvin's initial introduction is followed by the statement that "we shall never be clearly persuaded . . . that our salvation flows from the wellspring of God's free mercy until we come to know his eternal election."[15] He then quotes from Rom 11:5–6 to substantiate this point. Calvin, however, does not explain how a text concerning the Jewish remnant applies to sixteenth-century gentiles. Calvin also does not reflect on how Paul has wrestled with the interplay between God's election and the people's behavior up to that point in his letter to the Romans. Instead, Paul's text is given a new context in Calvin's *Institutes*, and its purpose is to convince all to humble themselves before God's grace as Calvin understood it. Lane rightly argues that Calvin's understanding was primarily drawn from Augustine,[16] as can be seen by the concentration of citations of Augustine in the chapters on predestination in the *Institutes*.

Calvin's understanding of the grace of God leads him to a strong statement of double predestination,[17] which would also be reflected in the title of chapter 21 in the 1559 edition of the *Institutes*. Calvin shows no awareness of the consistent rejection of this extreme form of predestination. Rather than provide an exegetical basis for his position, he simply declares that no one who wants to be thought of as religious would disagree with him. He writes as if this aspect of his doctrine is accepted and uncontroversial and does not need substantiation.

Instead of providing biblical warrant for his presentation of predestination in this opening chapter, Calvin moves on to explain why

---

12. Calvin, *Institutes* 3.21:1.
13. Niesel, *Theology of Calvin*, 166.
14. Calvin, *Institutes* 3.21:6, 7.
15. Calvin, *Institutes* 3.21:1.
16. Lane, "Augustine and Calvin," 178–79, 191.
17. Calvin, *Institutes* 3.21:5.

predestination is not based on divine foreknowledge of human merit.[18] Given the long tradition in parts of the Church to the contrary, it is not surprising that Calvin ended up in public disputes on this matter and he was forced to include a more robust argument in later editions. Calvin expanded chapter 21 by drawing on several passages from Deuteronomy to show that the character of God is not to choose on the basis of human merit, but rather on the basis of divine love.[19] The point is initially well made, however Calvin goes on to refer to the Israelite rebellion at Mount Sinai, where God's electing love turned into rejecting hate in response to the Israelites' behavior (Deut 9:6). The reader is left with the impression that there is more to be understood about God's love, because while positive merit may not earn God's love, divine rejection on this occasion is clearly in response to human sin. Calvin's argument in chapter 22 is more secure. By referring to Eph 1:4-9, 1 Tim 2:19, Rom 9, and select citations from the Gospel of John concerning the election and preservation of Jesus's disciples,[20] Calvin argues that God's choice is not based on merit, and that what God foreknows is that individuals need election.[21]

In the second half of his opening chapter on election, Calvin uses further examples from the history of Israel to argue that it is the character of God to elect and reject solely based on his special grace.[22] This exposition also shows how Calvin's interpretation is driven by his theology because he makes being part of the covenant people of Israel equivalent to salvation, describing individuals as either rejected or "kept . . . among his sons."[23] Calvin does not take into account the biblical data that the rejected Ishmael would also be blessed by God (Gen 21:18), and that there are honored priests outside the covenant (Melchizedek in Gen 14 and Jethro in Exod 2 and 18). Also conspicuous by his absence from Calvin's argument is David, who is chosen by God based on merit to be anointed as the future king.[24] Calvin's argument appears to be a conclusion looking for illustration, not a thorough analysis of the nuances of the biblical material.

---

18. Calvin, *Institutes* 3.21:5.

19. Deut 4:37; 7:6-8; 10:14-15; 23:5; 32:8-9.

20. John 15:16 in particular, but also John 6:37, 39, 44-45, 70; 10:28-29; 13:18; 17:6-12.

21. Calvin, *Institutes* 3.22:1-3.

22. Calvin, *Institutes* 3.21:6.

23. Calvin, *Institutes* 3.21:6.

24. 1 Sam 16:7.

Calvin eventually attempts to provide a biblical basis for the election of individuals to salvation at the end of chapter 21, quoting from Rom 9 to support his thesis that "God by his secret plan freely chooses whom he pleases, rejecting others."[25] While on the surface he appears to be on sound ground, he still makes no effort to explain how a passage about the rejection of Jesus Christ by many of Paul's fellow Israelites is to be applied to sixteenth-century gentile Christians, nor how God's choices in human history support a doctrine of what God decides before the foundation of the world.[26]

The subsequent three chapters of the *Institutes* focus on objections to Calvin's understanding of the doctrine of predestination and election. Calvin refers to Scripture extensively in his defense, especially Rom 9–11, although he continues his practice of reading straight from the text into his context and tries to silence objections by referring to Paul's admonition in Rom 9:20–21. Calvin's defense is awkward at times, such as when he argues against the plain reading of the parable of the sower which places some responsibility on the recipient (Matt 13:5, 7),[27] and when he has to concede that Adam's sin was not his own choice but God's will.[28] Calvin explains away competing texts by forcing them to be understood within the context of his preferred solution. The critical reader is left with the impression that the reverse argument could just as easily be made and be just as compelling.

In his commentary on Eph 1:3,[29] Calvin focuses on what is meant by "spiritual" blessings, leading Calvin to overlook how the topic sentence of Eph 1:3–14 concerns what God has done for believers in Christ. Thus, Calvin does not explain why he understands each phrase in Eph 1:4–14 as a statement of what God has done to believers rather than as a blessing for believers. This continues through the rest of his exegesis of Eph 1. Calvin's tendency is to focus on parts of a passage and to be distracted by sub-issues. He does not take care to stand back and make sure that his exegesis is reflective of the broader flow of the argument. Calvin's stated preference for brevity in his commentaries and his desire to let the text

---

25. Calvin, *Institutes* 3.21:7.

26. Calvin offers a more extensive argument based on Rom 9–11 in 3.22.4–6 of the *Institutes*, but still does not deal with this hermeneutical issue.

27. Calvin, *Institutes* 3.22:10.

28. Calvin, *Institutes* 3.23:8.

29. Calvin, *Galatians and Ephesians*, 196.

speak for itself may have been a factor in his analysis of Eph 1,[30] but it does him a disservice. In contrast, Aquinas was much more disciplined in stepping from the whole to the parts and then back to the whole again. In Calvin's commentary on Romans, Calvin shows how much his theology affects his biblical interpretation. On Rom 8:28–29, Calvin takes no time to consider why Paul felt it so necessary to introduce predestination into the sequence so awkwardly, and instead Calvin discusses election without explaining how it is connected to predestination.[31] On Rom 9, Calvin appropriately begins by noting that the chapter concerns Jews who have rejected God and his gospel in Paul's day, but when Calvin comes to the exegesis of Rom 9:12 concerning God's preference for Jacob, he does not interpret it within the broader concern of Rom 9 but seamlessly applies it to gentile Christians throughout the ages. Calvin's commentaries on key passages concerning predestination and election show more extensive exegesis than the *Institutes*, but they lack the precision of Aquinas's commentaries and don't answer the questions that are raised by the *Institutes*.

Calvin ends up both narrowing and heightening Augustine's theology. As with Augustine, the words "predestination" and "election" are used interchangeably to refer to the same doctrine.[32] Predestination is of the individual and determines that individual's eternal destiny. Calvin, however, does not take up Augustine's secondary references to the predestination of Jesus Christ or the election of the church. Calvin's strong doctrine of double predestination also goes well beyond Augustine's more tentative position. Like Augustine, Calvin relies heavily on Eph 1:1–14[33] and Rom 9–11,[34] but he also adds extensive support from the Gospel of John,[35] and he refers to many instances of election in both the Old and New Testaments. In this sense, Calvin attempted to put the doctrine of predestination and election on a sounder footing, but his sloppy reasoning at times ended up raising further questions about this doctrine's validity.

---

30. Parker, *Calvin's New Testament Commentaries*, 50.
31. Calvin, *Romans*, 315.
32. Calvin, *Institutes* 3.21:1.
33. Calvin, *Institutes* 3.22:1, 2, 3, 6, 10; 23:12; 24:8.
34. Calvin, *Institutes* 3.21:1, 7; 22:3, 4, 6, 8, 11; 23:1, 4, 5, 11, 12, 13; 24:1, 4, 5, 6, 13, 14, 16, 17.
35. Calvin, *Institutes* 3.23:7, 8, 10; 23:13; 24:1, 5, 6, 7, 9.

5

Karl Barth: The Attempted Save

Karl Barth covers the doctrine of election extensively in his prime theological work, *Church Dogmatics*, and like Aquinas, Barth locates his exposition of election within his volume on the doctrine of God following a discussion on providence.[1] Barth, however, places more importance on the doctrine of election, regarding it as "the sum of the Gospel"[2] because it is the best expression of the gospel, in that it declares that God freely loves, is for people, and chooses people. It makes grace truly grace.[3] Barth entitles this chapter "The Election of God" and breaks it up into four sections, the first of which redefines the doctrine of election and the subsequent three sections address respectively the election of Jesus Christ, the community, and the individual.

In the opening section on election, Barth explains that election is focused on God, because Jesus Christ "is both the electing God and the elected man in One."[4] To Barth it is the premier doctrine, logically prior to creation[5] and having "precedence over all other tenets of the Christian faith relating to God's work."[6] Barth disagrees with Aquinas that predestination is a subset of providence and therefore deterministic.[7] Instead,

---

1. Barth, "Perfections of the Divine Freedom," in *Church Dogmatics* 2.1:440.
2. Barth, *Church Dogmatics*, 2.2:3.
3. Johnson, *Essential Karl Barth*, 183.
4. Barth, *Church Dogmatics*, 2.2:3.
5. Gunton, "Salvation," 156.
6. Barth, *Church Dogmatics*, 2.2:76.
7. Barth, *Church Dogmatics*, 2.2:45.

Barth declares predestination to be God's plan for creation, and first and foremost a predestination of himself, thereby providing the rationale for subsuming providence within the doctrine of predestination.

For Barth, the context of the doctrine of election is that God in Trinity wills and acts within the Godhead to come to us graciously in Jesus Christ.[8] It is free love, uninfluenced by any claim or merit.[9] It is in God's essential nature for the Son to be sitting at the Father's right hand, and for the Son to be uniting the people with him and through him to God.[10] While Augustine also referred to the predestination of Jesus Christ and the Church, Barth reverses Augustine's emphasis and makes the election of Christ and the Church primary and logically prior to the election of individuals.

Barth continues to link predestination and election as a single doctrine with the terms being interchangeable.[11] Unlike Aquinas, he doesn't question whether this is valid. Instead, Barth accepts the understanding that has been handed down and attempts to recast it in a more acceptable light. Given Barth's extensive reworking of the doctrine, it will be of interest to see if he can convincingly hold predestination and election together or whether he exposes further cracks.

From early in his opening section on election, Barth acknowledges that a major motivation for the complete recasting of the doctrine of predestination and election is the widespread resentment toward it.[12] The Enlightenment brought a strong belief in human autonomy, and within that framework predestination was not only unwelcome, it was despised. To address that resentment, Barth first acknowledges that Luther and Calvin went too far in making election and rejection equivalent. Election is a positive act of grace and the focus of the doctrine. Rejection is subordinate and an absence of grace rather than the presence of reprobation. There is only a Book of Life and not a corresponding Book of Death.[13]

Barth is adamant that Scripture must be the basis of the doctrine of election. Neither Church tradition (including the Reformed tradition) nor the doctrine's usefulness in pastoral ministry were a legitimate basis

---

8. Barth, *Church Dogmatics*, 2.2:47. See also Busch, *Great Passion*, 126.
9. Barth, *Church Dogmatics*, 2.2:19. See also Johnson, *Essential Karl Barth*, 185.
10. Johnson, *Essential Karl Barth*, 178.
11. Barth, *Church Dogmatics*, 2.2:3, 13.
12. Barth, *Church Dogmatics*, 2.2:13.
13. Barth, *Church Dogmatics*, 2.2:16. To make his case, Barth refers to Exod 32:32; Ps 69:29; Phil 4:3, Rev 3:5; 17:8; 20:12, 15.

for the doctrine.[14] Election can also not be established by theological reasoning about the nature of God or the experience of the Christian life, although a properly established doctrine of election can be informed by them.[15] Thus Barth has set a clear standard by which his reasoning is to be judged.

Turning to Scripture, Barth observes the tendency in the OT to focus on the one elected man in whom people become elected.[16] He sees this first in Jacob-Israel, secondly in David and his successors, and finally in the one anticipated in the prophets.[17] This is the foundation on which Barth bases his key premise. Barth, however, does not reference an explicit Scripture to substantiate this point, and there is a sense of him imposing his theological framework onto the text. The OT refers to the blessing of the nations rather than them becoming elect in Jacob-Israel. The office of king which David occupied was initially an affront to God, and while God moved to make something positive of it, David does not become the basis of Israel's election. Barth seems to have started with his conclusion that election is about the one encompassing the many and then looked to find examples of that in the OT, rather than wrestling with how the OT authors understood the concept of election.

Having presented his opening point of the elect man in whom people become elect, Barth turns to find that concept in the NT. He references Eph 1:4–5, 11; 3:10; and Rom 8:29–30 to show that election is focused on Jesus Christ.[18] In so doing, Barth moves election from being a decree of God to being intrinsic to God's nature. As McCormack puts it, God is essentially and not consequentially the elector and the elected.[19] By this Barth undercuts the speculation about the sequence of divine decision-making and moves election into God's prime being.

Barth then seeks to use this new locus of election to find an alternative to both human-dependant Pelagianism and human-independent Absolutism. While he admires the Lutheran position, Barth ultimately sees it as God simply validating human decisions and hence a form of Pelagianism.[20] Pelagianism fails to realize that the human will without

---

14. Barth, *Church Dogmatics*, 2.2:36–38.
15. Barth, *Church Dogmatics*, 2.2:38–51.
16. Barth, *Church Dogmatics*, 2.2:55.
17. Barth, *Church Dogmatics*, 2.2:55–56.
18. Barth, *Church Dogmatics*, 2.2:60.
19. McCormack, "Grace and Being," 93.
20. Barth, *Church Dogmatics*, 2.2:63.

God is captive to its own corruption, and individuals need God to bring them to freedom.[21] Absolutism, however, is unnecessarily offensive to the modern mind because it totally removes individuals from involvement in their salvation or damnation.[22] Barth rejects Absolutism on the basis that it tries to pry into God's decisions in the abstract, undermining both revelation and salvation.[23] Calvinism had come to characterize God as an absolute sovereign, effectively indifferent to created beings.[24] Barth tries to avoid both Pelagianism and Absolutism by reasserting his principle that Jesus Christ is both the electing God and the elected man, but this does not resolve whether individuals have a role in their salvation. Effectively he postpones resolution of this core problem.

In the next section, Barth attempts to establish a biblical basis for Jesus Christ as the elected one. His argument is unconvincing, with McCormack going so far as to say there is "no direct confirmation in the New Testament."[25] Barth relies on John 1:1–18 and interprets the passage's description of the Word's essential eternal being to be an election of the Word.[26] This is consistent with Barth's theological framework, but it is not exegesis. Further on, Barth does identify biblical texts which refer to Jesus as chosen (Luke 23:35; 1 Pet 1:20),[27] but Barth uses these to support the fore-planning of Jesus's mission rather than to establish the election of Jesus Christ as Barth conceived it. Perhaps if Barth had started with these verses, he may have avoided the worst of McCormack's criticisms.

Barth makes another attempt to establish John 1 as a definitive text on the election of Jesus Christ in volume 4 of *Church Dogmatics* (§64 "The Exaltation of the Son of Man"). He does this by presenting Col 1:15–20 as another example of a passage on the predestination of Christ as both Son of Man and Son of God.[28] As with John 1, Barth does not show how the biblical text establishes his point but rather uses the passage to illustrate how election and predestination can be a state rather than an action. Barth goes on to show how Heb 1:2–3, 1 Pet 1:29, Eph 1:4, 7, and Rev 13:8 also fit in with his construct, but while the argument has

---

21. Busch, *Great Passion*, 117.
22. Barth, *Church Dogmatics*, 2.2:65.
23. Barth, *Church Dogmatics*, 2.2:80. See also Johnson, *Essential Karl Barth*, 194–95.
24. Busch, *Great Passion*, 113.
25. McCormack, "Grace and Being," 94.
26. Barth, *Church Dogmatics*, 2.2:95.
27. Barth, *Church Dogmatics*, 2.2:102.
28. Barth, *Church Dogmatics*, 4.2:33.

an intriguing internal coherence,[29] it lacks a sound basis to support the redefinition of election.

Barth is on firmer ground in using the Gospel of John to show that Jesus Christ chooses his disciples,[30] but this only serves to emphasize how explicit and prevalent the language of Jesus as the elector is in John, in contrast with the complete absence of any language of Jesus being elect. As a result, it would seem safer to conclude that John did not intend that Jesus be thought of as elect. Rather than supporting Barth's thesis, the Gospel of John may teach that the Father's eternal plan for the Son and the election of the disciples are not to be confused.

In the section on the election of the community, Barth characterizes Israel as elect for judgment and the Church as elect for mercy.[31] Barth may only be using the term "Israel" to refer to those Jews who reject the Messiah but, if so, it is a poor choice of language. There are both faithful and unfaithful Israelites, with numerous examples of that in the Pentateuch (e.g., Num 25) and the Former Prophets (e.g., 1 Kgs 19:18). This is also reflected in many of the psalms and in the Latter Prophets' remnant motif. Barth continues to paint Jews in a poor light by condemning them corporately for handing Jesus over to the gentiles to be put to death,[32] ignoring that it was a particular subset of Jews responsible for this.

Barth goes on to conduct a detailed exegesis of Rom 9–11 to establish his doctrine of the election of the community, but it suffers from Barth reading his theology into the text. Initially Barth does well to point out that those NT passages describing evangelism of Jews do not refer to them being called out of Judaism in the way gentiles are called out of paganism. Instead, Jews are called to be obedient to their election.[33] When it comes to Rom 9–11, however, Barth assumes that it concerns the election of the Church and he reads a Church-Israel dichotomy into the text. Barth turns Paul's angst for those Jews who had not received the Messiah into a Church-Synagogue confrontation.[34] Rather than finding Paul's sympathy for unbelieving Israelites, Barth sees condemnation of them and joy for members of the church. Barth's exegesis of Rom 9–11 appears to be unduly affected by his own context.

---

29. Barth, *Church Dogmatics*, 4.2:34.
30. Barth, *Church Dogmatics*, 2.2:106.
31. Barth, *Church Dogmatics*, 2.2:198.
32. Barth, *Church Dogmatics*, 2.2:200.
33. Barth, *Church Dogmatics*, 2.2:204.
34. Barth, *Church Dogmatics*, 2.2:205.

Barth treats the election of the individual last. He argues that it can only be understood in the context of the election of Jesus Christ and the Church, and he hopes that by doing this he can avoid Absolutism. To this end, he makes it clear from the start that it is the godless person's own choice that leads to rejection by God.[35] With respect to election, Barth continues to emphasize that it is fundamentally located in Christ, so much so that the individual's election is only relevant for Christ and does not infer eternal consequences for that individual. As Barth puts it, "Not everyone who is elected lives as an elect man. Perhaps he does not yet do so. Perhaps he does so no longer. . . . Perhaps he never does so."[36] For Barth, election of the individual does not represent an end state but an invitation. Later on, when writing about human sloth, Barth once again emphasizes that it is actually all of humanity that is elected in Jesus Christ as "the Representative and Head and Lord of all other men."[37] Everyone is invited to join in the covenant relationship. How one comes to take up that invitation is an enigma to Barth that needs to be left to rest in the freedom of God.[38] In the end, rather than finding an alternative to Pelagianism or Absolutism, Barth declares the matter to be an irresolvable mystery.

Barth begins his discourse on election in *Church Dogmatics* by stating that the doctrine needed to be founded in Scripture, and Barth does reference and dwell on biblical passages extensively. Barth's exegesis, however, is overly affected and constrained by his theology. In his survey of the OT, Barth selects passages and then construes them to support his thesis rather than carefully exegeting them, all the while ignoring counterarguments and contrary passages. His use of the prologue of John to establish Jesus Christ as the elect one also flounders due to the lack of exegetical support. Regarding Rom 9–11, Barth shifts the context from a first-century Jew's passion for his fellow countrymen to European frustration with the twentieth-century synagogue. This theological perspective is also evident in Barth's use of 1 Peter 2:9 to present Christians as the new elect, "the new and true Israel."[39] Barth's theological construct is not without merit, but it lacks the exegetical foundation to be adopted as is.

---

35. Barth, *Church Dogmatics*, 2.2:306.
36. Barth, *Church Dogmatics*, 2.2:321.
37. Barth, *Church Dogmatics*, 4.2:382.
38. Barth, *Church Dogmatics*, 2.2:343.
39. Barth, *Church Dogmatics*, 2.2:15.

There is much to be gained from reflecting on Barth's re-characterization of the doctrine of predestination and election. His shift of focus from the election of the individual to the election of Jesus Christ warrants consideration, and his broad engagement with the biblical text is informative. Barth, however, did not begin by examining how and why the concepts of election and predestination emerged in the biblical literature. Instead, he reacted to the Augustinian tradition handed down. Consequently, predestination and election become further strained, with a poorly substantiated commitment to the election of Jesus Christ, an unexplained and unsatisfying election of the individual, and a very awkward expression of the election of the community. The reader is once again left with the impression that something is fundamentally awry.

6

The Need for Reappraisal

Augustine's doctrine of predestination and election was the product of circumstance rather than of careful exegesis. Prior to Pelagianism coming into his orbit, Augustine maintained the then-common belief that predestination and election were separate concepts in Scripture, with election being both an encouragement and challenge for godly living, and predestination referenced rarely and being on the basis of foreknowledge of the individual's life. As the debate over Pelagianism developed, Augustine began to leverage election and predestination rhetorically more and more, and it was in this context, rather than from biblical exegesis, that the doctrines developed in Augustine's mind and eventually merged. Augustine was well into the debate before he began looking for a scriptural basis for his new understanding, but rather than engage in detailed exegesis and careful research of all of Scripture, he simply cited texts that superficially seemed to endorse his thoughts. This new doctrine of predestination was not universally welcomed, but such was the force of Augustine's rhetoric, the weight of his work, and respect for his reputation that his innovation set the agenda in the Western Church.

By the time of Aquinas, predestination had become a doctrine worthy of discussion in its own right. Rather than being a means to affirm unmerited grace, as it had been for Augustine, the discussion in the Middle Ages centered around how predestination impacted on individual agency and divine decision-making. This was reflected in Aquinas locating his section on predestination adjacent to his discussion of providence in *Summa Theologiæ*. Despite this prominent treatment, it is apparent that there had not been a detailed investigation into the way the concept of predestination was used throughout Scripture. Aquinas based his reasoning in *Summa Theologiæ* mostly on a single verse (Rom 8:29), and even then his argument was as much informed by Augustine's construct as it was from the actual wording of the text. While Aquinas entertained the possibility that election and predestination were not connected, he only did so within the constraints of how Augustine conceived of the terms and not how they were used more broadly in the biblical literature. Aquinas's exegetical work in his commentary on Ephesians was more considered and shows how Augustine's doctrine of predestination and election could be established. Nevertheless, that work also stayed within Augustine's understanding of the concepts, so ended up only considering a narrow range of possibilities.

Calvin was drawn into discussing predestination and election somewhat reluctantly. When he belatedly introduced Augustine's understanding of the doctrine into the *Institutes*, it stirred up such a controversy that he was forced to defend it vigorously. Calvin only did so because he considered the doctrine to be biblical, but he counseled against exaggerating its importance or engaging in extrabiblical speculation. Calvin's defense of the doctrine was weak, with Scripture used to support the Augustinian viewpoint rather than being thoroughly reappraised from the ground up. Calvin read Augustine's understanding of Rom 9–11 and Eph 1 back into the rest of Scripture when it would seem more appropriate, especially with respect to Rom 9–11, that the reverse should be the primary approach. Calvin's commentaries similarly suffer from too hastily finding Augustine's concepts in the text and not working carefully through the text and exploring other possible influences.

Barth attempted to quell the virulent opposition to Augustinian predestination and election that had only heightened since the Enlightenment. The way predestination attacked human autonomy was intolerable to many because it trapped individuals in their predetermined fate, whether that be condemnation or salvation. Barth attempted to solve this by making Jesus Christ the focus of the doctrine. Barth declared that it is Jesus Christ who is elected and rejected, not the individual. It is Jesus Christ who is predestined, not the individual. The implications of the doctrine only flow through to the individual on the basis of that individual's acceptance or rejection of Christ. Barth remained agnostic about whether the individual participated in joining the elect or whether it was solely God's action. That question was left shrouded in mystery. Given the degree of human autonomy is the very problem that Barth set out to address, his conclusion is somewhat disappointing and unsatisfying. Barth's exegetical efforts show that he too was working within the framework of Augustine's definition of predestination and election, and Barth read that understanding into Eph 1 and Rom 9–11 and then back onto the rest of Scripture.

What is needed is a fresh appraisal of key biblical texts that does not begin with the Augustinian understanding of predestination and election. Augustine's doctrine of predestination/election was poorly established, arising primarily from his rhetoric and only illustrated superficially in Scripture. Such was Augustine's influence, however, any subsequent discussion of the doctrine in the Western Church effectively began with how Augustine defined the terms. As such, while Aquinas, Calvin, and Barth wrestled with predestination/election, they stayed within the bounds of Augustine's basic understanding. Instead, there needs to be a broader consideration of how these terms are used in Scripture and in relevant extrabiblical literature in order to appreciate what meanings might be possible in specific passages. The key texts then need to be interpreted within their own original context before considering what value they may offer for the present context. The reappraisal of the texts will need to take recent scholarship into account and be exegetically grounded in inductive and contextually sensitive exegesis.

PART 2

Ephesians 1:3–14

A re-evaluation of predestination and election in Ephesians 1:3–14

The doctrines of predestination and election have been debated extensively since the days of Augustine, with Eph 1:3–14 being a key text in that debate. Augustine did not conduct a detailed exegesis of this text when he developed his joint doctrine of predestination and election, yet his understanding of those terms has set the agenda for many prominent Christian thinkers, leading to a concern that Augustine's definitions have been read into the text rather than from it. In the New Testament, predestination is presented as a reason for Christian joy, with the opening of Ephesians a prime example of that, whereas an Augustinian understanding of predestination produces stoic confidence at best and more often sadness and aversion. What is needed is a reappraisal of this text grounded in inductive and contextually sensitive exegesis without being haunted by the specter of fifth-century Pelagianism. The first section of part two surveys and critically assesses recent scholarly literature concerning issues that impact the study of Eph 1:3–14. This then informs an exegesis that considers the text in its first-century context, with a view to understanding how this passage ought to contribute to the doctrines of predestination and election.

7

Methodology and Background

The method chosen for the exegesis of Eph 1:3–14 is the inductive hermeneutical method put forward by Bauer and Trainer,[1] informed by comparable techniques proposed by Fee, Gorman, and Brown.[2] This supports the goal of conducting a fresh exegesis of the text in its first-century context that is uninfluenced, as far as practicable, by subsequent theological reflections. Inductive reasoning aims to infer probable conclusions, rather than seeking the certainty that deductive reasoning claims to achieve. Possible interpretations are assessed against the available evidence to arrive at a likely outcome that does not go beyond what can reasonably be supported. This involves engaging primarily with the implied author so that the exegesis is rooted in the text. The study is still informed by the historical context of the actual author and occasion, but it does not engage in historical speculation that distorts the text.[3] In a similar fashion, higher critical techniques are used only when relevant to the text. The exegesis is sensitive to the genre and structure, makes logical inferences from the grammar and terms, and integrates that interpretation with the broader literary context. The focus of the study is the text in its final form, with the biblical book being the basic literary unit and the canon being the broader

---

1. Bauer and Traina, *Inductive Bible Study*.
2. Fee, *New Testament Exegesis*; Gorman, *Elements of Biblical Exegesis*; Brown, *Handbook to Old Testament Exegesis*.
3. Bauer and Traina, *Inductive Bible Study*, 42.

context with a view to arriving at an interpretation that informs a religious perspective.

Following these principles, the following will be explored inasmuch as they help prepare for a detailed exegesis of Eph 1:3–14:

- the authorship and occasion of Ephesians;
- significant themes and motifs of the letter, including any relevant historical background;
- the genre of Eph 1:3–14; and
- the literary structure of Eph 1:3–14.

AUTHORSHIP AND OCCASION

The questions concerning the authorship and occasion of Ephesians can occupy a large part of any commentary, with scholars since 1800 split approximately 50/50 on whether the letter was written by Paul or even addressed to the church in Ephesus.[4] Nevertheless, such questions are of limited interest to this study, because the consensus is that:

- if the author was not the apostle Paul, then it was a devoted disciple who represented Paul's thoughts well;
- if Ephesians was not written to the church at Ephesus, it was likely written to a church or churches nearby that would have had a similar context; and
- if Ephesians was not written in Paul's lifetime, it was written shortly thereafter in a similar theological context.[5]

As such, the exegesis of Ephesians tends not to be greatly affected by the contested issues of authorship and occasion, and it is only when the text of Ephesians is in tension with other Pauline works that the commentator's view on authorship influences how that is dealt with.

Of the four key arguments for non-Pauline authorship identified by Lincoln,[6] only two significantly affect this study: the different literary style and different theological emphases of Ephesians when compared with the undisputed Pauline epistles. The variance in style can lead to the

---

4. Hoehner, *Ephesians*, 6–20.
5. Longenecker and Still, *Thinking Through Paul*, 244.
6. Lincoln, *Ephesians*, 42.

same word or phrase being used in a different sense from other Pauline epistles, although this difficulty should not be overstated since examples of the Ephesian style can be found throughout the Pauline corpus.[7] Colossians, whose authorship is also disputed, is the most similar in language and substance.[8] Ephesians also shares a number of traits with 1 Peter, with the common formulation at the beginning of each epistle being a prime example (cf. Eph 1:3–14 and 1 Pet 1:3–12).[9] Consequently, Colossians and 1 Peter in particular may provide helpful commentary on the concepts expressed in Ephesians. With respect to the supposed theological differences of Ephesians with the undisputed Pauline epistles, this also turns out to be more one of emphasis than actual difference, with most if not all of the ideas in Ephesians found elsewhere in Paul's writings.[10] In the main, these different emphases make sense in the Ephesian context.[11] I personally find the argument for non-Pauline authorship weak and unnecessary. Nevertheless, given its significant scholarly support, I will retain open the possibility of authorship by a Pauline disciple and address any relevant issues in the exegesis.

The most significant effect of the dispute over authorship for this study is that it has led to Ephesians being less prominent in discussions of Pauline theology.[12] This includes the doctrine of election, which has been reconsidered independently of the term's possibly idiosyncratic use in Eph 1:4, resulting in several perspectives quite different from the Augustinian understanding. Ephesians tends to be studied more on its own terms, with interpreters able to consider whether Paul had specific pastoral concerns that affected his choice of expression. This respects the now widely recognized principle that the meaning of a word is primarily derived from its context and that it is unwise to import developed concepts into a text without clear justification.[13]

---

7. Markus Barth, *Ephesians*, 4–6; Hoehner, *Ephesians*, 24–9.

8. Lincoln, *Ephesians*, xlvii.

9. Mitton, "Relationship Between 1 Peter and Ephesians," 67; Dunn, *Theology of Paul*, 396; Lincoln, *Ephesians*, 11; Talbert, *Ephesians and Colossians*, 6. These similarities may be due to some form of literary dependency or Peter's scribe, Silas, being the same Silas who accompanied Paul on his second missionary journey.

10. Hoehner, *Ephesians*, 49–58.

11. Keesmaat, "Colossians and Ephesians," 136.

12. Dunn, *Theology of Paul*, xxvii.

13. Patrick, "Election: Old Testament," *ABD* 2:434.

PREDESTINATION AND ELECTION

Summaries of the development of the doctrine(s) of election and predestination through history can be found in the works of G. C. Berkouwer and P. K. Jewett, among others,[14] to which I have added my own critical analysis in part one. Levering identifies five distinct perspectives on predestination over the centuries, ranging from the unconditional predestination of both the saved and the damned (Calvin) to some form of universal salvation (Origin).[15]

In more recent times, the tomes on Pauline theology by James D. G. Dunn and N. T. Wright have recast election as corporate rather than of individuals. Following the new perspective on Pauline theology ushered in by Ed Sanders' *Paul and Palestinian Judaism*,[16] Dunn and Wright place Paul firmly in his Jewish context and focus on Romans as the key Pauline text.[17] Dunn follows F. C. Baur in understanding election in a national sense.[18] While initially election was of historical Israel, ultimately election is of eschatological Israel, with participation being on the basis of a positive response to God's call.[19] Wright sees it slightly differently, with Israel's election in the OT being for the purpose of ushering in the Christ,[20] while election under the new covenant is achieved by becoming one of the Messiah's justified people in the inaugurated eschatological age.[21] Both Dunn and Wright continue to conflate predestination with election without justification. Their insights into the meaning of election in Rom 9–11 will be evaluated in part three, but they leave open that Paul may have something different in mind in Ephesians.

Thornhill documents a further shift among scholars from the national and unconditional view of election expressed in the works of G. F. Moore, W. D. Davies, and E. P. Sanders, all of whom relied on later Rabbinic writings, to the conditional election of the remnant that has

---

14. Berkouwer, *Divine Election*, 28–52; Jewett, *Election and Predestination*, 5–21.
15. Levering, *Predestination*, 1–12.
16. Yinger, "Interpretation," 516.
17. Wright, *Paul and the Faithfulness of God*, 774–1042; Dunn, *Theology of Paul*, 500–13.
18. Dunn, *Theology of Paul*, 501.
19. Dunn, *Theology of Paul*, 504.
20. Wright, *Paul and the Faithfulness of God*, 815.
21. Wright, *Paul and the Faithfulness of God*, 912.

been found to be prominent in the Second Temple period literature.[22] While physical descent from Jacob is still a factor in the Second Temple period, the elect are also defined by their personal behavior and attitude, particularly in remaining true to the law and not defecting to a Greek way of life.[23] What also emerges is the vision of an elect one who would draw together the elect ones (1 En. 39:6). The degree to which the Essenes further developed this line of thinking is debated by scholars. Broshi discerns in the Dead Sea Scrolls' *Manual of Disciple* a firm belief in double predestination that differentiated the Essenes from "normative Judaism,"[24] whereas others believe the text may merely be referring to classes of people rather than individual predestination.[25] For this second group of scholars, election in the Second Temple literature is a minor side issue that does not warrant extensive comment.[26]

Timo Eskola in *Theodicy and Predestination in Pauline Soteriology* also bases his understanding on Jewish writings in the Second Temple period. Like Broshi, Eskola prefers predestination as the key term, however Eskola argues that while there is the occasional reference to the lack of control people have over their general circumstances (e.g., Sir 33:11–15),[27] the consistent refrain through all the Second Temple texts regardless of genre is that individuals are accountable to God for their behavior. For Eskola, predestination is God's predetermined consequences for behavior rather than a specified outcome for every individual. This served as a theodicy in light of the continued suffering and struggles both of the nation and of individuals at the hand of unfaithful Jews.[28] Eskola argues that the apostle Paul follows the same line of thought in Romans, but Paul replaces allegiance to the old covenant regulations with responding to God's call to faith.[29] This thread of a theodicy is interesting, but Eskola's choice of predestination as the controlling term does not sit easily with the Second Temple literature not containing the Greek word for predestination (προορίζω) or with the peculiar way προορίζω is

---

22. Thornhill, *Chosen People*, 17–18.
23. Thornhill, *Chosen People*, 28, 39; Qimron, "Dualism in the Essene Communities," 195–6; Klein, *New Chosen People*, 20.
24. Broshi, "Predestination in the Bible," 235, 238.
25. Nickelsburg, *Jewish Literature*, 132.
26. Embry et al., *Early Jewish Literature*, 474.
27. Eskola, *Theodicy and Predestination*, 44.
28. Eskola, *Theodicy and Predestination*, 49.
29. Eskola, *Theodicy and Predestination*, 186.

deployed in Romans and Ephesians. As with Dunn and Wright, Eskola subsumes predestination within election rather exploring election in its own right. It would be better first to analyze how predestination is used in the NT before exploring potential precedents that might nuance that understanding.

Another significant factor in the scholarly treatment of the doctrines of predestination and election has been the waning of the biblical theology movement in the 1960s following the criticisms of James Barr in *The Semantics of Biblical Language*.[30] Barr's criticisms led to a loss of confidence in there being a comprehensive, synthetic concept of election. Subsequently few articles have been written on the subject of election, and those that have been published tend to look at the specific perspective of one passage. Summary articles on OT election are devoid of links to the NT and focus on the earthly reality of God's choices of people, places, and things for his purposes.[31] The classic formulation of the election of the nation of Israel is still presented, but it is then contrasted with alternate perspectives inside and outside the OT canon.[32] Shogren reflects this splintered approach in his summary article on election in the New Testament, describing many voices on the subject.[33] The Synoptic tradition, the Gospel of John, and Pauline theology are treated separately, as are the elections of Jesus, angels, Israel, the church, and individuals. Shogren identifies that Paul's emphasis regarding election is on God as the one who chooses, with the discussion of the purpose of that election containing the only citation from Ephesians.[34] Similarly, Hartman documents the many different uses of election in the NT, although he also separates out what he regards as deutero-Pauline letters such as Ephesians for their emphasis on the election of the church.[35]

Nevertheless, in some circles the combined doctrine of predestination and election continues to be a subject of general interest, and Eph 1:3–14 has come even more to the fore in those scholarly discussions owing to Rom 9–11 being reappraised as concerning the fate of unbelieving Jews rather than pre-creation divine decision-making.[36]

---

30. Patrick, "Election: Old Testament," *ABD* 2:434–35.
31. Patrick, "Election: Old Testament," *ABD* 2:436.
32. Seybold, "Election: Old Testament," *RPP* 4:393.
33. Shogren, "Election: New Testament," *ABD* 2:441–44.
34. Shogren, "Election: New Testament," *ABD* 2:443.
35. Hartman, "Election: New Testament," *RPP* 4:394.
36. Dunn, *Theology of Paul*, 500.

Newman credits Berkouwer and Jewett among others for contributing to the doctrine's vitality and controversy.[37] Jewett relies on Ephesians to establish the election of the gentiles and acknowledges the prominent role of Eph 3:8–12 in the debates on supra- and infralapsarianism.[38] Berkouwer references Eph 1:4–6 early in his work on election,[39] and goes on to wrestle with the debate as to whether Christ is the cause or the basis of election.[40] Berkouwer discounts the former because that would imply that the Father was reluctant or not directly involved.

Newman wades into the controversy himself, rejecting, along with most commentators, that Eph 1:4–6 implies double predestination.[41] Universalism, such as that proposed by W. Michaelis,[42] is also ruled out. For his part, Newman follows Karl Barth in interpreting Eph 1:4 as referring to the election of Jesus Christ before the foundation of time as the one in whom all believers would be found. It is then through Christ's earthly ministry, as described in the ensuing verses, that the corporate body of believers is united with him to share jointly in his election and its purposes.[43]

Hoehner takes this Barthian conception of election to task, primarily by refuting how Markus Barth expresses it in his commentary on Ephesians. Like his father, Markus Barth describes Jesus Christ as the prime object and subject of election. Christ is the revealed secret and the instrument of God's election, representing all those elected. Election is not about fixing someone's future.[44] For Hoehner, this does not respect the text, which he argues clearly has believers as the object of God's election.[45] Separately, Carson also rejects Barthian election because it relies on the "us" in Eph 1:4 referring to all people, when in context "us" is referring to the faithful in Christ Jesus.[46] Both Carson and Hoehner, however, have less exegetical support for their claims that Eph 1:4 concerns divine election of individuals. Furthermore, while Hoehner's survey of the OT use of

---

37. Newman, "Election and Predestination," 237.
38. Jewett, *Election and Predestination*, 33, 88.
39. Berkouwer, *Divine Election*, 15.
40. Berkouwer, *Divine Election*, 132.
41. Newman, "Election and Predestination," 237.
42. O'Brien, *Colossians, Philemon*, 56.
43. Newman, "Election and Predestination," 238–39, 243.
44. Markus Barth, *Ephesians*, 108.
45. Hoehner, *Ephesians*, 188–92.
46. Carson, *Divine Sovereignty*, 216.

election identifies that election is at God's initiative and prerogative, is of known options, and does not imply dislike for those not chosen,[47] that does not imply that each of those aspects can be read into Paul's expression in Eph 1:4.

Several other scholars also continue to defend a version of Augustinian predestination and election. Douglas Moo believes that Eph 1:4–6 unavoidably concerns the pre-creation selection of individuals,[48] and W. A. Elwell in the first edition of the *Dictionary of Paul and His Letters* leans in that direction as well, expressing it as the election of a group of individuals.[49] Elwell emphasizes that election is in Christ, but does not explain the significance of that. Both regard election and predestination as synonyms, and both see them as setting a certain outcome for individuals, although only in a positive sense. Levering holds a similar position, stressing that God lovingly seeks to save all people while permitting the rebellion and loss of some.[50] These scholars present neat constructs, but their case for individual election based on Eph 1:4–6 is weak. Thornhill challenges individual election in the second edition of the *Dictionary of Paul and His Letters*, in which Paul's understanding of election is presented as collective or corporate, whether in the old covenant national sense or in the new covenant sense of the collective people of God in Christ.[51] The individual enters the elect people by responding to the call to faith. While Thornhill's presentation perhaps better respects the Pauline texts, there is still a sense that a doctrine of election is being read into the Bible. Klein's work, *The New Chosen People*, also suffers from this because, having determined that election is being used corporately of the nation of Israel in the OT, he interprets all NT passages through that lens.[52] "Election" is just a word, and its particular usage does not necessarily bring with it concepts that are developed elsewhere. Thornhill also continues to run predestination and election together on the basis of an unspecified logic, despite noting their distinct usage.

Recent scholarly discussion on election and predestination has roughly divided into two streams. Those who follow the new perspective on Paul focus on Rom 9–11 and regard election as national and

---

47. Hoehner, *Ephesians*, 185–86.
48. Moo, *Theology of Paul*, 272.
49. Elwell, "Election and Predestination," 225–29.
50. Levering, *Predestination*, 177–201.
51. Thornhill, "Election and Predestination," 238–41.
52. Klein, *New Chosen People*, 10, 149.

ultimately eschatological. Prior to Christ, individuals would be born into the potentially elect people of God, among whom a remnant would show themselves as the true elect. Under the new covenant, individuals join the elect collective by some contemporary means such as responding to the call to believe (Rom 9:24–26; 10:12–21). Those scholars who take the more traditional line that election is of individuals for salvation tend to include Eph 1 in their reasoning and consider election to be either a predetermined outcome for individuals or the choice of Jesus Christ to be the vessel through whom individuals will be saved.

Despite this considerable scholarly research and debate, election and predestination continue to be used interchangeably, usually without explanation. This treatment of the two terms as synonyms is most surprising in the discussions of Second Temple period literature, in which election is arguably a significant doctrine and the word "predestination" does not appear. It is also surprising that the fresh appraisals of election in Romans have not led to some separate consideration of predestination, given the terms do not appear together in the same sub-argument in Rom 8–11 and appear to be used for different purposes by Paul. Predestination needs the same fresh appraisal that election has received, including an assessment of whether it is merely a synonym for election, and Eph 1:3–14 is the ideal place to commence that reappraisal.

ESCHATOLOGY

Election and predestination are the first brushstrokes of the picture of realized eschatology painted by Paul in Eph 1–3. Paul builds on the idea of the two ages first introduced in Jewish apocalypses in the Second Temple period, when a hope developed that the corrupt and failing world would be replaced by a new, holy, and glorious age.[53] Paul understands that in Christ the new age has begun and that believers experience the blessings of that new realm now while still enduring the struggles of the old. Lincoln follows Ridderbos, E. P. Sanders, and Beker in seeing Christ-centered eschatology at the core of Paul's thought.[54] Longenecker and Still, following J. C. Beker, describe Paul's eschatology as the narrative substructure upon which all of Paul's thinking is based.[55] One of the

---

53. Rowland, "Eschatology of the New Testament Church," 62.
54. Lincoln, *Ephesians*, lxxxix.
55. Longenecker and Still, *Thinking Through Paul*, 301.

distinctives of Ephesians, which it shares with Colossians, is that it places a greater emphasis on the realized aspect of that eschatology. Ephesians opens with an effusive description of the blessings already obtained in Christ, beginning with what has been achieved through election and predestination and going on to include the only explicit reference to both ages in the NT (1:21). Ephesians characterizes the present experience in the church as a foretaste of God's eternal promise.[56]

While realized eschatology is very much in the foreground in Ephesians, the understanding expressed in the epistle is still consistent with Paul's expression elsewhere.[57] Contrary to Lincoln, Paul's description of Christians being seated with Christ in the heavenly realms (2:6) does not include any additional sense of rule (cf. Col 3:1),[58] and is comparable to living in the Spirit in Rom 8. The heavenly/worldly dichotomy in Ephesians is similar to Paul's use of the spirit and the flesh elsewhere, and the characterization of the two realms as light and darkness in Eph 4 is like the expression in 2 Cor 4.[59] As Lincoln acknowledges, Ephesians maintains a strong distinction between what is received now and what is still to come.[60] The persistence of the old age is alluded to in chapter 1, identified in chapter 2, and becomes the focus from halfway through chapter 4.

The eschatology of Ephesians is a reflection of Paul the expert missionary, as Longenecker and Still describe him, tailoring his message to the peculiarities of the Ephesian region.[61] Ephesus was renowned for its heightened focus on magic, worship, and power,[62] and Paul's eschatological expression in Ephesians directly challenges the claims made by the pagan cults.[63] By describing the eschatological outcome for Christians as neither new nor reactionary but preplanned and prior to all else (Eph 1:4–5), Paul's establishes the superiority of the gospel of Jesus Christ over the Ephesian pantheon.

---

56. Rowland, "Eschatology of the New Testament Church," 67.
57. Markus Barth, *Ephesians*, 115–19.
58. Lincoln, *Ephesians*, xc.
59. Moo, *Theology of Paul*, 511.
60. Lincoln, *Ephesians*, xc.
61. Longenecker and Still, *Thinking Through Paul*, 299.
62. Campbell, *Ephesians*, 15.
63. Campbell, *Ephesians*, 15.

CHRISTOLOGY AND "IN CHRIST"

The Christology of Ephesians, like its eschatology, is more exalted when compared with other Pauline literature. Paul's description of Christ emphasizes those aspects that are of the new age, however Paul does not go beyond what he has written elsewhere. Christ's cosmic lordship (1:20–22) is also found in Phil 2:6-11 and Rom 14:11, and his headship of the church is described in 1 Cor 12:27.

Longenecker and Still's suggestion that it is ecclesiology rather than Christology that drives Ephesians seems to put the cart before the horse because it is the conquering Christ who creates the church.[64] Ephesians 1:3–14 lays out what Christ has achieved for believers here and now and points forward to the more to come. Christ's work for and through the church are understood in that context, and any glory for the church is subsequently redirected back to Christ and God (3:11).

The cosmic Christology of Ephesians is epitomized in 1:10, with everything in heaven and on earth placed under Christ's headship. This exalted Christology is the basis of most if not all of Paul's theology, including his eschatology. Predestination in Christ is an important part of this construct because predestination establishes that Christ has always been the focal point for the Father's actions, and hence Jesus Christ's proper place is at the head of all the church both now and in eternity.

Campbell notes that while union with Christ is prevalent in Paul's letters, it is particularly prominent in Ephesians, being used more frequently and being integrated with every other major theme.[65] In addition to the regular references to in/with/through Christ, Paul makes use of the metaphors of body, temple, building, armor, and marriage to describe the believers' relationship with Christ. At the beginning of the twentieth century Deissmann understood union with Christ in a mystical sense, and subsequently Bultmann attempted to connect it to the Hellenistic mystery religions and Gnosticism.[66] In more recent times, scholars consider a Rabbinic background as being more likely, describing union with Christ as participation in the eschatological reality and an expression of solidarity in the new realm.[67] Dunn categorizes union with Christ as either the benefit of an objective achievement or a subjective experience, and he

---

64. Longenecker and Still, *Thinking Through Paul*, 341.
65. Campbell, *Ephesians*, 21.
66. Dunn, *Theology of Paul*, 390; Markus Barth, *Ephesians*, 69.
67. Cohick, *Ephesians*, 92; Talbert, *Ephesians and Colossians*, 35.

also notes that Paul refers to his own work being done in Christ, suggesting that "in Christ" can also be a context or basis.[68] Campbell uses similar expressions when he describes union with Christ as mutual indwelling, participation in Christ's narrative, and association with Christ's realm, depending on the context.[69] Witherington goes so far as to describe Christ as a divine person who could incorporate others into himself.[70]

Thus, there is general agreement among scholars that the phrase "in Christ" can be used in either a locative or instrumental sense,[71] but given the lack of agreement on any particular use,[72] it is apparent that it is not possible to be certain on how each occurrence should be understood. This is not a major concern, however, because to be in the realm of Christ is to experience all the benefits of that realm and, conversely, experiencing the benefits of Christ puts the believer in Christ's realm. Whichever way a commentator might lean on the interpretation of "in Christ," the other perspective is effectively present as well. It is a matter of emphasis, not strict alternatives.

MYSTERY

Paul's choice of the word "mystery" (μυστήριον) has generated much commentary dating all the way back to the third century AD.[73] It is another concept that rose to prominence in the Second Temple period, being used in the Greek translation of Daniel eight times, and a further ten times in the noncanonical books of the LXX. As such, it is not likely that Paul borrows the term from pagan mystery cults or Gnosticism.[74] Paul is following the Jewish belief that God has plans for the future which have been kept secret, but which will one day be revealed. The expectation was that the revelation of the secret would come through a seer or prophet, and Paul discerned that it had been done through Jesus Christ.[75] Of the twenty-seven occurrences of μυστήριον in the NT, twenty are in

---

68. Dunn, *Theology of Paul*, 398.

69. Campbell, *Ephesians*, 22.

70. Witherington, *Philemon, Colossians, and Ephesians*, 235.

71. Harris, "Appendix: Prepositions and Theology in the Greek New Testament," *NIDNTT* 3:1171–215; BDAG 258–61; Talbert, *Ephesians and Colossians*, 35.

72. Contrast Hoehner, *Ephesians*, 173, and Talbert, *Ephesians and Colossians*, 38.

73. Hoehner, *Ephesians*, 428.

74. Campbell, *Ephesians*, 53.

75. Hoehner, *Ephesians*, 432; Markus Barth, *Ephesians*, 123.

the Pauline corpus and six are in Ephesians (1:9; 3:3, 4, 9; 5:32; 6:19). Paul primarily describes the secret as the inclusion of the gentiles in the people of God through Christ (Rom 11:25; Eph 3:3–6),[76] although other extraordinary aspects of Christ's mission are also referred to in this way (1 Cor 2:7). Describing Christ's mission as a planned event that had been kept secret prior to its enactment makes it comparable to military planning, which was one way the word μυστήριον was used in the LXX.[77] The added certainty of success provided by it being God's plan would make it reasonable to describe Christ's secret mission as predestined. As such, it will be interesting to see whether Paul's use of μυστήριον and προορίζω are interrelated in some way.

GENRE AND STRUCTURE

Aune observes that Paul's dialogical style is quite different from anything found in papyrus letters, so he classifies Ephesians as an epistle, that is, an artistic address that is intended to be public.[78] Lincoln rejects Käsemann's suggestion that Ephesians is a theological tract framed within a basic Pauline greeting and salutation because that does not adequately address the liturgical elements in chapters 1–3, nor the structural similarities with 1 Thessalonians.[79] What is different about Ephesians is the lack of any apparent personal connection between the author and the recipients. Unlike Colossians, which is otherwise very similar in structure, style, and content, Ephesians does not appear to address any obvious pressing issue, nor does it identify any recipients by name, showing a greater interest in the universal church than the local church. Despite this, the epistle is still crafted as if it is to be read aloud in church and it makes Paul present with the hearers.[80] The epistle represents Paul, as the apostle to the gentiles, expressing his understanding of the gospel to the whole church, adapted to reflect the general Ephesian context. Thyen's description of Ephesians as a liturgical homily delivered in letter form is not wide of the mark.[81]

---

76. Dunn, *Theology of Paul*, 526.
77. Finkenrath, "Secret, Mystery," *NIDNTT* 3:502.
78. Aune, *New Testament in Its Literary Environment*, 160.
79. Lincoln, *Ephesians*, xxxvii–xxxviii; Aune, *New Testament in Its Literary Environment*, 192.
80. Seal, "Role of the Letter," 108–9; Heil, *Ephesians*, 2.
81. Lincoln, *Ephesians*, xxxix.

The letter to the Ephesians falls into two parts, with a focus on foundational teaching in chapters 1–3 followed by ethical teaching in chapters 4–6, possibly following the pattern of covenant speech as seen in Deuteronomy.[82] While the two parts are distinct, they are nevertheless tightly integrated, with each part having elements of the other and both sharing common themes. Scholars describe the overarching theme variously as the new Christian identity,[83] the privileges and status in Christ,[84] union with Christ,[85] and unity through love.[86] In Ephesians, Paul describes a new reality created by Christ, which involves a new Jew-gentile church with a renewed ethic.

Within the letter, Eph 1:3–14 is broadly recognized as a distinct literary unit on the basis of both grammar and content. This unit is a continuous exclamation of praise of God that is clearly distinct from the preceding greeting and the following thanksgiving.

The form of Eph 1:3–14 is comparable to an extended blessing or *berakah* as found in the psalms and OT prophetic works (1 Kgs 8:15–21; Ps 144).[87] There are, however, features of Eph 1:3–14 which vary from a *berakah*, such as distinctive Christian titles for God and regular references to Christ, so the unit can also be usefully compared with the other two NT blessings in 2 Cor 1:3–4 and 1 Pet 1:3–12.[88] The Ephesian Blessing (as it will now be called) has no corresponding section in Colossians, however Lincoln notes several ways in which the two epistles share language and ideas.[89] Ephesians 1:3–14 is also referred to as a doxology,[90] although it lacks the brevity and formula of a typical doxology.[91] DeSilva, who insightfully refers to the Blessing as a "Celebration of God's Favor," observes that it does not so much advance an argument as outline a narrative of the Christian experience which the readers are invited to appreciate and live out.[92] It is an invitation for believers to be swept up in the excitement

---

82. Lincoln, *Ephesians*, xl.
83. Talbert, *Ephesians and Colossians*, 14.
84. Lincoln, *Ephesians*, xxxvi.
85. Campbell, *Ephesians*, 21.
86. Hoehner, *Ephesians*, 106.
87. Lincoln, *Ephesians*, 10; Talbert, *Ephesians and Colossians*, 42.
88. Abbott, *Ephesians and Colossians*, xxiv; Cohick, *Ephesians*, 83.
89. Lincoln, *Ephesians*, lii.
90. Campbell, *Ephesians*, 41.
91. Aune, *New Testament in Its Literary Environment*, 193.
92. deSilva, *Ephesians*, 52, 81.

of what God has done for them. This sense of joy is important to retain in the detailed exegesis of the Blessing because the detail is so intriguing that it is easy to lose sight of the wood for the trees.

The style of Eph 1:3-14 is similar to that of the rest of the epistle, except that certain aspects are heightened. The long sentence with its many dependent clauses draws the reader through what can initially feel like a kaleidoscope of ideas, but upon reflection the text paints a rich and profound picture.[93] While it is not a literary masterpiece, it is comparable in style to classical Greek rhetoric and not a monstrous conglomeration as some have suggested.[94] The repetition of key words and the use of multiple epithets have the effect of slowing the reader down, filling out the picture being painted, and encouraging reflection tinged with emotion rather than mere intellectual assent. Van Roon describes Paul's poetic technique well as the "rhyming of thoughts."[95] The similarity of vocabulary and style with the Qumran texts suggest that Paul shares a similar world of thought,[96] but there is sufficient divergence to make dependency unlikely.

There is no scholarly consensus on the structure of Eph 1:3-14. A summary of the options can be found in Hoehner's commentary.[97] Discourse analysis has suggested a breakup of 1:3, 1:4-6 (Father), 1:7-12 (Christ), 1:13-14 (Holy Spirit), with each part focusing not only on a different subject but also on a different temporal aspect of salvation's blessings.[98] Each of these sections concludes with the repetition of εἰς ἔπαινον δόξης (to the praise of his glory) (1:6, 12, 14). While this description looks neat on paper, it does not account for 1:4-6 naming only Christ and not the Father, 1:7-12 having as many pronouns referring back to the Father as there are in 1:4-6, and 1:13-14 referring to both the Father and the Christ more than the Holy Spirit. Furthermore, the subunits are unbalanced, and the multiple themes in 1:7-12 do not naturally form a coherent whole.

From a rhetorical perspective, there is a titular introduction in 1:3, an elaboration of the blessings in Christ in 1:4-8, a discussion of God's preplanning of those blessings in 1:9-13a, concluding with an

---

93. Robinson, *Ephesians*, 19.
94. Robbins "Composition of Eph 1:3-14," 677; Hoehner, *Ephesians*, 153; Witherington, *Philemon, Colossians, and Ephesians*, 230.
95. Lincoln *Ephesians*, xlv.
96. Kuhn, "Ephesians in the light of the Qumran texts," 116-19.
97. Hoehner, *Ephesians*, 160-61.
98. Larkin, *Ephesians*, xxi.

announcement of the certainty of reception of the full blessings in 1:13b–14. It has also been noted that Eph 1:3–14 includes parallelism, with the descriptions of God's blessings in the first half being partially restated from a different perspective in the second half, leading some to identify a chiasm hinged on 1:10.[99] Fitting the Blessing to a rigid chiastic structure, however, sits awkwardly with the content of the text. The Blessing is at best a weak and rough chiasm, and it is more likely that a linear train of thought was influenced by chiastic thinking.

From a grammatical perspective the structure is:

- 1:3—a sentence fragment formed around the implied verb "to be";

- 1:4–13a—a sentence governed by the main verb ἐξελέξατο (choose), under which there are two aorist participle clauses governed by προορίσας (predestine) and γνωρίσας (made known) respectively, each of which supports a series of relative and infinitive clauses;[100] and

- 1:13b–14—a clause governed by the main verb, ἐσφραγίσθητε (sealed).

Taking all of these considerations into account, it would appear that the Blessing does not have a clearly discernible structure, but to assist the exegesis an arrangement has been chosen that balances content, poetic markers, and syntax. Both 1:4–6 and 1:7–8 culminate by marveling at God's wisdom and grace, and each develops a single coherent idea, so these could be regarded as two subsections of an initial stanza. Ephesians 1:9–13a does not have the same strong poetic markers. The repetition of "to the praise of his glory" in 1:12 attracts the eye, but on this occasion the phrase is being used as content rather than a flourish, so it would not appear to be a subsection break. On the basis of content, Eph 1:9–11 can loosely be held together as concerning the revelation of God's plan for Christ, and Eph 1:12–13a is more clearly a single subsection which explores people coming to believe in the gospel. Ephesians 1:13b–14 is a distinct unit grammatically and in content and also finishes with a flourish. On this basis, the proposed structure can be summarized as follows.

---

99. Larkin, *Ephesians*, xxii; Heil, *Ephesians*, 17–19.

100. Hoehner, *Ephesians*, 214; Larkin, *Ephesians*, 11.

1:3	Thesis—The Father blessed us in Christ
1:4–8	Stanza 1—Blessings in Christ
	1:4–6 Christ's predestined acts
	1:7–8 Christ's redemptive acts
1:9–13a	Stanza 2—The secret revealed
	1:9–11 The predestination of Christ's acts
	1:12–13a For Jew and gentile
1:13b–14	Epilogue—The guarantee of redemption

The choice of "predestined" in the subheadings is explained in the detailed exegesis in the next chapter.

8

Exegesis of Ephesians 1:3–14

My translation and exegesis are based on the most recent critical edition of the United Bible Societies' *The Greek New Testament* (UBS[5]). The full translation follows. The detailed exegesis is divided up into convenient subunits, with each headed by the Greek text with translation.

TRANSLATION OF EPHESIANS 1:3–14

3 Blessed is the God and Father of our Lord Jesus Christ,
     who blessed us with every spiritual blessing in the heavenly realms in Christ,
4 because he chose us in him before the foundation of the world,
     to be holy and blameless before him in love,
5 and he predestined us for adoption through Jesus Christ into him,
     according to the good favor of his will,
6 to the praise of the glory of his grace,
     with which he graced us in the Beloved,
7   in whom we have redemption through his blood,
       for the forgiveness of sins, in accordance with the riches of his grace,
8   which he has lavished upon us, with all wisdom and insight.
9 He made known to us the secret of his will according to his good favor,
     which he pre-planned in him,
10   to order all the ages, and bring together everything in Christ,
       both what is in the heavens and what is on the earth in him,

11 in whom even we were apportioned what was predestined,
    in accordance with the plan of him who is doing everything
    according to the resolution of his will,
12 so that we, who first hoped in Christ, are to the praise of his glory,
13 in whom you also heard the word of truth, the gospel of your
    salvation,
    in which even you believed.
  You are sealed by the Holy Spirit of promise,
14 who is the first instalment of our inheritance,
    for the redemption of his possession, to the praise of his glory.

1:3 THESIS STATEMENT—THE FATHER BLESSED US IN CHRIST

The pair of clauses that crown the Blessing are the key to understanding Eph 1:3–14.[1] They form the thesis statement, establishing the framework of Paul's thoughts upon which the remainder of the Blessing is assembled.

> 1:3a Εὐλογητὸς ὁ θεός—Blessed is God . . .

Paul opens with a declaration that God is blessed. The predicate adjective εὐλογητός acts as the verb, in the same way it does in the LXX when used to translate the Hebrew passive participle *berakah*.[2] In this context, "bless" means something like "praise," but like a Jewish *berakah*, the text describes how God's actions bring him praise and glory rather than drawing it from the readers.[3] Instead the readers are invited to marvel at that praise.

> 1:3a Εὐλογητὸς ὁ θεὸς καὶ πατὴρ τοῦ κυρίου ἡμῶν Ἰησοῦ Χριστοῦ—Blessed is the God and Father of our Lord Jesus Christ,

The "article—substantive—καί—substantive" structure indicates that ὁ θεός and πατήρ are the same entity.[4] This makes the Father the God of the Lord Jesus Christ. Normally Paul refers to God generally or addresses the Father and Jesus distinctly, as in the epistle's greeting, but

---

1. Hoehner, *Ephesians*, 98.
2. Larkin, *Ephesians*, 5.
3. Campbell, *Ephesians*, 162; Abbott, *Ephesians and Colossians*, 3.
4. Larkin, *Ephesians*, 6; Hoehner, *Ephesians*, 164.

Paul also refers to the God of Jesus at times.[5] Throughout the NT this tends to occur when Jesus's unity with believers is emphasized, either in suffering or glory,[6] with the latter being the case here.

Paul introduces Jesus with three attributes: "our," "Lord," and "Christ." Believers in Christ are an integral part of this celestial masterpiece, not as actors but on the basis of their allegiance to their Lord. "Christ" evokes the OT Messianic promises, but rather than allude to specific OT texts, the Blessing expounds new revelations concerning the Christ that are grounded in broad scriptural principles.[7] Paul's constant reference to Christ is a reminder to both Jew and gentile that the nations are blessed by the gospel through Israel, a point Paul elaborates on in 2:11–22.

> 1:3b ὁ εὐλογήσας ἡμᾶς ἐν πάσῃ εὐλογίᾳ πνευματικῇ—who blessed us with every spiritual blessing

The action that brings God praise and glory is God's blessing of believers with every spiritual blessing. The aorist participle is translated as the simple past tense in an effort to keep the focus on God as the subject of the action. Using the English perfect tense would introduce an interest in the present effects of the action, and draw attention away from God and onto "us." Paul's focus at this point is on the blesser, not the blessed. Larkin notes Porter's proposed correlation between verb tense/aspect and prominence, but Eph 1:3 is an example of an aorist being used in a prominent position rather than for background material.[8] Larkin notes that Eph 1:3–14 is a known exception to that theory of tense prominence.[9]

Ἡμᾶς (us) would naturally be read as including all of Paul's readers, especially since Paul is the sole sender of the letter (1:1). Later on, Paul singles out a subset of his readers by addressing them as "you" (1:13; 2:11; and through 2:1–10) and distinguishes them from the group Paul is in, which he addresses as "we." It is not likely, however, that "we" and "you" are being used in that vein from the start of the letter. Paul has just referred to "our Lord Jesus Christ," which can only be inclusive of all Christians, and he does not caveat his words in 1:3 as he does in 1:13. As

---

5. Eph 1:17 in particular. Compare also Rom 15:6; 2 Cor 1:3; 11:3. Larkin, *Ephesians*, 6.

6. 1 Pet 1:3; John 20:17; Heb 2:17.

7. Cohick, *Ephesians*, 55–57; Lincoln, "Use of the OT," 49.

8. Larkin, *Ephesians*, xxiii–xxiv; Hoehner, *Ephesians*, 162.

9. Larkin, *Ephesians*, xxiv.

such, "us" in 1:3–14 is taken to be referring to all the holy and faithful in Christ Jesus (1:1), unless it is qualified otherwise.

Ἐν πάσῃ εὐλογίᾳ πνευματικῇ (with every spiritual blessing) is the first of three phrases governed by ἐν. These three phrases can be understood as a whole or as three distinct qualifiers.[10] The former is a more natural reading of the text and is consistent with the Blessing's style of using sequential phrases to build and refine the meaning. Each of the three phrases can also be understood as either locative or instrumental. As stated above, this concern may not be overly significant, as one implies the other, but it is likely that locative is intended on each occasion. The blessings are not external objects but whole of life changes in which one is immersed. My translation follows most in using "with" for the first phrase and "in" for the subsequent two so that it reads easily in English, but even in English "with every spiritual blessing" still has a locative sense because the blessings do not achieve something but are the end in themselves.[11] Hoehner interprets πάσῃ εὐλογίᾳ πνευματικῇ to mean that believers have everything they need for their spiritual wellbeing,[12] and while that is true it does not go far enough. Believers do not just have the spiritual blessings they need. They have *every* spiritual blessing. This shows the extraordinary generosity of God and how incredibly rich believers in Christ are.

1:3c ἐν πάσῃ εὐλογίᾳ πνευματικῇ ἐν τοῖς ἐπουρανίοις—with every spiritual blessing in the heavenly realms

Paul uses ἐν τοῖς ἐπουρανίοις (heavenly realms) five times in Ephesians (1:3, 20; 2:6; 3:10; 6:12) to refer to the spiritual realm where God reigns and deals with other spiritual forces,[13] and in which all people also struggle whether they are aware of it or not.[14] This apocalyptic perspective is typical of Paul generally, and is at the forefront in Ephesians. Käsemann detects a Gnostic influence, but Paul's apocalyptic has much more

---

10. Campbell, *Ephesians*, 42.

11. Hoehner, *Ephesians*, 166; Cohick, *Ephesians*, 83; Lincoln, *Ephesians*, 9; Campbell, *Ephesians*, 41.

12. Hoehner, *Ephesians*, 168, 172.

13. MacDonald, *Colossians and Ephesians*, 199. Paul also uses οὐρανός four times in Ephesians (1:10; 3:15; 4:10; 6:9), but this tends to be more general and has less of an apocalyptic sense.

14. Eph 2:2; 6:12. Gorman, *Apostle of the Crucified Lord*, 506; Robinson, *Ephesians*, 21–22; Witherington, *Philemon, Colossians, and Ephesians*, 232.

in common with Jewish tradition.[15] Moritz compares Paul's perspective with the vision of God enthroned in glory in 1 Enoch, although he notes that Paul has a greater focus on God's grace.[16]

While Paul draws his theology from his Jewish heritage, his emphasis on ἐπουρανίοις in Ephesians suggests that he perceives this to be a particular concern for his readers. Moritz identifies the dominance of the cult of the goddess Artemis in Ephesus and the surrounding region as a significant factor because Artemis was worshiped as savior, lord, and superior to all other powers.[17] Paul's focus on God's work ἐν τοῖς ἐπουρανίοις addresses that front on.

1:3d ἐν Χριστῷ—in Christ

The significance of the phrase ἐν Χριστῷ can lead to commentators examining it in isolation, as is notionally being done here. This risks the error identified by James Barr of failing to appreciate that meaning occurs at the sentence level and not in individual words.[18] Childs cautions that Barr overstates his case because Barr does not fully appreciate the effect of oral tradition,[19] something that may be in play with the phrase ἐν Χριστῷ. Both perspectives need to be considered, with weight placed where the ground is firmer.

Ἐν Χριστῷ is likely to be locative because that is how the phrase is used in both 1:1 and 1:4, and in 1:3 it is grouped with two other phrases that likely have a locative sense. If so, Paul is praising Christ's achievements in the heavenly realms, which have made available every spiritual blessing to believers in Christ (1:22).[20] Alternatively, if Christ is the instrument of God's blessing, that could simply be in the sense of the preaching of the word (1:13), or it could come through mystical union, as Campbell's studies into union with Christ have led him to believe.[21]

The details of the spiritual blessings follow in a series of clauses, but what must not be lost is that the blessings are from the Father, are in the spiritual realm, and are found in Christ. Believers are the beneficiaries of them, but they are not things done to believers. They are things done

---

15. Lincoln, *Ephesians*, 20; Markus Barth, *Ephesians*, 13.
16. Moritz, "'Summing Up All Things,'" 97.
17. Moritz, "'Summing Up All Things,'" 90.
18. Barr, *Semantics of Biblical Language*, 270.
19. Childs, "Semantics of Biblical Language," 376.
20. Larkin, *Ephesians*, 6; Abbott, *Ephesians and Colossians*, 7.
21. Campbell, *Ephesians*, 44.

for them in Christ in the spiritual realm.[22] These prime concepts need to be maintained through the detail of the exegesis to avoid distorting the interpretation.

1:4–8 STANZA 1—BLESSINGS IN CHRIST

1:4–6 Christ's predestined acts

1:4a καθὼς ἐξελέξατο ἡμᾶς ἐν αὐτῷ πρὸ καταβολῆς κόσμου
because he chose us in him before the foundation of the world

The conjunction καθώς (because) is likely being used in the causal sense[23] because it is the details of the blessing that lead to God being blessed. Reading καθώς in the sense of comparison or degree can be ruled out because Paul is describing every spiritual blessing and not comparing one with another or referring to a subset.

The first blessing referred to is the Father's choice of believers in Christ before the foundation of the world. This is the Blessing's main clause, which establishes the primary idea, and the rest of the text expands on this and explores its consequences. The use of the aorist ἐξελέξατο (chose) continues the sense that Paul is considering actions that are complete and set, an impression that is confirmed by the action being located before the foundation of the world. Paul's choice of the middle voice reminds readers that their attention should be on the subject, God. Larkin describes it as a cognitive middle or a thinking within oneself.[24] Καταβολῆς κόσμου (foundation of the world) is a common phrase in the NT, which refers to time since creation when used with ἀπό,[25] and to things before creation when used with πρό.[26]

Paul usually refers to the elect in noun form and only uses the verb ἐκλέγομαι here and in 1 Cor 1:27–28. In the OT, the verb is preferred,[27] which had the effect of emphasizing the subject, God, the object of his

---

22. Aquinas, *Galatians and Ephesians*, 182.
23. BDAG 391.
24. Hoehner, *Ephesians*, 187; Larkin, *Ephesians*, 11, quoting Kremmer.
25. Matt 13:35; 25:34; Luke 11:50; Heb 4:3; 9:26; Rev 13:8; 17:8.
26. John 17:24; Eph 1:4; 1 Pet 1:20.
27. The Hebrew *bāchar*, translated mostly by ἐκλέγομαι in the LXX. Schrenk, *TDNT* "ἐκλέγομαι," 5:145.

choice, and the purpose for which the object was chosen,[28] which is how ἐκλέγομαι functions in Eph 1:4. The sense of those chosen having status and privilege developed late in the Second Temple period,[29] and this may be so to a degree in Paul's writing when he uses the noun form.[30] The use of the verb in 1:4, however, likely indicates that Paul is implying the earlier OT sense, with the emphasis on God and God's purpose for the object chosen.

The expression of the chosen object is unusual and is an innovation by Paul, a point that is missed by most commentators. The object of the choosing is believers in him, with "in him" referring to Christ, because the pronoun is not reflexive and parallels the reference to "in Christ" at the end of 1:3. Nowhere else does Paul describe God choosing people "in Christ,"[31] nor does any other biblical writer, nor is there any comparable expression with respect to election in the pre-NT Jewish literature. The closest comparable text is 1 En. 39:6, which describes an Elect One who will draw together the elect ones, but in that text the parties remain distinct. Many commentators look at the words ἐξελέξατο ἡμᾶς (he chose us) in isolation from ἐν αὐτῷ (in him) and conclude that Paul is referring to God's direct choice of individuals or of Christians collectively,[32] and that "in Christ" is the destination for which believers have been chosen.[33] Other commentators follow Karl Barth in regarding Christ as the object of God's choice, with believers subsequently participating in Christ.[34] Barth's explanation is consistent with the high concentration of references to Christ in the Blessing and the comparable expression in 1 Pet 1:20, but it does not do justice to the almost equally frequent and prominent first-person pronoun in the Blessing. The object of the verb is ἡμᾶς in a particular context, namely ἐν αὐτῷ, and separating these two aspects distorts the meaning.[35] The emphasis in the phrase ἡμᾶς ἐν αὐτῷ is on

---

28. Hoehner, *Ephesians*, 186.

29. Pannenberg, *Human Nature*, 54.

30. 1 Thess 1:4; Rom 8:33; 9:11; 11:5, 7, 28. Coenen, "ἐκλέγομαι," *NIDNTT* 1:540.

31. In Rom 16:13, it is the elect Rufus himself who is located in Christ, rather than God's act of choosing.

32. Calvin, *Galatians and Ephesians*, 197; Campbell, *Ephesians*, 45; Hoehner, *Ephesians*, 176; Whiteley, *Theology of St Paul*, 94.

33. Calvin, *Galatians and Ephesians*, 198.

34. Barth, *Church Dogmatics*, 2.2:3; Karl Barth, *Ephesians*, 96.

35. Witherington, *Philemon, Colossians, and Ephesians*, 233; pace deSilva, *Ephesians*, 60.

Christ because that is where Paul placed the spotlight in 1:3, and because the Father's achievements in Christ are of prime interest throughout the Blessing.[36] Paul is describing what God decided to achieve in Christ for the people of God.[37] This understanding aligns with the principles established in 1:3 and compares favorably with 1 Pet 1:20, which makes the same point as Eph 1:4 but without any direct reference to believers.

A review of Coenen's and Schrenk's respective articles on election shows that Eph 1:4 is also the first time that the divine choice of the people of God is located before the foundation of the world.[38] Paul is not writing of election in the normal sense, which otherwise is always of people who exist (taking conception as the beginning of existence).[39] Instead Paul is writing of what God decided prior to creation to achieve "in Christ" for future believers who are now present in the text. Paul in 1:4 is not writing of God's choice of specific believers, whether individual or corporate, but for Christ to be the one in whom believers would one day be and now are. This understanding is consistent with the two other occasions in which πρό is used with καταβολῆς κόσμου (John 17:24; 1 Pet 1:20),[40] both of which concern the Father's interaction with Jesus Christ. How believers come to enjoy what the Father has predetermined would be available for them in Christ is made clear at the end of the Blessing (1:12–13).[41]

Ephesians 1:4 has been used historically to inform the understanding of Rom 9, but Paul's expression here is atypical for him and is unique in its construct, strongly indicating that he has a specific objective for his Ephesian audience. I suggest that Paul's use of ἐκλέγομαι here is not to expand or redefine the concept of election coming from the OT, but to introduce a new idea that becomes explicit from 1:5.

> 1:4b εἶναι ἡμᾶς ἁγίους καὶ ἀμώμους κατενώπιον αὐτοῦ ἐν ἀγάπῃ—to be holy and blameless before him in love,

---

36. MacDonald, "Biblical Doctrine of Election," 222.

37. Pannenberg, *Systematic Theology*, 3:437; Lincoln, *Ephesians*, 23; Witherington, *Philemon, Colossians, Ephesians*, 234.

38. Coenen, "ἐκλέγομαι," *NIDNTT* 1:536–43; Schrenk, "ἐκλέγομαι," *TDNT* 5:174–75. Schrenk notes that subsequent Rabbinic literature does refer to God contemplating Israel prior to creation.

39. Hoehner, *Ephesians*, 187.

40. Compare also 1 Cor 2:7 and 2 Tim 1:9, which have similar expressions using αἰώνων. Trinidad, "Mystery Hidden in God," 7.

41. Pannenberg, *Systematic Theology*, 3:454; Witherington, *Problem with Evangelical Theology*, 62.

Following the OT pattern of election being for a purpose, an infinitive purpose clause describes God's intent for the elect in Christ, which is for believers to be holy and blameless before him in love. Paul's shift to the present tense indicates he has moved his attention from the preconceived election to its present realization. Ἅγιος (holy) is Paul's default term for believers (1:1, 15, 18; 2:19; 3:8, 18; 4:12; 6:18). Holiness means to be dedicated to God. Although it had implications for behavior (5:3), there are not degrees of holiness based on that behavior. Holiness is not achieved by merit, but by the application of Christ's sacrifice (5:27; Col 1:22). Ἄμωμος (blameless) is a cultic term,[42] referring to the purity of the sacrifice (Heb 9:14; 1 Pet 1:19), and in both Eph 5:27 and Col 1:22, it is something achieved for believers by Christ. Ἄμωμος is also used once by Paul in a behavioral sense (Phil 2:15), and it is a common theme in the NT that being made holy must lead to holy living (Eph 4:1; 1 Pet 1:15; Jas 2:17), but that is not on view here contrary to Lincoln and others.[43] The way in which ἅγιος and ἄμωμος are paired in Eph 5:27 and Col 1:22 strongly suggests that they should be read the same way in 1:4. Paul's argument is that it was always God's intent that people would stand before him in Christ's purity.[44]

"Before him" refers to God the Father rather than to Christ because believers are already referred to as being in Christ. Some suggest that this is the end of the thought and that ἐν ἀγάπῃ (in love) belongs to προορίσας (he predestined) in 1:5.[45] While there may be comparable examples of such a structure, it is at odds with the normal rhythm of the Blessing, which typically completes each thought with multiple prepositional phrases, often ending with "in" something, and is also not reflective of Ephesians generally, which consistently uses "in love" to complete rather than commence thoughts.[46] Retaining ἐν ἀγάπῃ (in love) with κατενώπιον αὐτοῦ (before him) softens a phrase that might otherwise evoke a sense of judgment. To enable believers to stand before God in Christ's holiness and blamelessness is truly an act of love.

1:5a προορίσας—he predestined

---

42. Abbott, *Ephesians and Colossians*, 7; Markus Barth, *Ephesians*, 113.
43. Lincoln, *Ephesians*, 24; Gorman, *Apostle of the Crucified Lord*, 506.
44. Chrysostom, *Hom. Eph.* 1 (*NPNF*[1] 13:116).
45. E.g., Cohick, *Ephesians*, 98.
46. Eph 3:17; 4:2, 15, 16; 5:2. Robinson, *Ephesians*, 27.

What seems to be missed by commentators is that predestination is a NT innovation. Προορίζω is not found in the LXX and is rarely used in classical literature. Claimed examples of predestination in Second Temple literature use different vocabulary and present concepts akin to election in Romans 9 rather than a pre-creation plan.[47] Προορίζω appears six times in the NT, two times clearly referring to God's plans for Jesus Christ (Acts 4:28; 1 Cor 2:7), another two times where the focus is on Christ's work for believers (Rom 8:29, 30), and twice in Ephesians (1:5, 11), again referring to Christ's work for believers.[48] The meaning of predestination has some overlap with that of election, such as the sense of purpose, but there are differences as well because other than for Jesus Christ, election consistently occurs within human history (other than as used in Eph 1:4).[49]

Jacobs and Krienke reason that the NT authors also used words related to predestination, such as "foreknowledge" and "providence," in a similar way.[50] The NT authors avoid the Greek philosophical sense of providence and fate either by using the words differently or by choosing different words to convey their ideas. The NT does share some common terminology with Second Temple literature, but whereas the latter had a strong sense of God being in control, only the NT authors perceive that God had a predetermined plan from the beginning.

1:5a προορίσας ἡμᾶς εἰς υἱοθεσίαν διὰ Ἰησοῦ Χριστοῦ εἰς αὐτόν—and he predestined us for adoption through Jesus Christ into him,

Paul returns to the aorist tense with προορίσας (predestined) to consider what has already been done. The connection of the participle προορίσας with the main verb ἐξελέξατο (chose) is variously suggested to be one of time, manner, means, or cause.[51] Because the two terms uniquely appear together here, it is proposed that the word "election" is being used to introduce the new concept of predestination, making the clauses complementary rather than sequential, and the relationship one

---

47. Talbert, *Ephesians and Colossians*, 45; Best, *Ephesians*, 124.
48. Jacobs and Krienke, "προορίζω," *NIDNTT* 1:695.
49. Hoehner, *Ephesians*, 193.
50. Jacobs and Krienke, "Foreknowledge, Providence, Predestination," *NIDNTT* 692–97.
51. Hoehner, *Ephesians*, 194.

of manner.[52] This is not needless duplication, as Hoehner suggests,[53] but a helpful way to introduce the new concept of predestination to readers.

As with election in Eph 1:4, what is predestined must be understood as a whole and in the context of the principle laid out in 1:3, that the blessings are from the Father, are located in Christ, are for believers, and not done directly to them. On this basis, what is predestined is that believers would be adopted through Jesus Christ into God's family.[54] Seen in context, predestination is not predetermining an individual's choice but predetermining what would be available for believers through Christ as the instrument of the Father's will.[55]

This interpretation aligns with how προορίζω is used elsewhere in the NT to declare that God's actions in Jesus Christ were not a reaction to what had happened in Israel but the divine plan all along. It is also consistent with Paul's epistles more generally, where the same concept is often expressed in other words. It is hinted at in Galatians, when Paul writes that God sent his Son ὅτε δὲ ἦλθεν τὸ πλήρωμα τοῦ χρόνου (in the fullness of time) (Gal 4:4; cf. Eph 1:10). First Corinthians is more explicit in its reference to God's secret wisdom which God predestined before the ages for our glory (ἣν προώρισεν ὁ θεὸς πρὸ τῶν αἰώνων εἰς δόξαν ἡμῶν) (1 Cor 2:7; cf. Eph 1:4, 5, 9). In Romans, Paul is concerned to anchor his argument within the timescale of Scripture, but there is still a thread of fore-planning (Rom 1:1–4) and an allusion to a long-intended plan (Rom 3:21, 25, 31), leading to God's predestined plan in Christ for foreknown believers being explicitly announced (Rom 8:28–29). Colossians and Ephesians are both more explicit about God's atemporal plans. The description of Christ as πρωτότοκος πάσης κτίσεως (the firstborn over all creation) (Col 1:15) sets up the expectation that God's plans have always been centered around Christ, which is what Paul goes on to explain (Col 1:15–20; cf. Eph 1:10, 22), later declaring it a secret that has been revealed (Col 1:26; 2:3). In Ephesians, in addition to 1:3–14, Paul writes of God's secret eternal purpose which was kept hidden but is now revealed through the preaching of Paul and its realization in the church (Eph 3:9–11). Paul even includes this theme in his pastoral letters, writing that πρὸ χρόνων αἰωνίων (before the beginning of time) God planned in Christ Jesus to save and call believers (2 Tim 1:9; cf. Eph 1:10), and

---

52. Campbell, *Ephesians*, 47.
53. Hoehner, *Ephesians*, 194.
54. Cohick, *Ephesians*, 97.
55. Thornhill, *Chosen People*, 219.

promised the hope of eternal life (Titus 1:2; cf. Eph 1:13). While God's predetermined plan revealed in Christ is not the main theme even in those Pauline epistles in which it appears, it occurs consistently enough and early enough for it to be regarded as core to Paul's theology, and προορίζω (predestine) is one of the words Paul used to describe it. These words and concepts are an innovation of the NT because it was only once God's plans were revealed in Jesus Christ that it became apparent that this was God's plan all along. It is also why Paul normally does not use election in this context (Eph 1:4 being the only exception) because in Jewish literature election had been used to refer to the choice of people in human history.

The reference to adoption is another NT innovation and is specific to Paul (also found in Rom 8:15, 23; 9:4; Gal 4:5).[56] It is not merely a metaphor for salvation as Larkin suggests,[57] but also includes participation in God's family and all that goes with that (e.g., Eph 3:14–21). The full background for Paul's thoughts in this regard is uncertain. The OT and Second Temple literature referred to God's people as sons,[58] but υἱοθεσία (adoption) does not appear in the LXX.[59] The OT focused on actual descendants, with adoption being rare among Jews.[60] Some scholars link Eph 1:5 to Ps 2:7, which does have a sense of adoption even if the specific word is not present.[61] Alternately Paul's expression may have been influenced by Roman law and practice.[62] Whichever the case, in Eph 1:5 Paul is peering back into God's decision-making pre-creation and sees that it was determined that Christ, the Son of the Father (1:3), would be the means through which all believers, Jews and gentiles, would be adopted into God's family (cf. Rom 3:25; 8:29). Εἰς αὐτόν (into him) is understood to be referring to the Father because it is the Father's family that is being joined.

> 1:5b κατὰ τὴν εὐδοκίαν τοῦ θελήματος αὐτοῦ—according to the good favor of his will,

---

56. Hoehner, *Ephesians*, 194.
57. Larkin, *Ephesians*, 8.
58. Thielman, *Ephesians*, 51; Gorman, *Apostle of the Crucified Lord*, 507.
59. Braumann, "υἱός," *NIDNTT* 2:287.
60. Cohick, *Ephesians*, 98.
61. Allen, "Old Testament Background," 108.
62. Hoehner, *Ephesians*, 196.

Predestination of the adoption of believers through Christ was all done according to the good favor of God's will, an expression also used by other NT authors (e.g., Matt 11:26; Phil 1:15), which underlines the purposeful kindness of God (cf. Eph 1:9). The repeated reference to God's will in the Blessing is a reminder that God planned these events. Εὐδοκίαν is taken to describe God's disposition towards people rather than God's character, so it is translated as "good favor" rather than "good will."[63] This is a synonym for grace in this context, one of the major themes of the Blessing.

1:6a εἰς ἔπαινον δόξης τῆς χάριτος αὐτοῦ—to the praise of the glory of his grace

The ultimate effect of the Father's work in Christ is to the praise of the glory of his grace, echoing the introduction to the Blessing (1:3). Paul's attention is on God, which is reflected in the interpretation thus far. Αὐτοῦ is taken to refer to the Father because it parallels the final phrase in 1:5 and is consistent with the Father being the ultimate focus of the Blessing (1:3). Χάριτος could be an attributive genitive,[64] but the translation has followed Hoehner in treating it as a genitive of quality, as this better aligns with the comparable phrases in 1:12, 14 where God's glory is also praised. Paul's characterization of God's gift as being nonreciprocal and for the unworthy is contrasted by Cohick with Roman gift-giving which was strategic in nature with an expectation of a return.[65]

1:6b ἧς ἐχαρίτωσεν ἡμᾶς ἐν τῷ ἠγαπημένῳ,
with which he graced us in the Beloved,

As in 1:3, Paul concludes the subunit by extolling Christ. The relative pronoun is likely genitive by attraction to χάριτος (grace),[66] which has also probably influenced the selection of the verb ἐχαρίτωσεν (graced). While Chrysostom understood ἐχαρίτωσεν as an adornment and clothing of the soul,[67] Hoehner argues that it is better understood as a granting of favor, given the context refers to specific gifts (1:4, 5).[68] This perspective is

---

63. BDAG 404.
64. Larkin, *Ephesians*, 9.
65. Cohick, *Ephesians*, 100.
66. Larkin, *Ephesians*, 9.
67. Chrysostom, *Hom. Eph.* 1 (*NPNF*[1] 13:118).
68. Hoehner, *Ephesians*, 202.

supported by continued use of the aorist tense, which points to it referring to Christ's completed earthly ministry rather than a present experience.

Paul then switches to the perfect tense to identify the one who was, is, and always will be the Beloved. The Beloved must be Jesus Christ, since Paul goes on in 1:7 to refer to the redemption through his blood. The Western tradition[69] includes υἱῷ αὐτοῦ (his son) after τῷ ἠγαπημένῳ (the Beloved), possibly as an explanatory note to this effect or to reflect the poetry of the passage.[70] "The Beloved" is likely derived from the OT designation of Israel as God's beloved people (e.g., Isa 5:1, 7), but Paul has refocused this on Christ in the same manner that the early Christian tradition referred to Jesus as ὁ υἱός μου ὁ ἀγαπητός (my beloved Son) (Mark 1:11; 9:7; 12:6).[71] The loving service of Jesus Christ is the epitome of the Father's grace.

The thesis statement of the Blessing established the principle that Paul is concerned with the Father's desire to bless believers in Christ in the spiritual realm. It was not about what would be done to believers, but what would be done for them in Christ. Both election and predestination are used in that vein in 1:4–6, referring to God's predetermined plan for bringing people before him in Christ.[72] That plan was that people would not stand before him by themselves but in the holiness and purity of Christ and that they would not be born into privilege but graciously adopted. Paul draws on aspects of the earlier OT concept of election to introduce this novel NT teaching of predestination, but it is not Paul's intent to do the reverse and redefine election. Predestination is developed as a concept distinct from Paul's references to the elect elsewhere, and Eph 1:4 should not be read back into those texts. Instead, Paul invites his readers to marvel with him at God's rich blessing of them.

1:7–8 Christ's Redemptive Acts

> 1:7a ἐν ᾧ ἔχομεν τὴν ἀπολύτρωσιν διὰ τοῦ αἵματος αὐτοῦ, τὴν ἄφεσιν τῶν παραπτωμάτων—in whom we have redemption through his blood, for the forgiveness of sins,

---

69. Unicals D*, F, G, and Old Latin. See UBS⁵ apparatus.
70. Larkin, *Ephesians*, 9.
71. Lincoln, *Ephesians*, 26; Robinson, *Ephesians*, 233.
72. Trinidad, "Mystery Hidden in God," 12.

Paul changes tense to the present because he is shifting from what Christ achieved in the past to what believers have now. It could be that ἐν ᾧ ἔχομεν (in whom we have) is an expression of the mystical union believers have with Christ, or it is a statement of their objective standing before God.

Redemption, while not a common term, would have been one that resonated with both Jew (from Egypt) and gentile (from slavery). God is often referred to as the Redeemer of Israel in the OT, and the reference to blood also suggests that the Passover may be informing Paul's thoughts.[73] Lincoln follows Dodd in arguing that redemption does not imply a payment, with the term sometimes used in biblical and related literature only with a sense of release from difficulty.[74] Hoehner responds that the NT regularly refers to a payment being made, and he contends that the following reference to blood with its cultic overtones points strongly in that direction.[75] Jesus himself was not averse to using payment language at times (Mark 10:45). Nevertheless, while the text raises the suggestion of a sacrificial payment, it ultimately leaves it hanging because the focus is on the benefit for believers rather than the details of the divine transaction.

Redemption is further explained by the appositional phrase "the forgiveness of sins." In the LXX, ἄφεσις (forgiveness) is used with a strong sense of release and liberty, which complements redemption well. Forgiveness of sins is a hallmark of Jesus's preaching of the gospel, and Paul follows suit by encouraging Christians to continue to hold their forgiveness as central to their faith.[76] The blood shed by Christ liberates believers in Christ from the consequences of their sins.

> 1:7b κατὰ τὸ πλοῦτος τῆς χάριτος αὐτοῦ—in accordance with the riches of his grace,

Having described the blessing of redemption, Paul adorns it with another flourish, which underlines both the generosity of God and how blessed believers are as a consequence.

> 1:8 ἧς ἐπερίσσευσεν εἰς ἡμᾶς, ἐν πάσῃ σοφίᾳ καὶ φρονήσει—
> which he has lavished upon us, with all wisdom and insight.

---

73. Robinson, *Ephesians*, 29.
74. Lincoln, *Ephesians*, 28.
75. Hoehner, *Ephesians*, 205, 207.
76. Lamerson, "Forgiveness," 325–27.

The grace is not only immensely valuable, but it was given with unstinting generosity. As in 1:7, the relative pronoun agrees with grace (genitive by attraction), further emphasizing grace as a key theme of the Blessing. God's blessings cannot be grasped at or pursued by humans. They come solely from God's good heart and mind, and the selection of another effusive verb such as ἐπερίσσευσεν (lavished) emphasizes the overwhelming nature of it. Ἐπερίσσευσεν is a return to the aorist, paralleling ἐχαρίτωσεν in 1:6, which suggests that the completed ministry of the Beloved is in mind, although Paul still locates the end purpose of that ministry εἰς ἡμᾶς (upon us), so it has been translated with the English perfect tense. As Campbell notes, while the perfective aspect of the aorist is usually employed to refer to past completed actions, when markers such as εἰς ἡμᾶς indicate a present event is in mind, the aorist can still be used where the author wants to consider the action as a whole.[77]

The inclusion of θελήματος (will) (1:5) and σοφίᾳ καὶ φρονήσει (wisdom and insight) (1:8) make it clear that God's grace is based on deliberate decisions and not capricious behavior, which aligns with the theme of predestination. The return of the word "πάσῃ" (all) links 1:8 back to 1:3, signifying that this is the completion of Paul's reflection on the content of the blessings. This weighs against Cohick's argument that the prepositional phrase belongs to 1:9.[78]

What God planned before creation and lavishly enacted in the ministry of Christ is now experienced by believers. The death of Christ provides redemption for believers and forgiveness from their sins. In the previous subunit, Paul established that this was God's plan all along, and he continues to emphasize this theme by referring to the wisdom and insight of God that lay behind Christ's redemptive act. As much as grace is a major theme of the Blessing, so too is the wisdom of God's plan.

1:9–13A   STANZA 2—THE SECRET REVEALED

1:9–11 The predestination of Christ's acts

> 1:9a γνωρίσας ἡμῖν τὸ μυστήριον τοῦ θελήματος αὐτοῦ, κατὰ τὴν εὐδοκίαν αὐτοῦ—He made known to us the secret of his will according to his good favor,

---

77. Campbell, *Ephesians*, 90; Young, *Intermediate New Testament Greek*, 122.
78. Cohick, *Ephesians*, 105.

Having twice lauded the mind of God in the previous stanza (1:5, 8), in this stanza Paul looks more closely at the nature of the divine will. The aorist tense of γνωρίσας (made known) conveys that the revelation is complete. To reflect this, the translation begins a new sentence using the simple past tense. The pronoun ἡμῖν (us) identifies believers as the recipients of the revelation.

Μυστήριον is translated as "secret" because, while the revealed secret is surprising, it is meant to be clearly understood and not remain mysterious.[79] Lincoln suggests that Paul's thoughts are influenced by the mystery cults of the Greco-Roman world,[80] however, if so, it is more by contrast than comparison because the revelations of those cults remained mysterious.[81] There is a stronger link with Second Temple literature, which had an expectation that God's secrets would be revealed through a prophet, although for Paul there is only one secret and that is the revelation of Jesus Christ.[82] The content of the secret is contained in the following relative clauses in 1:9b–11, although the repetition of θελήματος (will) and εὐδοκίαν (good favor) from 1:5 indicates that the first part of the Blessing is also in mind. The content of 1:4–5 is the things that God knew from the beginning but which he had not disclosed to people until Paul's day, so they were by definition part of God's secret prior to Christ. As such, it is proposed that προορίζω (predestine) and μυστήριον (secret) are used for the same purpose in Ephesians, with the former emphasizing God's determination and the latter emphasizing the hiddenness of that preplanning until it was revealed in Christ.[83] These were things neither anticipated nor understood by God's people prior to and even during Jesus Christ's earthly ministry (cf. 1 Pet 1:10–12). Paul's following words confirm this understanding.

1:9b ἣν προέθετο ἐν αὐτῷ—which he pre-planned in him,

Ἣν agrees with εὐδοκίαν. God preplanned his good favor. Προέθετο is translated "pre-planned" to better represent the contextual connection with predestination in 1:4–5 and 1:11. Προέθετο also carries with it a

---

79. Markus Barth, *Ephesians*, 124; Campbell, *Ephesians*, 53; Robinson, *Ephesians*, 240.

80. Lincoln, *Ephesians*, 30. For a discussion of the translation options and the preference for "secret," see BDAG 661–62; Abbott, *Ephesians and Colossians*, 15.

81. Keesmaat, "Colossians and Ephesians," 137.

82. MacDonald, *Colossians and Ephesians*, 201; Talbert, *Ephesians and Colossians*, 47.

83. Whiteley, *Theology of St Paul*, 95.

sense of plans to be revealed,[84] which makes it an appropriate choice in this context. The aorist indicates that the planning is viewed as done and not in progress. Ἐν αὐτῷ (in him) is taken to refer to Christ because the pronoun is not reflexive. Ἐν αὐτῷ is in parallel with 1:10 where Christ is also likely the referent, and this matches the model of 1:3–4 of things being done in Christ.

> 1:10a εἰς οἰκονομίαν τοῦ πληρώματος τῶν καιρῶν—to order all the ages,

Εἰς οἰκονομίαν (to order) is difficult to translate. It is likely introducing a purpose clause,[85] with οἰκονομίαν referring to the administration or management of a household. Interestingly οἰκονομίαν is used in contemporary literature with respect to inheritance and adoption.[86] Οἰκονομίαν could be understood as a noun (plan) or more likely an activity (ordering).[87]

The Father's ordering in Christ is applied to τοῦ πληρώματος τῶν καιρῶν (all the ages). This and Gal 4:4 are the first time this phrase appears in Greek literature, although it can also be favorably compared with Mark 1:14. Ephesians 1:10 is the only reference that has "time" in the plural.[88] Translating this as "the fullness of time" or similar might suggest that Paul is concerned with when the order will occur,[89] but Lincoln argues that the apocalyptic background of the text suggests Paul is referring to where the order is applied,[90] and the plural καιρῶν likewise suggests Paul has the totality of history in mind.[91] This is consistent with the thrust of 1:10, that God acted on all things in Christ. Barth favorably compares Paul's words to the idea within Second Temple apocalyptic writing of consecutive periods of history being crowned and completed by an era that surpassed them all.[92]

---

84. BDAG 889.
85. Hoehner, *Ephesians*, 216.
86. Kim, "God's Household Management," 389, 409.
87. Markus Barth, *Ephesians*, 86.
88. Rambiert-Kwaśniewska, "Paul's 'Fullness of Time' (Gal 4:4) and 'Fullness of Times' (Eph 1:10)," 199.
89. Campbell, *Ephesians*, 54.
90. Lincoln, *Ephesians*, 32; Hoehner, *Ephesians*, 219; Thielman, *Ephesians*, 64.
91. Rambiert-Kwaśniewska, "Paul's 'Fullness of Time' (Gal 4:4) and 'Fullness of Times' (Eph 1:10)," 216.
92. Markus Barth, *Ephesians*, 128.

1:10b ἀνακεφαλαιώσασθαι τὰ πάντα ἐν τῷ Χριστῷ, τὰ ἐπὶ τοῖς οὐρανοῖς καὶ τὰ ἐπὶ τῆς γῆς ἐν αὐτῷ—and bring together everything in Christ, what is in the heavens and what is on the earth, in him,

Typical of the Blessing, Paul repeats and expands on the previous idea, this time with a participle clause. Paul declares that the Father brought all of creation together in Christ, both heavens and earth, spiritual and material. Paul again chooses the aorist middle to convey that the action is complete and that the attention is on the subject.

The scope of God's plan is more than astronomical. It is also not merely to help people's standing before him, nor just for the church as Whiteley argues.[93] It brings together the earthly and the heavenly in Christ. "Heavens and earth" is a way of referring to all of creation (Gen 1:1), but in Ephesians it also includes the spiritual realm where God resides (3:15; 6:9).[94] Without Christ, things on earth follow their fleshly desires, encouraged by a sympathetic spirit (2:1–3). They are dislocated from God and under God's wrath. The Father undid that in Christ. Hoehner considers the timing of this event, and prefers the future messianic age,[95] but the use of the aorist points to it already being complete, suggesting that Paul has in mind Jesus's death (1:7), resurrection (1:20), and glory (1:20–22). Paul's line of thought is an expression of realized eschatology. The lack of any reference to judgment in Paul's words does not imply universal salvation because the focus here is on what Christ achieved, not on how people participate in it. Paul will go on to make clear that the benefits in Christ need to be accessed through faith.

1:11a ἐν ᾧ καὶ ἐκληρώθημεν προορισθέντες—in whom even we were apportioned what was predestined,

From this point, Paul begins to descend from the climax by restriking some key notes of the Blessing. Having painted the big picture of Jesus Christ's mission for the universe and beyond, Paul turns to the benefits for believers. "In whom" refers to Christ and could be incorporative union, or a simple locative. Paul switches to the passive voice for ἐκληρώθημεν (were apportioned) because "we," the recipients, now take prime focus rather that the giver, God. Καί is used three times in three verses (1:11–13) to create a sense of surprised excitement at our

---

93. Whiteley, *Theology of St Paul*, 95.

94. Yates, "Principalities and Power," 521.

95. Hoehner, *Ephesians*, 224.

inclusion. Ἐκληρώθημεν is a rare word and difficult to translate. In the active voice it means to appoint by lot, and so in the passive can mean to receive what was apportioned.[96] The immediate context explains what was allocated, and it is not necessary to import the idea of inheritance.[97] What was apportioned is what was predestined (also in the passive), which was stated in 1:5 to be adoption into God's family through Christ. The return of the verb προορίζω reinforces that God's pretemporal plan for believers in Christ is a consistent theme throughout the Blessing.

> 1:11b κατὰ πρόθεσιν τοῦ τὰ πάντα ἐνεργοῦντος κατὰ τὴν βουλὴν τοῦ θελήματος αὐτοῦ—in accordance with the plan of him who is doing everything according to the resolution of his will

The next clause uses the noun form of προέθετο (plan) from 1:9 to further reinforce that predestination is about God's plans. Paul's selection of the present tense for the participle ἐνεργοῦντος (doing) echoes the use of ἔχομεν in 1:8, reminding the reader that God is now enacting those pretemporal plans. θελήματος (will) is used for the third time in the Blessing, this time adorned with βουλή (resolution), which introduces the sense of deliberation. The essence of Paul's argument is that God thought about how to bless people, planned it, enacted that plan in the ministry of Jesus Christ, and is purposefully applying those blessings to believers in Christ. This work in Christ was not plan B, or responsive to events on earth. It was the plan all along.[98]

1:12–13a For Jew and Gentile

> 1:12 εἰς τὸ εἶναι ἡμᾶς εἰς ἔπαινον δόξης αὐτοῦ, τοὺς προηλπικότας ἐν τῷ Χριστῷ—so that we, who first hoped in Christ, are to the praise of his glory,

Paul uses the present tense for εἶναι (are) (cf. 1:4) to indicate his mind is on the present effect on believers. Εἰς τὸ εἶναι introduces a purpose clause, meaning the consequence of putting one's hope in Christ is the

---

96. Abbott rejects Bauer's extension of this to "inheritance." Abbott, *Ephesians and Colossians*, 20; BDAG 548.

97. Lemmer, "Reciprocity Between Eschatology and Pneuma," 171; *pace* López, "Study of Pauline Passages," 449.

98. deSilva, *Ephesians*, 59; Gorman, *Apostle of the Crucified Lord*, 506.

praise of God's glory (cf. 1:3). It is a reminder to believers not to be self-focused, but God-focused.

Paul changes tense to the perfect with προηλπικότας (who first hoped) to describe how some have entered this new state with God by having already placed their hope in Christ (locative).[99] At this point Paul starts to distinguish two groups in the text: those who have been Christian for some time (1:12) and those who have recently heard and believed the gospel (1:13). The stated distinction is only one of time in the faith here, although 2:11 distinguishes Jews and gentiles using a similar expression, so that is probably what is intended in 1:12–13. While it is not explicit, it would be natural for gentiles to hear it that way and newly believing Jews would also naturally feel affinity with those Jews who first believed.

> 1:13a ἐν ᾧ καὶ ὑμεῖς ἀκούσαντες τὸν λόγον τῆς ἀληθείας, τὸ εὐαγγέλιον τῆς σωτηρίας ὑμῶν, ἐν ᾧ καὶ πιστεύσαντες—in whom you also heard the word of truth, the gospel of your salvation, in which even you believed.

Paul now addresses recent converts/gentiles by switching to ὑμεῖς (you). It is tempting to consider ἐν ᾧ (in whom) as referring to incorporative union, but it is probably only meant in a general locative sense given how the verse ends. Paul refers to the gentiles hearing the word of truth, a common phrase in the NT for evangelism,[100] and Paul makes that explicit in the following words, τὸ εὐαγγέλιον τῆς σωτηρίας ὑμῶν (the gospel of your salvation). The double use of ἐν ᾧ καί . . . ἐν ᾧ καί ties the hearing and believing together. The use of the aorist tense expresses Paul's confidence in the fullness of their Christian conversion.

1:13b–14 Epilogue—The Guarantee of Redemption

> 1:13b ἐσφραγίσθητε τῷ πνεύματι τῆς ἐπαγγελίας τῷ ἁγίῳ—
> You are sealed by the Holy Spirit of promise,

Ἐσφραγίσθητε (sealed) is a main verb that is not in a subordinate-clause construction. Lincoln argues that it is coincident with the preceding clause,[101] but the content of this clause connects better with the follow-

---

99. Lincoln, *Ephesians*, 37. Lincoln counsels against over emphasizing the prefix πρό in προελπίζω.

100. Lincoln, *Ephesians*, 38.

101. Lincoln, *Ephesians*, 39.

ing verse, so I have taken it to be the introduction to the epilogue of the Blessing. God is the implied agent. Marking possessions with a seal was a common practice at the time, and Paul uses that image to convey God's interest in those who have faith in Christ.[102] The verb is aorist, painting the picture of a completed action. The language of "inheritance," "redemption," and "possession" in the surrounding verses may also indicate that Paul is suggesting that being filled by the Holy Spirit replaces the seal of circumcision.[103] The placement of the genitive τῆς ἐπαγγελίας (promise) between the noun and its adjective is unusual and raises the question as to whether the Holy Spirit was promised, or the Holy Spirit brings believers to what was promised.[104] Since the following relative clause focuses on the gift of the Spirit, it is probably the former.

> 1:14a ὅ ἐστιν ἀρραβὼν τῆς κληρονομίας ἡμῶν—who is the first instalment of our inheritance,

The relative pronoun refers back to the Spirit, who is (present tense) the first installment of our inheritance. Ἡμῶν (our) is not qualified, so Paul has probably reverted to referring to the common experience of all Christians. This is the first hint of unrealized eschatology in Ephesians. Believers do not yet have it all. Great things have been achieved for them in Christ, but there is still more to come. This is the already/not-yet eschatological tension typical of Paul. Nevertheless, the reception of the Spirit is a key part of the eschatology already realized by being both the means by which the promised spiritual blessings are brought to effect in believers in Christ and also a key part of that eschatological experience.[105]

> 1:14b εἰς ἀπολύτρωσιν τῆς περιποιήσεως, εἰς ἔπαινον τῆς δόξης αὐτοῦ—for the redemption of his possession to the praise of his glory.

The purpose of God marking believers with his seal (1:13) is "for the redemption of his possession." Paul previously used "redemption" for the forgiveness of sins, and now he uses it to refer to the future act of God to bring believers into the full inheritance. There is no pronoun to identify the owner of the possession, but given the seal metaphor in 1:13, it would seem clear that God has claimed possession of each believer (cf. Mal 3:17;

---

102. Cohick, *Ephesians*, 110; Lincoln, *Ephesians*, 39.
103. Ferde, "'Sealed' with the Holy Spirit," 576.
104. Campbell, *Ephesians*, 59.
105. Lemmer, "Reciprocity Between Eschatology and Pneuma," 177.

1 Pet 2:9). The Blessing finishes with a typical *berakah* phrase.[106] Everything that God does enhances his glory.

---

106. Lincoln, *Ephesians*, 42.

9

Synthesis

The Blessing's repeated references to the will of God (1:5, 8, 9, 11), the love and grace of God (1:4, 5, 6, 7, 9), the praise of his glory (1:6, 12, 14), and "in Christ" (1:3, 4, 6, 7, 9, 10, 11, 12, 13) point to the central theme of the passage.[1] Ephesians 1:3–14 is a celebration of God's gracious foundational plan to redeem people in Jesus Christ, a truly surprising and exhilarating revelation, which Paul enthusiastically shares with his readers in the form of a *berakah* of praise. This was God's plan from before creation but had been kept secret until it was revealed in Jesus Christ and in the preaching of the gospel. To introduce this new idea, Paul takes the old, understood concept of election and uses it to introduce the new concept of predestination by embellishing election as being in Christ and before the foundation of the world. Paul is not redefining election, so Eph 1:4–5 should not be read back into other Pauline expressions specifically about election. Paul uses the new vocabulary of "predestination," "purpose," and "secret" to paint the complete picture of the revelation of the Father's predetermined eschatological blessings. While faithful Jews in the Second Temple period still had a strong belief that God was in control and would win out in the end, what predestination added was that the end had been worked out in detail from the beginning. God was not responding to human events, but at just the right time the Father enacted his secret plan to provide redemption, forgiveness, and holiness in Christ, uniting heaven and earth in Christ. This realized eschatological vision presents Jesus Christ as the true Lord of all that is. The gift of the

---

1. Robinson, *Ephesians*, 19.

Holy Spirit is definitive evidence that this new reality has begun and will just as certainly be brought to its full conclusion.

This grand vista has been obscured since the days of Augustine by the belief that predestination is not for us, but actually of us, and that predestination is a synonym of election of the people of God. For many, Augustine's interpretation changed the passage from a song of victory to a dirge of defeat. As Pannenberg laments, the classical doctrine of election abstracts and depersonalizes the individual.[2] In recent times, however, speculation about Pauline authorship, the demise of the Biblical Theology movement, and the new focus on the Jewish origins of Pauline theology has allowed a fresh appraisal of Ephesians independent of the particular theological interests of Romans. Within the historical context of Ephesians, Paul is refuting a pagan spiritual triumphalism epitomized in the Artemis cult, and in its place announcing God's eternal glorious divine plan for humanity. He is also giving both Jews and gentiles a way of understanding the place of the old covenant in the new church. The old covenant structures were not being replaced by something new, because the new covenant structures were the original plan, for which the old covenant was set up to prepare.

In Eph 1:3–14, Paul does not describe anyone's predetermined future other than Jesus Christ's. Modern arguments about whether predestination is individual or collective are unnecessary. Predestination is of what is available for believers in Christ, and it is accessed through faith in the gospel and sealed by the Holy Spirit. That Paul and all fellow believers in Christ are beneficiaries of God's plan for Christ from the beginning brings nothing but praise and wonder in response.

---

2. Pannenberg, *Human Nature*, 47.

PART 3

Romans 8:18—9:29

A reevaluation of predestination and election in Romans 8:18—9:29

In part 1 we saw that Rom 8:29–30 and 9:1–29 featured heavily in the establishment and maintenance of Augustine's combined doctrine of predestination and election. That the two terms became combined is surprising because the relevant Greek terms are used sparingly in Rom 8–11, and they are not used synonymously in the epistle. The doctrines of predestination and election have been reappraised in recent times, but the words continue to be treated as synonyms and are often jointly regarded as a key theme of Rom 9. This intertwining of predestination and election is due to a particular interpretation of Eph 1:3–14, which is being read into the text of Rom 8:18—9:29. In part 2, I proposed an alternate understanding of Eph 1:3–14, showing that while the verb ἐκλέγομαι (choose) is in that text, Paul is not writing about the election of God's people as first introduced in the OT, but using that term to help introduce the new concept of the predestination of the ministry of Jesus Christ for the people of God. With that in mind, we are now in a position to re-examine Paul's argument in Romans and look closely at how the terms are being used in this context.

10

Methodology and Background

A SOCIO-RHETORICAL APPROACH

As with Eph 1:3-14, the detailed exegesis will follow the inductive hermeneutical method, but the peculiarities of Paul's letter to the Romans suggest that it would also benefit from the application of the socio-rhetorical method. Socio-rhetorical criticism was developed by Vernon Robbins to enhance rhetorical criticism with the recent insights from anthropology and sociology. Socio-Rhetorical Interpretation (SRI), as Robbins now refers to it, views the text as a form of persuasive communication that is shaped by the social and cultural context of the author and the reader.[1] It seeks to explore the values, convictions, and beliefs in the text in a manner that is sensitive to how they vary from our own. The meaning of the text, according to Robbins, is found in the tapestry created by five interwoven layers or textures.[2]

1. The inner texture resides in the features of language and the way in which the words are used as tools of communication. It is examined through literary and rhetorical criticism.

2. The inter-texture is made up of the influence of other texts and cultural expressions on the passage under study. Citations, allusions,

---

1. Robbins, *Invention of Christian Discourse*, 1:xxvii.
2. Robbins, *Exploring the Texture of Texts*, 3-4.

and background material give insight into the author's insights and way of thinking.

3. The social and cultural texture explores how the text reinforces or subverts cultural norms in its day, and how societal biases have affected interpretation.
4. The ideological texture is formed by the viewpoint of the text evoking and interacting with different points of view through the ages.
5. The last layer, the sacred texture, considers how the text explores the relation of humans with the divine.

Robbins has continued to develop this critical approach, emphasizing that it is not a new method but an interpretative analytic that brings together a variety of relevant methods, allowing the interpreter to bridge ancient, modern, and postmodern thinking.[3] Sub-textures have been identified, and the way in which the textures interrelate has been mapped out, making it easier to see how various approaches to a text interact with SRI. This more extensive application of SRI is exemplified in Ruth Christa Mathieson's work on the parable of the banquet (Matt 22:1–14).[4]

SRI is particularly useful for approaching Romans. Paul is known for his close familiarity with Jewish Scripture and tradition, as well as for his ability in Greek rhetoric,[5] producing a rich inner texture and sophisticated inter-texture within his letters. Examining these layers will clarify how Paul employs predestination and election in Rom 8:18–9:36. Paul is also respected for his ability to adapt his theological expression to connect with the society and culture he is addressing,[6] which can lead to a well-developed sociocultural texture. This is where Paul's rationale in writing can be explored and further insights into his purposes in Rom 8:18–9:36 gained. The rich history of interpretation of the Pauline letters results in complex ideological textures, which has had a significant influence on the understanding of the doctrine of predestination. The sacred texture is ever present in Paul's writings and is at the heart of the significance of predestination and election to the reader. SRI will allow the influence of each these layers on the interpretation to be appreciated

---

3. Robbins, "Socio-Rhetorical Interpretation," 192–219.
4. Mathieson, *Matthew's Parable*, 33–35.
5. Witherington and Hyatt, *Romans*, 19.
6. Longenecker, "What Do We Find," 3–22.

and analyzed, with a view to understanding how they might support or distort the exegesis.

SRI has not had such an impact that it warrants specific acknowledgement by Michael Gorman in his survey of perspectives on Pauline theology.[7] Nevertheless, the terminology has been adopted by various Pauline commentators. Ben Witherington III has produced several commentaries which he describes as socio-rhetorical, including one on Paul's Epistle to the Romans.[8] David deSilva also uses SRI in one of his commentaries on Hebrews.[9] Aune, however, criticizes both those authors for hijacking the term "socio-rhetorical" and regards their work as having little in common with the methodology promoted by Robbins.[10] Gowler agrees and goes further, claiming that Witherington merely uses some rhetorical and social-science insights to support his conservative historical agenda in contrast to Robbins's sophisticated multidimensional approach.[11] These criticisms, however, go too far because at its heart SRI is not a rigid methodology but rather aims to be open to making use of a range of approaches to explore the meaning of the text. Even within Robbins's works there is variation and development in how SRI is applied. Robbins, for his part, commends deSilva for his work in this field.[12]

Robbins himself is criticized by Peter Lampe of misusing the term "rhetorical," with Lampe describing Robbins's seminal work on the Gospel of Mark as narrative criticism.[13] While this may be technically correct, Robbins uses the term "rhetoric" to refer to all performed speech and not just a particular style defined by classical or modern rhetoricians. Despite his criticisms, Lampe acknowledges the high value of Robbins's work.

Because I am making use of SRI for a particular purpose rather than seeking to be an exemplar of the full method as articulated by Robbins, I will not attempt to resolve these scholarly tensions. My implementation sits between the narrower focus of Witherington and deSilva and the detailed application of SRI by Mathieson, and is guided principally by Robbins's 1996 work, *Exploring the Texture of Texts*, rather than his

---

7. Gorman, *Apostle of the Crucified Lord*, 1–4.
8. See Witherington, *Acts of the Apostles*; Witherington, *1 and 2 Thessalonians*; Witherington and Hyatt, *Romans*.
9. See deSilva, *Hebrews*.
10. Aune, "Introduction," 4.
11. Gowler, "Socio-Rhetorical Interpretation," 193.
12. Robbins, "Socio-Rhetorical Interpretation," 193.
13. Lampe, "Rhetorical Analysis of Pauline Texts," 8–10.

later works. Beginning with a translation of the Greek text, I step through each of the five textures to explore what the passage may have meant in its original setting and how different social and ideological contexts may have influenced subsequent interpretations.

In keeping with SRI, it is appropriate to acknowledge my own context as an interpreter.[14] I put my faith in Jesus Christ in my mid-teens from a socialist agnostic background in which faith and religion were not discussed. I was initially nurtured in an Australian evangelical Protestant context, in which I do not recall predestination and election being discussed, although in hindsight that community likely leaned toward Arminianism. At university, I joined a church that strongly held to Reformed theology and over time I tried to adopt that position, eventually attending a theological college noted for being in the Reformed tradition. Nevertheless, I continued to perceive a tension between the Bible and the Reformed doctrine of predestination and election. That and the frustration the doctrine can bring to people led me to work harder to make sense of the relevant texts in their original contexts. Ten years later, here I am. I am open to whatever the text may mean, as I do not feel allegiance to any point of view, and I am comfortable being uncomfortable with what is in the Bible.

THE OCCASION OF WRITING

To appreciate the complexity of each of the textures of Rom 8:18–9:29, it is necessary to consider how the selected text fits within the epistle, beginning with what led to the letter being written. For a long time, Romans was read as a timeless theological treatise, but it is now appreciated that it needs to be understood in its historical context.[15] There is broad agreement that the letter was written by Paul to Christians in Rome from Corinth or nearby just before his final visit to Jerusalem in the late 50s, but there is still uncertainty regarding Paul's reason(s) for writing and whether the letter was written to Jews, gentiles, or both.[16] From an innertextual perspective, Paul addresses the letter to all Christians in Rome

---

14. Robbins, *Exploring the Texture of Texts*, 96.

15. Donfried, *Romans Debate*, xli; F. F. Bruce, "The Romans Debate—Continued," 334; Longenecker, *Romans*, 2.

16. Longenecker, *Romans*, 5; Matera, *Romans*, 4, 6; Witherington and Hyatt, *Romans*, 8.

without discrimination (Rom 1:7).[17] This is reflected in Paul addressing both Jews and gentiles directly at times (1:6; 2:17; 9:24; 11:13, 22) and greeting both Jews and gentiles in his closing remarks.[18] A combined Jew and gentile audience is consistent with what is known of the sociocultural context of Christianity in Rome. The Christian faith was likely established in Rome by Jews but came to have significant gentile leadership owing to the occasional expulsion of Jews from the capital.[19] Paul is clear that he has only been commissioned to minister to gentiles (1:5, 13-14), which leads some to conclude that the letter is only intended to be read by gentiles.[20] Such an inference is unnecessary because Paul is known to have spoken to Jews about his ministry to the gentiles (e.g., Gal 2:1-2; Acts 22). Longenecker acknowledges that a mixed audience is most likely, but he considers the connection between Roman Christians and the Jerusalem church to be the more significant factor.[21] While this hypothesis has circumstantial support, Paul does not refer to the Jerusalem church until the end of the letter and then does not acknowledge any such special connection in Rom 15:25-27. On balance, it seems more likely that Paul is addressing a relatively independent audience of both Jews and gentiles in Rome,[22] even if at times Paul may have one or the other particularly in mind. The reason why the apostle to the gentiles would include Jews among his addressees is explained by Paul in his rationale for the letter.

Ann Jervis rightly points out that Paul's purpose in writing should be discerned primarily from his explicit statements in 1:8-15 and 15:14-32, with inferences from the letter body being interpreted in the light of those statements.[23] Starting again with the inner texture, Paul states that his letter was in preparation for a long-hoped-for visit to Rome, so that Paul could share his spiritual insights (1:11), give and receive encouragement (1:12), and preach the gospel to the gentiles in Rome (1:13-15). From this viewpoint, 1:16-15:13 would serve to persuade the Roman

---

17. Staples, *Paul and the Resurrection*, 21.

18. Rom 16:7, 11; Cranfield, *Romans*, 1:18; Witherington and Hyatt, *Romans*, 9; Donfried, "Short Note," 48.

19. Dunn, *Romans*, 1:xlv-liii; Longenecker, *Introducing Romans*, 63.

20. Klein, "Paul's Purpose in Writing Romans," 36. Miller notes that Elliott and Stanley Stowers, among others, also hold this view. Miller, "Romans Debate," 310, 317.

21. Longenecker, *Romans*, 9.

22. Miller, "Romans Debate," 327; Moo, *Romans*, 11; Matera, *Romans*, 7; Longenecker, *Romans*, 9.

23. Jervis, *Purpose of Romans*, 29.

Christians that Paul is a visitor whom they would like to receive and to partner with in outreach to gentiles. In 15:14–32, Paul fills out his purpose further. He explains that his intent in writing was not to tell the Roman Christians something new (15:14; cf. 1:8, 12), but to remind them of some points important for the mission to the gentiles and of Paul's key role in that mission (15:15–16; cf. 1:1, 5). By these words, Paul is not so much asserting his apostolic authority over gentile Christians in Rome as Jervis proposes,[24] but prompting his readers to recognize and respect his divine commission for further work (cf. 15:20–22). This may suggest that Paul is concerned that support for his ministry may waiver in Rome, hence the need to include such an extensive exposition of his gospel message in the body of the epistle. Paul goes on in 15:17–19 to explain that he has achieved as much as he could to the east of Rome and, not wanting to build on other people's work (15:20–22), Paul advises that he hopes to stay only briefly in Rome and that he is actually seeking the support of the Roman Christians for a mission to Spain (15:23–24, 28–29).[25] Jewett explains at some length why the language and cultural barriers that Paul would face in such a mission would necessitate strong support from the full Christian body in Rome, in addition to that of his new patron, Phoebe (16:1).[26] While a surprising development, the mission to Spain is an expansion of Paul's motivation revealed in 1:8–15 and does not contradict his earlier statements.[27]

It is not until Paul discusses his intervening visit to Jerusalem that there is an indication of another sociocultural context and another ideological group that may be influencing the scope and nature of the epistle. This is not so much the Jerusalem church, as suggested by Dunn.[28] In 15:25–27, Paul's language describing his impending visit to the Jerusalem church is matter of fact and the paragraph ends positively (15:28–29). The conflict that concerns Paul is with τῶν ἀπειθούντων ἐν τῇ Ἰουδαίᾳ (the disobedient in Judea, whom I understand to be those who oppose the gospel), and how that conflict might affect the response of the church in Jerusalem (15:30–31). Paul's expression shifts from businesslike to being

---

24. Jervis, *Purpose of Romans*, 159.

25. Jewett, "Ecumenical Theology," 104–5.

26. Jewett, *Romans*, 74–79, 89–90; Longenecker and Still, *Thinking Through Paul*, 171.

27. Wedderburn, "Purpose and Occasion," 139; Peter Stuhlmacher, "The Purpose of Romans," 236.

28. Dunn, *Romans*, 1:xlii.

seriously concerned with a hint of desperation. The words "urge" and "struggle," the reference to potentially needing rescue, and Paul's plea for prayer all point to this not being a trivial matter. The threat is so severe that it may interfere with Paul's reception by the Jerusalem church (15:31) and prevent Paul from coming to Rome (15:32). It would make sense in these circumstances that Paul would want to ensure that those whose support he needed were not put off by this opposition and his potential suffering at their hands.[29] This is consistent with Paul's more general aim of gaining Roman support for his mission to Spain, but if the opposition in Judea is relevant, it would lead to the letter being more focused on convincing the Roman Christians that Paul's preaching stands up against his opponents' accusations. Thus, rather than the epistle being a summary of his ministry,[30] Romans would be an argument aiming to extend his ministry in the face of specific objections. This is not to suggest that Paul is crafting the defense he would deliver to a hostile audience in Jerusalem. What it does suggest is that Paul is providing a preemptive explanation of the soundness of his position in order to shore up his support in the Christian community in Rome.

The arrangement and content of the central teaching section of the epistle is consistent with this rationale. Romans 1:16–15:13 systematically responds to a series of distinctly Jewish objections to the gospel (e.g., that the gospel nullifies the law; it excuses sin; it makes the law out as sin; it contradicts God's promises) before finishing with a description of a life of faith that could be regarded by all as commendable before God. The lack of any discussion of some core doctrines such as the resurrection discounts the epistle from being a summary of Paul's theology.[31] Neither is the sociocultural context of Rome likely to be Paul's primary concern, because there are only minor references to points of tension with Roman society such as false worship, attitudes to civic authority, and setting aside of personal honor for kindness.[32] The genre of the epistle is more like a λογός προτρέπτικος, that is a speech to win adherents to a philosophical

---

29. Jervell, "Letter to Jerusalem," 66. Richard Longenecker acknowledges this motivation but argues that it is only a subsidiary purpose on the grounds that it is only inferred from the text rather than explicitly stated. That is a reasonable point, but without this motivation it is difficult to justify the extensive scope of Paul's argument. See Longenecker, *Romans*, 11.

30. E.g., Bornkamm, "Romans as Paul's Last Will and Testament," 14.

31. Longenecker, *Romans*, 2.

32. Jewett, *Romans*, 46–53; Ascough, "What Kind of World," 52.

school,[33] or possibly a *paraenesis* (exhortation) as proposed by Elliott.[34] Paul is concerned with persuading his readers of a position rather than providing general instruction.

Many scholars argue that Romans is targeted not at a potential problem, as I have proposed, but at actual friction within the Roman Christian community, such as over food laws or attitudes to civic authority.[35] It is argued that the multiplicity of household churches in Rome (Rom 16) is evidence of a lack of unity, and that the well-documented civic tension between gentiles and Jews in Rome had spilled over into the church.[36] Haacker characterizes the entire epistle as a peace memorandum designed to address conflicts between Jewish and gentile Christians and between Christians and unbelieving Jews.[37] Romans 11:13–24 and 14:13 fit this narrative well. Weighing against this position is that most of Rom 12–15 is in the vein of general advice,[38] and Paul does not rebuke or commend behavior by specific individuals in Rome, which is his normal practice when he is aware of actual problems (e.g., 1 Cor 1:10; 5:1; Gal 1:6; Phil 4:2; 1 Thess 4:13; etc.). In contrast, in Rom 1:12; 15:14; and 16:17–20, Paul states that he is unaware of any current troubles in the Roman Christian community. Rather than a sign of disunity, it is more likely that the multiplicity of churches is due to the size of rooms available for meetings due to the low socioeconomic status of Jewish and gentile Christians.[39] Rather than addressing manifest tensions, Rom 12–15 is more likely part of the argument that the gospel is for both Jew and gentile, is supported by Scripture, and results in godly behavior, and thus is not antinomian.

As such, it appears that Paul is primarily concerned with maintaining the commitment of Jewish and gentile Christians to the mission to

---

33. Aune, "Romans as a Logos *Protreptikos*," 278–96.

34. Miller, "Romans Debate," 310.

35. Longenecker, *Romans*, 11; Watson, "The Two Roman Congregations," 211; Stuhlmacher, "Purpose of Romans," 239; Gorman, *Romans*, 24; Matera, *Romans*, 9; Timmins, "Why Paul Wrote Romans," 394; Fitzmyer, *Romans*, 79.

36. Wiefel, "Jewish Community," 94; Watson, *Paul, Judaism and the Gentiles*, 94–105.

37. Haacker, "Der Römerbrief als Friedensmemorandium," 39; Haacker, *Theology of Paul's Letter*, 20.

38. Karris, "Romans 14:1–15:13," 155–78; Longenecker, *Romans*, 11.

39. Ascough, "What Kind of World," 54; Witherington and Hyatt, *Romans*, 10; Longenecker and Still, *Thinking Through Paul*, 171.

the gentiles in light of an impending mission by Paul to Spain.[40] The church in Jerusalem is hovering in the background, but Paul's thinking appears to be more affected by opponents of the gospel in Judea. While the epistle may be influenced by the Roman sociocultural context or rival internal groups among the Roman Christian community, I suggest that Paul's concern with the level of opposition he might face in Jerusalem from those outside the church is underappreciated as a factor in the scope of the epistle. This is consistent with Luke's record of Paul at this time. On Paul's return journey to Jerusalem, which follows shortly after he wrote Romans, he acknowledges that he has been aware of the trouble that awaits him in Jerusalem for some time (Acts 20:22–24). Thus, when Paul addresses suffering in Rom 8:18–39, he may be thinking not only of what the Roman Christians might be facing, but also of how they might react to what might happen to Paul in Jerusalem. When Paul addresses the failure of many of his kin to embrace the gospel in Rom 9–11, he may have in mind not only how the believers in Rome might be affected by unbelieving Jews around them, but how the saints in Rome might feel about unbelieving Jews in Judea should the worst of Paul's fears eventuate.

GENRE AND STRUCTURE

Genre

To determine which SRI literary and rhetorical tools might be useful, it is necessary to understand the nature of the literature under study.[41] There is clear evidence of Romans being an occasional letter, and yet it is dominated by a sustained argument that is not easily connected to the occasion. This is not only unusual for Paul because there are few comparable examples in ancient letter writing.[42] Much of the epistle is a refined and less passionate restatement of material in Galatians, 1 Thessalonians, and 1 and 2 Corinthians,[43] which leads to some regarding Romans as Paul's summation of his theology, but that suggestion belies the rhetorical nature of the epistle. Moo reviews the many genre classifications applied to Romans, including those by Aune and Elliott referred to above, but concludes that while they offer interesting comparisons, none is a perfect

---

40. Moo, *Romans*, 19.
41. Robbins, *Exploring the Texture of Texts*, 7.
42. Longenecker, *Romans*, 3.
43. Fitzmyer, *Romans*, 73; Witherington and Hyatt, *Romans*, 24.

fit.⁴⁴ Longenecker rejects the genre of "literary epistle" as too general and "letter of recommendation" as inappropriate because Romans does not focus on Paul's credentials nor contain third party endorsements.⁴⁵ Longenecker prefers the term "letter essay," as proposed by Martin Stirewalt and practiced occasionally by Epicurus and Dionysius among others, but this may also fall short of fully representing the strong rhetorical character of Romans.⁴⁶

Romans, however, does not neatly fit classical rhetorical classifications either. As Duane Watson notes, the epistle exhibits some characteristics of epideictic (ceremonial), deliberative (persuasive), and judicial (legal argument) rhetorical styles, but it is not distinctly representative of any particular category.⁴⁷ Jewett prefers to classify Romans as epideictic, with the epistle most closely representing an ambassadorial letter, but he acknowledges that the epistle also contains several subgenres.⁴⁸ There are some similarities with Hellenistic forms such as protreptic speech (exhortation), but there are significant differences as well, which Longenecker argues is due to Paul blending in Jewish remnant rhetoric.⁴⁹ Robbins, too, regards early Christians as more influenced by Jewish than classical Greco-Roman rhetoric.⁵⁰ Robbins identifies the emergence of six Christian rhetorical dialects in the NT, of which he regards apocalyptic rhetoric as being the most prevalent in Romans,⁵¹ because Paul is visualizing a new way of looking at life and his Jewish heritage in light of the Christ event. This Jewish flavor is reflected in the letter's inter-texture, with extensive OT citations and allusions. Paul has artfully blended Jewish and Greco-Roman techniques in developing his unique masterpiece.

Nevertheless, reasonable comparisons can be made between the epistle's structure and Greco-Roman rhetoric. Dunn counsels against being overly prescriptive because to do so does little to advance understanding of the letter and risks obscuring what is distinctive about the text.⁵² A survey of proposed rhetorical structures by Witherington and

---

44. Moo, *Romans*, 14.
45. Longenecker, *Romans*, 13.
46. Longenecker, *Romans*, 14.
47. Watson, "Three Species of Rhetoric," 34.
48. Jewett, *Romans*, 43–44.
49. Longenecker, *Romans*, 15–16.
50. Robbins, *Invention of Christian Discourse*, 1:2.
51. Robbins, *Invention of Christian Discourse*, 1:406.
52. Dunn, "The Formal and Theological Coherence of Romans," 246. Watson

Wuellner demonstrate Dunn's point by their lack of convergence on a rhetorical arrangement or even rhetorical vocabulary.[53] Jewett uses the teachings of Aristotle, Cicero, and Quintillian to classify the text and derive a structure for the epistle,[54] but this too leaves questions. Jewett spends some time debating with Kennedy on what part of the epistle is the *narratio*, but by Cicero's definition of *narratio*, the events that set the context for the dispute,[55] it is questionable whether a *narratio* even exists or needs to exist in Romans. Lampe cautions against drawing solely on ancient rhetorical handbooks, arguing that comparisons should also be made to real speeches which often deviated from the theory.[56] Nevertheless, Lampe advises against a purely oratory analysis as well because ancient schools recognized both similarities and differences in epistolography and rhetoric, and authors of letters were free to draw from either or to be inventive.[57] Because there is no obvious reference for the form of Romans, I will use Cicero's terminology to help explain how Paul is using rhetoric to persuade his audience, without constraining the text to fit neatly into Cicero's proposed structures, nor suggesting that Paul is following Cicero's methodology.

From a literary perspective, Cranfield notes that Romans is described as competent but not outstanding, with the strength of the letter being its content rather than its artistry.[58] This may be a bit harsh, since Paul uses a wide range of figures of speech such as metaphor, parallelism, antithesis, chiasm, repetition, anticipation, apostrophe, rhetorical questions, and personification.[59] At times, Paul's expression is uplifting and worth savoring (e.g., Rom 8:38–39). The unusual literary structure is also intriguing, with the central treatise-like body (1:16—15:13) being sandwiched between two passages that are more typical of ancient letter

---

likewise cautions against rigidly defining Paul's epistles, noting that Paul easily moves from style to style as it suits his purposes. See Watson, "Three Species of Rhetoric," 42.

53. Witherington and Hyatt, *Romans*, 16–21; Wuellner, "Paul's Rhetoric of Argumentation," 331. Witherington describes Hyatt's contribution to the Romans commentary in the dedication as "helping by providing some of the application materials in this commentary." On that basis, I only refer the ideas in the commentary as being Witherington's unless I am addressing application material.

54. Jewett, "Following the Argument of Romans," 265–77.

55. Cicero, *De Inventione*, 61.

56. Lampe, "Rhetorical Analysis of Pauline Texts," 11.

57. Lampe, "Rhetorical Analysis of Pauline Texts," 14.

58. Cranfield, *Critical and Exegetical Commentary*, 1:25.

59. Watson, "Role of Style," 133–35; Jewett, *Romans*, 30–40.

writing.[60] Nevertheless, other than identifying Romans as an epistle, these literary characteristics appear to serve the rhetorical nature of the epistle rather than help to identify the genre further.

In light of the lack of agreement on genre, it is probably best to settle for a more general term such as "letter essay" but to modify it slightly to reflect its rhetorical nature and the occasion proposed above. Romans may be best understood as a defense of the gospel, noting Paul at times explicitly addresses misrepresentation (e.g., 3:8; 6:1; 9:14), so "letter apology" may be a better description. Following Dunn's guidance, this proposed genre will be used to inform rather than to drive the exegesis.

Literary Structure

The Greeting

One of the distinctive characteristics of Paul's letter writing is his use of the greeting to establish how he intends to relate to his readers and to foreshadow the issue(s) he wishes to address.[61] This is particularly the case for Romans, which has the longest greeting of all his extant letters. Paul identifies himself as a servant of Christ Jesus and an apostle to the gentiles (1:1, 5). That gospel is first and foremost about who Jesus Christ is and what he has achieved (1:3-4). Although the letter is written to all God's people in Rome without distinction (1:7), Paul acknowledges that he only has standing to minister to gentiles, with the aim of his ministry being to elicit from the gentiles ὑπακοὴν πίστεως (an ambiguous term that could mean obeying the call to faith and/or an obedience that comes from faith; cf. 6:16; 10:21; 15:18).[62] By emphasizing the scriptural origins of the gospel as key to the inter-texture (1:2), Paul foreshadows his argument that the gospel does not subvert the law but is the fulfilment of it. The reference to the resurrection alerts readers that it is this astounding event that has led to Paul's radical reinterpretation of Scripture. With respect to Rom 8:18–9:29, it is worth noting the following features of Paul's greeting:

- the repetition of κλητός (called) (1:1, 5, 6) and the absence of ἐκλογή (elect);

---

60. Dunn, "The Formal and Theological Coherence of Romans," 245.
61. Dunn, *Romans*, 1:26; Longenecker, *Romans*, 47.
62. Moo, *Romans*, 51.

- that the gospel was promised beforehand (προεπαγγέλλω) through the prophets (cf. 8:29), which may indicate the time frame Paul has in mind when using other words prefixed by προ- later in the epistle;
- the focus on the Son of God and the Holy Spirit;
- the use of the word σπέρμα (seed) to refer to Jesus Christ's human origins, noting σπέρμα reappears in Paul's argument in Rom 9; and
- the use of the verb ὁρίζω (determine) with respect to Christ and ἀφορίζω (appoint) with respect to Paul, noting the related form προορίζω (predestine) appears in 8:29.

Exordium

Romans 1:8–15 serves to establish rapport between Paul and his readers and, as such, acts like an *exordium*.[63] Paul writes of his desire to visit Rome but at this point there is no hint of the long-term strategy articulated in 15:23–33. Paul simply wishes his readers to be aware they are dearly loved, and that Paul is delighted to be engaging with them with a view to partnering with them in the mission to the gentiles. His closing words, that he is eager to preach the gospel in Rome, flow naturally into the argument that follows.

Constitutio

Romans 1:16–17 is like a *constitutio* in that it specifies the controversial issue that is at the heart of Paul's concerns.[64] At issue is the nature of the gospel, which Paul has introduced in some detail in 1:1–6, and to which Paul now adds is the δικαιοσύνη θεοῦ (righteousness of God) for the Jew first and then for the gentile.

---

63. Cicero, *De Inventione*, 41; Matera, *Romans*, 31; Witherington and Hyatt, *Romans*, 40.

64. Longenecker, *Romans*, 147; Matera, *Romans*, 34. Witherington labels these verses the *propositio*, but defines *propositio* as Cicero defines *constitutio*. Witherington and Hyatt, *Romans*, 47; Cicero, *De Inventione*, 21.

Partitio

Romans 1:18—3:8 acts as a *partitio* in that it lays out the problem that needs to be addressed.[65] Because the controversy that Paul is addressing is ideological and Paul's opponents are not present, there is no content for a *narratio*. In good rhetorical style, Paul begins the *partitio* with a point of agreement with his audience, namely the rampant sinfulness of the gentile world,[66] which is rightly condemned by God. Paul then gradually moves on to the point of contention, that Jews are similarly facing God's judgment for their own moral failings. Paul uses a variety of rhetorical devices to challenge, persuade, and lure his audience to acknowledge that Jews cannot rely on their religious culture for their standing with God (3:1–8).

Confirmatio

Romans 3:9–30 can be understood as a *confirmatio* or proof of thesis.[67] In a rapid series of scriptural quotes, Paul drives home his opening argument on the sinfulness of all people and then demonstrates how the gospel addresses that universal sinfulness, delivers salvation, and reveals the righteousness of God. In his conclusion, Paul acknowledges a key objection of his opponents, that the gospel is a threat to the law (3:31).

Challenges and Refutationes

The implied objection in 3:31 begins a pattern that continues through to 11:36 of Paul raising a rhetorical challenge to his argument which he then addresses in a following *refutatio*.[68]

---

65. Matera, *Romans*, 41; Cicero, *De Inventione*, 63.

66. Although Paul does not specify that he is exclusively referring to gentiles, Paul's appeal to general revelation in 1:20 rather than the law makes it highly likely. See Moo, *Romans*, 104; Materia, *Romans*, 43.

67. Cicero, *De Inventione*, 69. It is debatable at which verse Paul moves from *partitio* to *confirmatio*. The sequence of rhetorical challenges from 3:1 is a significant shift in style, but 3:1–8 can reasonably be seen as still laying out the "why" of the debate, so I have retained it as part of the *partitio*. Equally 3:10–20 could be taken as part of the argument for universal sinfulness beginning at 1:18 or separated out as its own section as several scholars choose to do. I have been guided by the rhetorical question in 3:9 that sets up the answer the gospel provides and therefore understand 3:10–20 as part of the proof of thesis or *confirmatio*. For alternate arrangements, see Matera, *Romans*, 89; Longenecker, *Romans*, 329.

68. Witherington proposes a similar rhetorical structure. See Witherington and

- 3:31 Challenge: Is the law nullified? *refutatio*: 4:1—5:20.
- 6:1 Challenge: Is sin excused? *refutatio*: 6:2—7:6.
- 7:7 Challenge: Is the law sin? *refutatio* 7:8—8:17.
- 8:18 Challenge: Christian suffering. *refutatio* 8:19-39.
- 9:1-5 aims to win good will and sympathy for the difficult issue that follows, so acts as another *exordium*.
- 9:6 Challenge: Has God's word failed? *refutatio*: 9:7—11:36.

Many commentators prefer a structure for Romans that is arranged around theological themes. The typical thematic structure is not significantly different from my rhetorical arrangement, with the main variance being that the thematic approach often identifies Rom 5:1—8:39 as a complete unit addressing the nature of the Christian life, as part of Paul's "two age" explanation of the gospel.[69] Dunn is one of the exceptions, regarding chapter 5 as the conclusion to the preceding argument, pointing out several literary and thematic connections with chapters 1-4.[70] From a rhetorical perspective, the themes of justification and faith from chapter 4 continue to be prominent in chapter 5 (5:1, 2, 9, 16, 17, 18, 19, 21), and my proposed *refutatio* is introduced and concludes with the purpose of the law (3:31; 5:20).[71] On this basis I have kept these chapters together in my structure, although my exegesis of 8:18—9:29 does not depend on it.

N. T. Wright prefers to view all of chapter 8 as a single unit sharing common motifs framed by a celebratory introduction and conclusion (8:1-11 and 8:31-39).[72] This proposal is undermined by the major theme of the sinful nature not being present from 8:18 onward, and for this reason 8:1-17 appears to be more strongly connected with 7:7-25. Furthermore, the literary style of 8:1-17, with its many short, sharp, and often verbless sentences, suggests a climax has been reached, whereas the long flowing sentences from 8:18 lead the reader to mull over the new ideas being presented.

Hyatt, *Romans*, vii-ix.

69. Cranfield, *Romans*, 1:xi; Gorman, *Romans*, xi; Longenecker, *Romans*, vi; Moo, *Romans*, 32, 532; Matera, *Romans*, vii.

70. Dunn, *Romans*, 1:242.

71. Dunn, *Romans*, 1:242.

72. Wright, *Into the Heart*, 10.

Most agree that Rom 8:18-39 is a distinct section,[73] although separating it as strongly from 8:1-17 as I have is not as common. This is understandable in view of the common motifs observed by Wright and others, however those common themes, such as the role of the Holy Spirit, appear to be serving different purposes in these sections. Furthermore, there is a significant shift at 8:17-18 to the issue of suffering. In any case, my arrangement will have a similar bearing on the exegesis as that of those commentators who prefer to regard 8:18-39 as more connected with the preceding material, because my proposed structure acknowledges how each *refutatio* is responding to a challenge that arises from the preceding one.[74]

Interestingly, Paul does not include a *peroratio* in the epistle. Nowhere does Paul draw the threads together of the sequence of issues he has addressed. It is possible that Paul considered that his introduction (1:1-7) performed this purpose. Some see 8:31-39 in this vein,[75] but that passage is more a celebration than a thorough conclusion. The doxology in 11:33-36 could be seen as acting as the inverse of a *conquestio*,[76] which Cicero advises can cap off a *peroratio*, but it is probably better not to force such terms on the text and allow Paul to present himself as he sees fit.

Romans 12:1—15:13

Romans 12:1—15:13 is of a different style. While it still contains rhetorical elements, it is not a reasoned defense of a theological position, but rather a sequence of exhortations to behave in accordance with God's will (part of the obedience of faith). Within the overall argument of Romans, this section shows how the gospel is not antinomian but produces admirable godliness, thereby countering accusations to the contrary. It has some similarities with a digression, as defined by Hermagoras,[77] in that it describes praiseworthy behavior that might win further support for Paul's position.

---

73. Longenecker, *Romans*, 715; Cranfield, *Romans*, 1:403; Moo, *Romans*, 530; Witherington and Hyatt, *Romans*, 220; Gorman, *Romans*, 34.

74. E.g., Campbell shows how Paul's argument from Rom 4:1 responds to the rhetorical question of 3:31 and connects to the Paul's solution in 3:21-31. Campbell, *Deliverance of God*, 326.

75. Gorman, *Romans*, 209.
76. Cicero, *De Inventione*, 157.
77. Cicero, *De Inventione*, 147.

Romans 15:14—16:27

In Romans 15:14-33, Paul reverts to more conventional letter-writing style and reveals further reasons for writing this epistle and how he hopes the addressees will respond to it. Romans 16:1-27, if it is original, which in the main seems likely,[78] is a typical Pauline valediction. It gives the reader insight into Paul's knowledge of the state of Christianity in Rome.

Summary

The rhetorical flow of Paul's letter apology can be summed up as follows.

The Rhetorical Flow of Romans	
• 1:1–15	An engaging introduction
o 1:16–3:30	The gospel of justification by faith
o 3:31–5:20	It does not overthrow the law, it fulfils the law
o 6:1–7:6	It does not encourage sin, it leads away from sin
o 7:7–8:17	It does not make the law the problem, it provides the solution to the problem that the law exposes
o 8:18–39	It is not put off by suffering, it elicits endurance and hope
o 9:1–11:36	It does not defy God's promises, it is God's promised word
o 12:1–15:13	The obedience that comes from faith in Jesus Christ
• 15:14–16:27	Closing encouragement

Looking more closely at the passage under study (8:18—9:29), it contains the whole of one *refutatio* and the first part of the subsequent one. The exegesis, therefore, will need to be conscious of how the argument has been introduced and developed in the preceding chapters and how 9:1-29 relates to the rest of its section.

---

78. Donfried, *Romans Debate*, 449; Lampe, "Roman Christians," 217; Jewett, *Romans*, 18.

11

Exegesis of Romans 8:18–39

In order to spend sufficient time on those verses pertinent to the topic while also ensuring that they are understood in their context, SRI will be used to explore the *refutatio* in full (8:18–39) before applying the inductive hermeneutical method (within an SRI structure) to select parts of the text. My translation and exegesis are based on the most recent critical edition of the United Bible Societies' *The Greek New Testament* (UBS[5]).

TRANSLATION OF ROMANS 8:18–39

[18]For I consider the sufferings of this present age are not worthy of the glory that is about to be revealed to us. [19]Even creation eagerly awaits the revelation of the children of God. [20]Creation was subjected to futility, not willingly, but because the one who subjected it hoped [21]that even creation itself could be set free out of the slavery to decay and into the freedom of the glory of the children of God.

[22]We know that the whole of creation has been groaning and suffering until now, [23]and not only creation, but also those of us who have the firstfruits of the Spirit. We too groan inwardly as we eagerly wait for adoption, the redemption of our bodies. [24]We were saved to hope. Hope that is seen is not hope. For who hopes for what can already be seen? [25]But if we hope for what we cannot see, then we persevere and eagerly wait for it.

[26]In this very matter the Spirit comes right alongside us in our weakness, so that, should we pray about things which we do not understand,

the Spirit himself pleads for us with sighs too deep for words. ²⁷God, who searches the heart, knows the mind of the Spirit and directs the Spirit to intercede on behalf of the saints.

²⁸We know that for the lovers of God, those called according to plan, all things work together for good ²⁹because God foreknew them and predestined them to be conformed to the likeness of his Son so that he would be the firstborn among many siblings. ³⁰Having predestined them, he called them, and having called them, he justified them, and having justified them, he glorified them.

³¹Therefore, what will we say concerning these things? If God is for us, who can be against us? ³²Indeed, if God did not spare his only Son, but gave him up for all of us, how will he not also freely give us everything that is on offer in him? ³³Who will bring charges against God's chosen? If God is the justifier, who is left to condemn? Christ Jesus died, and even more was raised from the dead, and is at the right hand of God to intercede for us. ³⁵What can separate us from the love of Christ? Can distress or trouble or persecution or famine or nakedness or danger or warfare? ³⁶It is written, "Because of you we are put to death every day. We are considered as sheep for the slaughter," ³⁷but in all these things we prevail through the one who loves us.

³⁸I am convinced that neither death nor life, neither angels nor demons, neither the present nor the past, neither spiritual powers ³⁹in the world above or the world below nor any other created thing will be able to separate us from the love of God that is in Christ Jesus our Lord.

ROMANS 8:18-39 OVERVIEW

The rhetorical flow that leads up to Romans 8:18-39 creates the expectation that there will be echoes of the prime issues Paul is addressing in the epistle, justification and faith (e.g., 8:30, 33). There will also be some carryover of ideas from the preceding *refutatio* because the counterpoint leading to each *refutatio* is itself a response to an issue that arose in what came before. In this case, the human-divine relationship, which was the answer in the preceding *refutatio*, becomes the point of tension in 8:18-39.[1]

The challenge that leads into the *refutatio* does not come from an external opponent as previously (3:31; 6:1; 7:7; 9:6), but from Paul himself in the condition of 8:17, "if we share in his sufferings so that

---

1. Dunn, *Romans*, 1:466; Jewett, *Romans*, 506.

we may share in his glory." The experience of suffering would naturally cause some to doubt the validity of the gospel,[2] and Paul understands the need to address this concern, especially after the triumphant tone of 8:1–17a. This different lead into the *refutatio* results in 8:18–39 being less argumentative and more encouraging, but the passage still fits neatly into the sequence of five challenges because it concerns a threat to the gospel that needs to be answered.

Inner Texture

The literary structure of Rom 8:18–39 appears to be based on declarative main verbs placed at the beginning of each paragraph as follows:[3]

- 8:18 λογίζομαι (I consider)
- 8:22 οἶδα (We know)
- 8:28 οἶδα (We know)
- 8:31–37 is a change in style using a series of rhetorical questions.
- 8:38 πείθω (I am convinced)

Ὡσαύτως (in this very matter) in 8:26 is another possible literary marker,[4] although because this expression refers to what has come before, 8:26–27 would still be linked closely with 8:22–25 rather than with 8:28–30.[5] Some commentators prefer alternate subdivisions based on key motifs such as suffering, creation, and hope, but most scholars agree that 8:28–30 is a distinct subunit.[6]

Repetition of words or concepts indicate the topics of interest and suggests the progression of thought.[7] Suffering is the premier concern, but rather than simple repetition, Paul uses a range of synonyms and related concepts to draw attention to his concern. Paul moves from suffering with Christ (συμπάσχω, 8:17) to the sufferings of this present age (πάθημα, 8:18), to creation being subjected to futility (ματαιότης, 8:20),

---

2. Moo, *Romans*, 531; Longenecker, *Romans*, 717.
3. Longenecker, *Romans*, 716.
4. Moo, *Romans*, 532.
5. Witherington and Hyatt, *Romans*, 221; Longenecker, *Romans*, 731.
6. For a similar structure to mine, see Matera, *Romans*, 187; Longenecker, *Romans*, 711.
7. Robbins, *Exploring the Texture of Texts*, 8–14.

to creation's slavery to decay (φθορά, 8:21), to creation groaning and suffering (συστενάζω, συνωδίνω, 8:22), to Christians groaning inwardly (στενάζω, 8:23), to our frailty (ἀσθένεια, 8:26), and finally to the Spirit interceding with deep sighs (στεναγμός, 8:26). Suffering is presented as God's purpose for all of creation in this evil age,[8] so it is shared by Christ and Christians, and they are helped in this respect by the Holy Spirit. Suffering is absent from 8:28 until 8:35–36, at which point seven catastrophes are listed in rapid succession followed by an intertextual reflection on Ps 44:22, but this time, rather than suffering being a threat, it appears defeated. Romans 8:28–30 begins this transition.

Glory also appears multiple times (8:17, 18, 21, 30) and, as with suffering, it is filled out with a range of related concepts (revelation of the children, adoption, redemption of our bodies). Glory is juxtaposed to suffering, although, unlike suffering, glory not only appears in 8:28–30 but is the climax of those verses, leading Moo to regard glory rather than suffering as the overarching theme of 8:18–30.[9] Cranfield prefers hope as the key motif, with 8:18, 19, 21, 23 giving some indication of the content of this hope,[10] but this is probably better seen as a subtheme filling out the main suffering-glory axis.

The rhetorical structure follows the literary structure. Paul contends (λογίζομαι), knows (οἶδα), knows (οἶδα), cannot conceive of a contrary argument (τίς), and is convinced (πείθω). A closer look shows that the first two sections work together, with Rom 8:18–25 being made up of four rhetorical antitheses, which provide an eschatological perspective on life and creation.[11]

- 8:18–19   suffering   glory
- 8:20–21   futility   freedom
- 8:22–23   groaning   redemption
- 8:24–25   seen   hope

These antitheses reflect the "now" and "not yet" nature of the Christian life. In Rom 8:15, Paul states that Christians have received a spirit of adoption, whereas in 8:23 Christians are waiting for adoption in the redemption of their bodies. Christians are both children of God now (8:16)

---

8. Longenecker, *Romans*, 723; Cranfield, *Romans*, 1:411.

9. Moo, *Romans*, 530.

10. Cranfield, *Romans*, 1:404.

11. Matera, *Romans*, 186, 199; Gorman, *Romans*, 205; Dunn, *Romans*, 1:488.

and at the same time waiting for that to be revealed (8:19). In the same vein, John Chrysostom understood glory as something Christians already have and yet also concealed awaiting revelation (8:18; cf. Col 3:3).[12] The saints are simultaneously heirs and awaiting their inheritance (Rom 8:17, 25). Paul makes use of the term "firstfruits" (ἀπαρχή) to convey that believers only have the first installment of what will eventually come in full (cf. 2 Cor 1:22; 5:5; Eph 1:14).

Romans 8:26–27 applies this series of tensions to a Christian's prayer life. Weakness becomes a strength through the aid of the Spirit and lack of understanding is transformed to insight by the Spirit's pleading on the believer's behalf.[13] There is some ambiguity as to whether the help is how to pray or what to pray, but the end is godly prayer that can be expressed from our deepest angst (cf. 8:22, 23).[14]

In Romans 8:28–30, Paul explains that his confidence in the face of suffering comes from knowing the full sweep of God's plan.[15] The divine plan provides a new value system which differs markedly from the surrounding culture, so it empowers an alternate frame of mind from which to consider present difficulties. This will be examined in detail below.

Romans 8:31–37 contains a series of rhetorical questions showing how incredible the suggestion is that Christian suffering might somehow invalidate the gospel.[16]

- 8:31: Who can question God's favor toward us? God gave up his Son for us.
- 8:33: Who can condemn us? Christ Jesus is our defender.
- 8:35: What can separate us from the love of Christ? Christ continues to love us.

This is a fine example of high rhetoric,[17] designed to win hearts and minds by showing how strong and beautiful the case for the gospel is and by exposing any challenge as futile. These verses are somewhat like a *peroratio* for this *refutatio* in the way they inspire enthusiasm for Paul's

---

12. Chrysostom, *Hom. Rom.* 8:12, 13 (NPNF[1] 11:793); Cranfield, *Romans*, 1:409.

13. Moo, *Romans*, 546; Gorman, *Romans*, 193; Longenecker, *Romans*, 730; Dunn, *Romans*, 1:492.

14. Longenecker, *Romans*, 733; Jewett, *Romans*, 524–25.

15. Matera, *Romans*, 203.

16. Gorman, *Romans*, 209.

17. Witherington and Hyatt, *Romans*, 231; Cranfield, *Romans*, 1:434.

perspective. The gospel perspective may be countercultural, but Paul shows that it is well founded and makes better sense.

Romans 8:38-39 is Paul's exalted conclusion. Nothing can challenge God's love for his people, which is found in Christ Jesus their Lord. Paul's poetic skill comes to the fore in a sequence of all-encompassing extremities conveying the universal reach of the love of God. The list of extremities is surprising because it has more of an apocalyptic feel in what is otherwise a grounded epistle.[18]

This rhetorical flow of Rom 8:18-39 can be outlined as follows.

The Rhetorical Flow of Romans 8:18-39
• 8:18-39 The gospel is not undermined by suffering
o 8:18-25   The gospel inspires living for the future
▪ 8:18-19   From suffering, it delivers glory
▪ 8:20-21   From futility, it delivers freedom
▪ 8:22-23   From groaning, it delivers redemption
▪ 8:24-25   It looks past the present to the future
o 8:26-27   Faithful sufferers are helped by the Holy Spirit
o 8:28-30   Faithful sufferers know God's plan for their good
o 8:31-37   Faithful sufferers know God's plan cannot be thwarted
o 8:38-39   Faithful sufferers know the glorious outcome is certain

Inter-Texture

Paul begins and ends this *refutatio* with personal reflections ("I contend," "I am convinced"). In between Paul switches to shared knowledge ("we know"), which is likely drawn from the well-known Jewish eschatological hope for God's people and all of creation.[19] Some have perceived the influence of the Hellenistic philosophy of the seen and the unseen on 8:24-25, but it is easier to find connections between Romans and Paul's other letters and OT Scripture. Paul's expression has more in common with the Jewish apocalyptic tradition.[20]

The interplay of suffering and glory was first raised in Rom 5:2-3, a chapter that subsequently harks back to Adam and the seminal sin. The

---

18. Gorman, *Apostle of the Crucified Lord*, 2, 30.
19. Dunn, *Romans*, 1:472.
20. Cranfield, *Romans*, 1:405, 420.

language of 8:20–21 is also reminiscent of references to the withering of the earth under the curse of God. This inter-texture of Gen 3 and OT commentary on that passage (Isa 24:4–7; 65:17–25; Hos 4:1–3) reminds readers of the link between human sin and the state of creation and points to a spiritual solution to those woes. Paul's comparison of momentary afflictions with eternal glory in 2 Cor 4:17 also likely lies behind the text. Wright draws connections to the Exodus story and the glory manifested in the tabernacle and by Moses, but the text lacks explicit cues to that effect.[21] Similarly, Wright's linking of 8:26–27 with the laments of the OT lacks clear direction from the text, suggesting that Wright is working more in the ideological layer.[22]

Paul's words in 8:27 are probably alluding to the numerous references in Scripture to God searching the heart and knowing our unspoken desires.[23] Central to Paul's argument is that Christians can draw confidence from knowing that God is aware of so much more than humans can comprehend, so God can act in a manner that is for the best.

In Rom 8:31–35, Paul rapidly alludes to several major OT images,[24] emphasizing the gospel's grounding in Scripture and reinforcing that, within Romans, Paul is considering God's actions within the biblical timeline. Some suggest these verses may be an early Christian hymn, but Dunn shows that this is unlikely in view of the many allusions and parallels to Paul's other letters.[25] The link between Isaac and Christ is not atonement, as some early Christians thought, but is found in the commitment of the offeror (Abraham/God) to the beneficiary (God/us) (cf. Gen 22:16).[26]

Paul concludes 8:31–37 with a quotation from Ps 44:22, a psalm to which Jews continue to turn in their suffering.[27] This shows that Paul is still on the central motif of suffering and is not offering a conclusion for the entirety of the epistle to this point, even if 8:31–38 may also allude to several themes from Rom 5–8.[28] Paul is theologically aligned with the psalm and yet also further developed in his thinking. Both the psalmist and Paul

---

21. Wright, *Into the Heart*, 110.
22. Wright, *Into the Heart*, 137.
23. Cranfield, *Romans*, 1:424.
24. Dunn, *Romans*, 1:499.
25. Dunn, *Romans*, 1:498.
26. Longenecker, *Romans*, 753.
27. Cranfield, *Romans*, 1:440; Dunn, *Romans*, 1:505.
28. *Pace* Witherington and Hyatt, *Romans*, 220; Moo, *Romans*, 560; Cranfield, *Romans*, 1:434.

are looking forward to God's redemption from a time of grave suffering, however, while the psalm is a desperate plea by someone perplexed by the suffering of God's people, Paul understands the present and is confident of the future. Rather than being a rerunning of the OT, the gospel completes the picture and therefore empowers the faithful to endure confidently.

Sociocultural Texture

Paul does not indicate that he has any particular incident of suffering in mind. He refers generally to suffering as a result of faith in Christ (8:17) and creation being subjected to futility (8:20).[29] Paul likely has in mind the general struggles of life or persecutions he and his readers were facing.[30] Rome was known for its anti-Semitism despite the general toleration of Judaism across the empire, and at this time Christianity was still regarded as a Jewish sect.[31] Suggestions, such as those by Gorman and Matera, that Paul was reflecting the Jewish belief in great suffering preceding the age of eschatological salvation is not well supported by the text.[32] While Rom 8:17 links Christ's sufferings to his glorification, the inter-texture at 8:36 suggests that Paul has in mind the global and long-running opposition to God, which inevitably extends to God's people. This is consistent with creation's labor pains in 8:22 being connected to creation's subjection to futility in 8:20, making that suffering characteristic of almost the entirety of the biblical timeline.

Even though Paul's terminology suggests that he has his Jewish heritage more in mind than Greco-Roman culture, his rich imagery can be applied to both contexts and serves to subvert common approaches to suffering in his day. Stoics turned to the unaffected inner self in the face of external suffering,[33] whereas Paul's confidence is not in human effort but in God's grace. Jewish writers in the late Second Temple Period understood that the suffering of the righteous was brought on by the enemies of God, who needed to be defeated.[34] In contrast, the gospel invites the faithful to share in Christ's suffering (8:17), to declare that God

---

29. Matera, *Romans*, 199.

30. Gorman, *Romans*, 212.

31. Wiefel, "Jewish Community," 86; Gorman, *Apostle of the Crucified Lord*, 33; Witherington and Hyatt, *Romans*, 12; Longenecker, *Introducing Romans*, 62.

32. Gorman, *Apostle of the Crucified Lord*, 442; Matera, *Romans*, 203.

33. Gorman, *Romans*, 211.

34. Avemarie, "Suffering," RPP 12:343.

remains present during suffering (8:26), and to anticipate confidently future relief. In this regard Paul shared more in common with OT prophets such as Isaiah (e.g., Isa 40—55).[35] Paul's approach to glory also challenged contemporary desires. Whereas Greco-Romans would seek glory and honor in the present that could only ever be temporary,[36] the gospel offers permanent glory that may be hidden now but will ultimately be revealed.

Ideological and Sacred Textures

Thus far, discussion of the ideological texture has been dominated by Paul's worldview, which he invites his readers to share. The brief reference to persecutions and the sword in Rom 8:35 hints at other groups, but they are not engaged in any detail. Not even unbelievers are acknowledged in Paul's reflections on the current state of creation in 8:19–23. As noted above, through the ages commentators have identified thematic interests of relevance to them, and variously found connections with Hellenistic philosophy, late Second Temple period literature, the OT, and Pauline literature. The ideological texture with respect to major writers on the doctrine of predestination will be explored further in the detailed exegesis below. The sacred texture of the divine plan for and aid to the children of God has been touched on in stride above and will be the focal point of the detailed exegesis below.

What this review of Rom 8:18–39 has shown is that Paul's purpose is to encourage suffering Christians to be certain of their eventual glory, release, and redemption, because of the present experience of the love of God for them in Christ Jesus. Any angst arising from the dissonance between experience and expectation is alleviated by prayer led by the Holy Spirit, knowledge of God's complete plan revealed in Jesus Christ, and experience of God's unchallengeable love. The primary intertextual connections are to Jewish Scriptures and culture, with secondary influences from Greco-Roman rhetorical style. The text subverts both Jewish and Greco-Roman cultures to varying degrees. For the Jew, it is a matter of moving on from the partial understanding of the Jewish Scriptures to the complete (fulfilled) revelation available in Christ. For the gentile, it may mean setting aside aspects of their culture's values and embracing the explanation of the gospel. Rather than being undermined by suffering,

---

35. Wright, *Into the Heart*, 19.
36. Gorman, *Apostle of the Crucified Lord*, 13.

the gospel of God's salvation for Jew and gentile provides understanding and an answer that surpasses all challenges. Within that context, it is time to turn to those verses that address predestination and election in detail.

ROMANS 8:28-30

The purpose of 8:28-30 in the broader argument is to encourage suffering Christians that God is for them and will follow through on the already-received firstfruits and deliver the promised redemption. Paul's aim is to convince his fellow believers that present suffering does not call into question the trustworthiness of the gospel. In Rom 8:28-30, he does this by drawing together several threads, including preplanning, justification, and glory, and by foreshadowing a major theme of the next *refutatio*, calling.

> 8:28a οἴδαμεν δὲ ὅτι τοῖς ἀγαπῶσιν τὸν θεόν—We know that for the lovers of God

The particle δέ makes a weak connection to the preceding verse. In 8:18-24, γάρ (for) is the more commonly used connector, because Paul is building his case. The use of δέ here suggests that Paul is expanding the consequences of his argument.[37] In the preceding verses Paul has explained how prayer with the support of the Holy Spirit sustains Christians through their trials. From 8:28, it is the understanding of God's overarching plan that enables Christians not to be discouraged by suffering.

The disclosure formula ("we know . . .") suggests that this is part of the heritage Paul shares with his readers, a heritage that comes from both ancient Jewish and recent Christian origins.[38] What Paul knows is not a secret to be revealed but readily available knowledge that supplies current and continuing encouragement to Christians.

The conjunction ὅτι (that) introduces the clause that acts as the object of the verb οἶδα (to know). The clause begins with its indirect object (for the lovers), as the substantive participle τοῖς ἀγαπῶσιν (the lovers) is in the dative case. The direct object of their love is τὸν θεόν (God). Bringing the indirect object forward in the clause has the effect of making the lovers of God the focus of attention.[39] Using the plural

---

37. Moo, *Romans*, 549; Longenecker, *Romans*, 736.
38. Dunn, *Romans*, 1:480; Cranfield, *Romans*, 1:424; Longenecker, *Romans*, 736.
39. Cranfield, *Romans*, 1:424.

"lovers" matches Paul's preferred use of the first-person plural pronoun in 8:18–39. As Gorman notes, in the Hellenized Mediterranean culture, people identified themselves as individuals within a group,[40] and Paul's description of Christians as lovers of God would have resonated with that perspective. The phrase possibly alludes to the call to love God in Deut 6:5,[41] although, as Dunn suggests, by not including a reference to keeping the commandments, Paul may be wanting to emphasize the distinctive Christian reliance on grace.[42] Jewett points to the Holy Spirit as the source of that love (from Rom 5:5 and 8:15–16).[43]

8:28b πάντα συνεργεῖ εἰς ἀγαθόν—all things work together for good

There is ambiguity as to the subject of the verb συνεργέω (work together).[44] The syntax and a variant reading leave open several possibilities, with πάντα (all things) or God (implied) being the most likely subjects. Cranfield considers the former to be almost certain, whereas Longenecker prefers the latter.[45] In any case, the difference in interpretation is marginal because Paul would have regarded God as being in ultimate control of "all things" to achieve the good.[46] What Paul is doing by this expression is heightening the widespread belief within Judaism that God-fearers could trust God for a good outcome amidst adversity.[47] "All things" includes present suffering (cf. 8:17),[48] as well as God's multiple acts in Rom 8:29 to achieve a glorious outcome for the lovers of God. Aquinas speculates that a believer's sin is also included in "all things,"[49] but such an interpretation could lead to lovers of God being less concerned with sin, so that is not likely to be Paul's intent.

---

40. Gorman, *Apostle of the Crucified Lord*, 12.

41. Wright, *Into the Heart*, 159. Cranfield documents the extensive OT and Jewish background behind this expression. See Cranfield, *Romans*, 1:424.

42. Dunn, *Romans*, 1:481.

43. Jewett, *Romans*, 526; Barth, *Romans*, 322.

44. Moo, *Romans*, 549.

45. Cranfield, *Romans*, 1:427; Porter and Yoon, *Romans*, 190; Longenecker, *Romans*, 738. BDAG 969, takes a more neutral stance on the options. Wright documents more recent speculation. See Wright, *Into the Heart*, 158.

46. Dunn, *Romans*, 1:481.

47. Cranfield, *Romans*, 1:429; Fitzmyer, *Romans*, 522.

48. Moo, *Romans*, 550; Cranfield, *Romans*, 1:428.

49. Aquinas, *Romans*, 232; Moo, *Romans*, 550.

The goal of all things working together is εἰς ἀγαθόν (for good). Aquinas, following Augustine, drew from this that God would permit no evil unless he could draw some good out of it.[50] While this is an interesting theological reflection, the text is more focused on the believer's experience of God's kind hand than on what is going on in the divine mind. Paul will elaborate on the content of the good in subsequent verses, but it is also informed by the preceding references to glory, freedom, adoption, and redemption. This suggests that Paul's mind is likely on eternal blessings in 8:28.[51] Quoted out of context, this verse can lead hearers to think of good things in a worldly sense and a realized eschatology. Jesus taught such things at times (Mark 10:29–30) and that sense may be behind Paul's words in Rom 13:1–7 (cf. 1 Cor 11:30; Phil 4:12–13) but the focus of 8:18–33 is on present suffering being relieved by a future glory.[52]

8:28c τοῖς κατὰ πρόθεσιν κλητοῖς οὖσιν—for those called according to plan

The article τοῖς agrees with the participle οὖσιν (those being), making κλητοῖς (called), as modified by κατὰ πρόθεσιν (according to plan), the attributive adjective of the noun clause.[53] Τοῖς . . . οὖσιν is effectively dative of apposition with τοῖς ἀγαπῶσιν despite not being immediately adjacent, so 8:28c provides further detail about that same group. Thus, the lovers of God are those called according to plan, allowing the two indirect objects to be brought together in the full translation to allow the English to flow more naturally. It is, however, "those called according to plan" that is of primary concern to this study. Κλητός is sometimes used in the NT in conjunction with election, and πρόθεσις (plan) is grouped by Jacobs and Krienke with the family of words that deal with divine foreknowledge and predetermination of future events.[54]

Paul introduces κλητός in the opening verse of the epistle, describing himself as called to be an apostle, and he uses this term two more times in the introduction to describe his addressees as called by Jesus

---

50. Aquinas, *Romans*, 231; Augustine, *Enchr.* (*NPNF*[1] 3:531).

51. Wright, *Into the Heart*, 163; Gorman, *Apostle of the Crucified Lord*, 443; Dunn, *Romans*, 1:481.

52. Witherington and Hyatt, *Romans*, 226; Moo, *Romans*, 551; Cranfield, *Romans*, 1:428.

53. Porter and Yoon, *Romans*, 190.

54. Jacobs and Krienke, "Foreknowledge, Providence, Predestination," *NIDNTT* 1:692–97.

Christ to be holy. The term "call" is not merely a beckoning but rather a commissioning to be molded to a new environment or to take on a divine task.[55] While Paul has traversed considerable ground since that greeting, his return to this term in 8:28 suggests that Paul is now arriving at his intended destination. Paul goes on to use "called" in noun or verb form eight times between 8:28 and 9:26, indicating that this part of Romans may be at the heart of Paul's purpose in writing.

In the OT, while the expectation was that people should hear and respond to a divine calling, it was not a compulsion.[56] People could refuse to listen (Isa 65:12; Jer 7:13), not answer (Isa 50:2), or seek to avoid it (Exod 3:11). This sense that a divine calling did not presume a positive response is reflected explicitly in some NT passages (Matt 22:1–14; 24:14; Luke 14:15–24), and nowhere do the NT authors describe those who are not believers as not having been called. Nevertheless, Rom 8:28 is interpreted by some scholars as an effectual call in that God evokes the faith required to respond to the call because God has predetermined that the person would be a believer.[57] In favor of this perspective, there is no sense of any residue of called people who are not also justified in 8:30. That inference, however, is unnecessary because Paul is only addressing those who are already lovers of God to encourage them, so his words only apply to those who have responded positively to the call of God. In Rom 10:16–21, when Paul reflects on those Israelites who have not responded positively to the gospel, Paul makes clear that the onus is firmly on them by citing Isaiah multiple times (Isa 53:1; 65:1, 2), a book that has God's call as a significant theme, including the failure of the people to respond appropriately to that call (Isa 43:22; 50:2; 65:12; 66:4). The biblical evidence suggests that κλητός in Rom 8:28 does not imply that God causes people to believe. Instead, the reference to their calling reminds lovers of God of God's love for them as shown in God's initiative to invite them.

Furthermore, their calling is part of a grander plan. This is the first time Paul uses πρόθεσις (plan) in Romans, however πρόθεσις occurs again in 9:11, and the related terms, προγινώσκω (foreknow, 8:29; 11:2) and προορίζω (predestine, 8:29, 30), pepper the text from here on.[58] Ja-

---

55. E.g., Rom 1:6–7; 1 Cor 1:9; Gal 1:15; 1 Thess 2:12.
56. Coenen, "Call," *NIDNTT* 1:272.
57. Moo, *Romans*, 552; Cranfield, *Romans*, 1:430; Barth, *Romans*, 322.
58. Jacobs and Krienke, "Foreknowledge, Providence, Predestination," *NIDNTT* 1:692–97; Cranfield, *Romans*, 1:430.

cobs and Krienke explain that the Jewish use of these terms differs from their meaning in classical Greek literature. For the Greek, these terms evoke a sense of fatalism and capricious determinism—a sense of lack of control that one must dishearteningly or stoically accept—and for that reason they were used sparingly by a philosophical culture that was biased toward human freedom.[59] Jewish writers did not use this terminology in the same way. Instead, they integrated these words into their theology of a loving, righteous, and deliberate God, who controls the mass of options with which a person might be presented, but who also carves out room for some human freedom within that divinely created context. God's control is not understood as capricious but caring, seeking to foster noble human responses and ultimately glorious outcomes.[60] By declaring that all things work together for good for lovers of God, Paul makes clear that he has adopted the Jewish and not the Greek perspective.[61]

Lovers of God can appreciate that all things work together for good because they can know that they are not the victims of random events but are within God's plan (πρόθεσις), in which God has invited them to participate (κλητός).[62] Rather than being overwhelmed with despair, lovers of God are invited to see God's good intent and to reevaluate their situation in the light of that divine intent.[63] That God had planned to call people does not imply that God had predetermined that they would be believers, as suggested by Calvin.[64] The direct connection by Aquinas of πρόθεσις in this verse to Augustinian predestination and Eph 1 is speculative.[65] All that is stated thus far is that it was part of God's plan to call those who are now lovers of God, and because of God's manifest commitment to them, they can be confident that God will continue to work for their good.

8:29a ὅτι οὓς προέγνω—because God foreknew them

The clause beginning with ὅτι mirrors the same conjunction in 8:28, indicating that Paul is elaborating on what we know, although the lack of an additional conjunction (e.g., "and") suggests that here ὅτι may be causal as it is commonly regarded and reflected in my translation. That still

---

59. Jacobs and Krienke, "Foreknowledge, Providence, Predestination," *NIDNTT* 1:692.
60. Jewett, *Romans*, 528.
61. Dunn, *Romans*, 1:482.
62. Cranfield, *Romans*, 1:430; Klein, *New Chosen People*, 137.
63. Cranfield, *Romans*, 1:431.
64. Calvin, *Romans*, 315.
65. Aquinas, *Romans*, 233.

results in awkward grammar, as the clause is then headless, with a loose connection to the substantive participles τοῖς οὖσιν or τοῖς ἀγαπῶσιν.[66] Either way, the meaning is similar whether 8:29 is regarded as the reason behind Paul's conclusion in 8:28 or a further expression of the thoughts in 8:28. Verses 28 and 29 an intricately linked.

The relative pronoun οὓς (those) also refers back to 8:28. The lovers of God are in the position of emphasis in the preceding clause, so they are the group Paul ultimately has in mind,[67] with the appositional τοῖς ... οὖσιν (those called according to plan) the immediate antecedent, especially since that clause introduces the concepts that are being explored in 8:29–30. As with 8:28, Paul brings the object (them) forward in the sentence, keeping the focus on the recipients of God's actions rather than on God. In order to improve the flow of the translation, I moved the object after the verb, although hopefully the overall translation of 8:28–29 reflects Paul's interests well.

Προγινώσκω (foreknow) is the first of a series of verbs in the aorist tense, which conveys a perfective aspect, including when referring to future events such as possibly with δοξάζω (glorify).[68] Paul is viewing these events as a completed whole rather than a sequence of emerging events. The verb is in the third-person singular form, which in context implies God is the subject of the verb.

While προγινώσκω suggested determinism in Greco-Roman society, in a Jewish context the term was neither mysterious nor foreboding. Προγινώσκω only implied that someone or something had been known to the subject for a long time (e.g., Acts 26:5). God knew Abraham would have descendants since the time of Abraham (Rom 11:2), and it was obvious to God for a long time how a rebellious world would treat the Christ (Acts 2:23). Peter's addressees had known for some time that God was holding off judgment day so that more might be saved (2 Pet 3:17). On the rare occasions προγινώσκω occurs in Second Temple Jewish literature, it is used in the same vein (Wis 6:13; 8:8; 18:6; Jdt 9:6; 11:19).[69] In Peter's first letter, προγινώσκω is qualified to refer to pre-creation (1 Pet 1:20), suggesting that the term on its own was not understood that way. In the case of Rom 8:29, Paul is likely referring to OT references to God

---

66. Porter and Yoon, *Romans*, 190.
67. Witherington and Hyatt, *Romans*, 227; Cranfield, *Romans*, 1:431.
68. Young, *Intermediate New Testament Greek*, 122.
69. Jacobs and Krienke, "Foreknowledge, Providence, Predestination," *NIDNTT* 1:692; Witherington and Hyatt, *Romans*, 230.

foreseeing the people of God,⁷⁰ such as the designation of Abraham as the "father" of both the circumcised and the uncircumcised who would have faith (Rom 4:16-17). The importation of a pretemporal sense along the lines of 1 Pet 1:20, as proposed by Cranfield and Moo, is unnecessary.⁷¹ Paul has firmly established in Romans that he is focused on the biblical timeline.

In Rom 8:29, what was it that God foreknew? Paul does not state that God foresaw faith or any merit, as was commonly believed in the church prior to the fifth-century Pelagian crisis and subsequently remained the case in the Eastern church.⁷² It is also not likely that foreknowledge refers to a person's love for God as per 8:28 because lovers of God are referred to in the present. Nor is it likely that it is foreknowledge of whom God would elect as Calvin understands election, given the word "elect" does not appear in 8:28-30.⁷³ Moo's argument that the knowledge is of the person rather than about the person has merit, but he too goes beyond the text to import a pretemporal perspective from Eph 1:4 and 1 Pet 1:20.⁷⁴ The lack of any qualification of προγινώσκω simply suggests that God foresaw people who needed his intervention,⁷⁵ and the most likely temporal reference point is within the biblical time span (cf. Rom 1:2; 11:1).

> 8:29b καὶ προώρισεν συμμόρφους τῆς εἰκόνος τοῦ υἱοῦ αὐτοῦ, εἰς τὸ εἶναι αὐτὸν πρωτότοκον ἐν πολλοῖς ἀδελφοῖς—and predestined them to be conformed to the likeness of his Son so that he would be the firstborn among many siblings

Commentators often consider the sequence of verbs in Rom 8:29-30 as being used in the same way and in a logical series, neglecting that προορίζω (predestine) is introduced and treated differently by Paul. Paul uses καί to join προγινώσκω and προορίζω, suggesting that these terms should be understood in parallel rather than in sequence. That allows οὓς at the beginning of the verse to act as the object of both verbs. The words

---

70. Wright, *Into the Heart*, 169.

71. Cranfield, *Romans*, 1:431; Moo, *Romans*, 555; Bultmann, "Προγινώσκω," *TDNT* 1:715.

72. Clement of Alexandria, *Miscellanies* 6.9, 7.17 (*ANF* 2:1041, 1170); So, too, Tertullian and Origen, according to Bromiley, "Predestination," *ISBE* 3:946. John of Damascus in the eight century is noted as maintaining this position in Aquinas, *Summa Theolgiæ* 1a.23.1.

73. Pace Calvin, *Romans*, 317; Cranfield, *Romans*, 1:432.

74. Moo, *Romans*, 555.

75. Luther, *Romans*, 75.

immediately following προορίζω make the most sense if they are taken as belonging solely to that verb because those words reflect decisions rather than knowledge, but once understood, this second clause should be interpreted together with προγινώσκω.

Προορίζω is rare in Greek literature and not found at all in Jewish writing prior to the NT.[76] Schmidt describes προορίζω as a stronger form of ὁρίζω (appoint, determine), and regards προορίζω as a predetermination of all things before time, of both persons and things.[77] Jacobs and Krienke prefer to think that what is predetermined is God's love and purpose for people,[78] and this seems a closer fit to the use of προορίζω in the NT. On two occasions προορίζω refers to God's plans for Jesus Christ (Acts 4:27; 1 Cor 2:7). The other four (Rom 8:29, 30; Eph 1:5, 11) describe God's plans for people through Jesus Christ. Often scholars use Eph 1:4–5 as the key text for aiding the understanding of Rom 8:29, however 1 Cor 2:7 is likely the more significant intertextual passage. First Corinthians was written earlier and only by a year or two,[79] and Romans was composed by Paul in the context of a visit to the Corinthian church. Having this in mind raises the expectation that in Rom 8:29–30 Paul may be thinking of God's plans for how Christ Jesus would benefit the people of God.

In Rom 8:29, the object of προορίζω, as with προγινώσκω, is those who love God. What is predestined is that those who love God would be conformed to the likeness of God's Son, building on the OT teaching of people as being created in the image of God. God's purpose is that Jesus Christ might be the firstborn among many siblings. This continues the family motif that has been running through chapter 8 (8:3, 15–17, 21, 23) and references the messianic credentials of Jesus to lead such a restoration (Ps 89:27).[80] This expansive qualification of the object of προορίζω raises a question. Does God predestine who would be in his family or does God predestine what Christ will do for those who are in his family?[81] The answer to that question is best informed by reviewing how Paul has prepared his readers for understanding his thoughts.

---

76. Schmidt, "Προορίζω," *TDNT* 5:456.

77. Schmidt, "Προορίζω," *TDNT* 5:456.

78. Jacobs and Krienke, "Foreknowledge, Providence, Predestination," *NIDNTT* 1:696.

79. Fee, *First Corinthians*, 5.

80. Jacob, *Conformed to the Image*, 187.

81. Interestingly, Aquinas describes predestination in both these senses. See

What precedes 8:29 is a series of pointed statements that the gospel was a long-considered plan by God for his people. In Rom 1:2 the gospel is described as having been promised (προεπαγγέλλω) through the prophets, and in 1:4 the gospel concerns the one determined (ὁρίζω) to be the Son of God. While ὁρίζω is linked temporally with Jesus's resurrection, its logical link with προεπαγγέλλω indicates that this was also part of God's long determined plan. Romans 3:25 states that God was only able to leave sins unpunished before Christ because he had preplanned (προτίθημι) Christ's sacrificial death for sins.[82] In Rom 4, when Abraham was told by God that he would be a father of many nations, God is presented as relating to Abraham in a manner that anticipated how God would ultimately relate to all his people through Christ (4:22–24). In 8:19, creation is personified as eagerly awaiting what it knows is going to happen, as are the saints themselves (8:23). Paul's epistle is peppered with descriptions of God's foreknowledge of his plans concerning what he is going to do for the saints through Christ. That is the expectation the attentive reader has when coming to 8:28–30.

This aligns with the flow of thought in 8:28–30. For people who love God, everything will turn out well because God has called them according to plan. God foreknew their need and therefore planned for them to be like Jesus. God's purpose for the lovers of God is conformity to the Son.[83] From 8:29–30, that likeness is achieved in the believers' justification and glorification.[84] Predestination is God deciding what God would do for his people, not God deciding who would be his people.[85] It is neither foreseeing a person's faith nor that the person is one of the elect. Predestination is God knowing humanity's future need and deciding how to meet that need in Christ. That is why predestination and election of believers are not synonymous. Once predestination is understood this way, there is no conflict, apparent or real, between predestination in 8:28–30 and the call for a human response in 10:13–17.[86] Furthermore, the text does not have

---

Aquinas, *Romans*, 234.

82. Jacobs and Krienke include προτίθημι in the same word group as προορίζω, which denotes divine control over future events. Jacobs and Krienke, "Foreknowledge, Providence, Predestination," *NIDNTT* 1:692.

83. Jacob, *Conformed to the Image*, 231.

84. *Pace* Cranfield, *Romans*, 1:432. Growing in conformity to Christ is an important teaching of Paul. It has come up in Rom 6 and Paul will return to it in Rom 12, but in 8:28–30 Paul is encouraging suffering Christians with what God is doing for them.

85. Thornhill, *Chosen People*, 219.

86. *Pace* Sanders, *Paul and Palestinian Judaism*, 447.

implications with respect to the predetermined rejection of individuals, nor whether believers could abandon their faith, other than declaring that nothing external can separate the believer from God's love.

While predestination concerns the people of God, it is important to understand that it is primarily about Jesus Christ.[87] Predestination is not recognition of God's establishment of love toward God, as Karl Barth suggests.[88] Predestination is God deciding in advance to establish his Son as the one on whom God's people would be modeled and the one around whom God's people would return to God as their Father. Predestination primarily concerns what would be done for and through the Son. Paul's breaking of the rhythm of 8:29–30 to refer twice to Christ belies Moo's suggestion that the text does not support a Christ focus.[89] Paul emphasizes that the divine goal was to make Jesus the firstborn among many children. This understanding is consistent with Paul's previous use of προορίζω in 1 Cor 2:7, which describes God's long-held plan for Jesus Christ and him crucified.

> 8:30a οὓς δὲ προώρισεν, τούτους καὶ ἐκάλεσεν—having predestined them, he called them

Although προορίζω is not qualified here, the qualification in 8:29 is implied. Augustine consistently failed to take this into account in his anti-Pelagian writings.[90] Even such a careful exegete as Aquinas acts at times as if the extensive qualification of προορίζω in 8:29 is a superfluous aside or not even there.[91] If προορίζω means what Augustine thought it meant, Paul's explanation of predestination in 8:29 is unnecessary and turns what would otherwise be a fine piece of rhetoric and poetry into an awkward and unnecessary excursus. That Paul needed to qualify προορίζω so extensively suggests it could not be applied to believers in the same way as the following verbs. Thus, when Paul commences 8:30 with οὓς δὲ προώρισεν, the reader is expected to keep in mind that Paul's understanding is "those for whom God had planned great things."

---

87. Thornhill, "Election and Predestination," 240.
88. Barth, *Romans*, 324.
89. Moo, *Romans*, 555.
90. Augustine, *Spirit and the Letter* (NPNF[1] 5:301, 333); *Against the Two Letters of the Pelagians* (NPNF[1] 5:1007); *Admonition and Grace* (NPNF[1] 5:1167–69, 1177); *Predestination of the Saints* (NPNF[1] 5:1247).
91. Aquinas, *Summa Theolgiæ* 1a.23.1; Aquinas, *Romans*, 233–35. So too Wright, *Into the Heart*, 10.

These, God called. The use of καλέω (to call) in the NT has been discussed above with κλητός (called). "Foreknew"/"predestined" being followed by "called" matches the construct τοῖς κατὰ πρόθεσιν κλητοῖς (those called according to plan) at the end of 8:28. God calls people to the family planned around the Son. As with 8:28, the text does not imply that this is an "effectual" or irresistible calling, as Moo argues,[92] but that it was part of God's plan to reach out to those who are now lovers of God.

> 8:30b καὶ οὓς ἐκάλεσεν, τούτους καὶ ἐδικαίωσεν—and having called them, he justified them

Paul cannot finish the sentence with καλέω because those who love God know that they cannot come to God in their own effort, as Paul established in the *partitio* (1:18–3:8). That is why Paul must go on to include their justification. It is beyond the scope of this study to engage with the extensive scholarly debate over the meaning of δικαιόω. It is enough to say that God justifies those who have faith in Jesus (Rom 3:26).

> 8:30c οὓς δὲ ἐδικαίωσεν, τούτους καὶ ἐδόξασεν—and having justified them, he glorified them

Those whom God justified, God also glorifies. Δοξάζω is also in the aorist tense, which may imply that Paul is thinking of glory already received by believers such as the gift of the Spirit as the firstfruits of glorification (8:23).[93] Alternately, Paul may be employing a futuristic aorist to consider the perfected glory to be revealed (8:18).[94] Cranfield views glorification as both now and not yet, with believers sharing in Christ's present glory.[95] Future glorification, however, has been a constant theme through the epistle. In 2:7, God will give glory, honor, and immortality to those who persistently do good. In 5:2 Paul invites his readers to rejoice in the hope of the glory of God. Romans 8:17 and 18 refer to the glory to be revealed in the saints, and in 8:21 creation longs to see that glory. Whether Rom 9:4 refers to past or future glory is considered below, but Paul returns to the future glory in 9:23 for which people are being prepared. It seems that 8:30 is best interpreted as focused on future glory as well.

---

92. Moo, *Romans*, 557; Cranfield, *Romans*, 1:432.

93. Matera, *Romans*, 205; Jewett, *Romans*, 530.

94. Gorman, *Apostle of the Crucified Lord*, 443; Young, *Intermediate New Testament Greek*, 125; Moo, *Romans*, 558; Dunn, *Romans*, 1:485.

95. Cranfield, *Romans*, 1:433.

Paul begins Rom 8:28–30 by referring to the saints as lovers of God, encouraging them to believe that their love has not been misplaced. Despite the hardships they may be facing, they are assured that they are firmly in the plan of God into which God has called them for their good. That plan was prepared long ago and is centered on God's Son, Jesus Christ, who is to be the firstborn of many who will be called to be the children of God and conformed to the Son by being justified and then glorified.

ROMANS 8:33

> τίς ἐγκαλέσει κατὰ ἐκλεκτῶν θεοῦ—Who will bring charges against God's chosen?

In Rom 8:33, Paul introduces the word ἐκλεκτός (chosen). This word is not common in the Pauline corpus, appearing only here and in Rom 16:13; Col 3:12; 1 Tim 5:21; 2 Tim 2:10; and Titus 1:1. On each occasion the significance of the term is assumed knowledge and there is no discussion of how one becomes elect. As Ridderbos notes, Paul uses "elect" like "saints," "beloved," and "called" as a customary expression which characterizes those in the church.[96] Ἐκλεκτός emphasizes God's commitment to believers (as in Rom 8:33) or points to a necessary response due to being called by God. Paul's broader use of the concept of the elect is discussed in more detail in the exegesis of 9:11, where the synonym ἐκλογή (elect) appears.

Stepping back to consider Rom 8:18–39 as a whole, some interim conclusions can be drawn with respect to predestination and election. Firstly, Paul does not use the terms synonymously. The two terms appear in different sections of the text for different purposes. Predestination is explained extensively without using election vocabulary (in contrast to Eph 1:4–5), whereas election appears incidentally as a reflexive description of God's people as is typical of Paul more generally. Predestination concerns God's plan for the Son to be the one through whom the people could join the family of God. Election implies that people are in God's family because God wants them there. In Rom 8, they are two very distinct ideas. Paul will has more to say on election in Rom 9, but for now it is important to see that in Romans, election is distinct from predestination.

---

96. Ridderbos, *Paul*, 330–333.

12

Exegesis of Romans 9:1–29

ROMANS 9:1–29 IN THE CONTEXT OF ROMANS 9—11

In the *constitutio* (1:16–17), Paul declares that the gospel is for the Jew first. In the epistle's final *refutatio*, Paul defends that statement in the face of so many Jews rejecting the gospel. Romans 9:1—11:36 is not an ungainly appendage to the epistle, as is sometimes thought, but is a deliberate part of the argument of the epistle.[1] It is probably an overreaction to refer to Rom 9—11 as the climax of the letter[2] because the *constitutio* and the *confirmatio* (3:9–30) are intended to be of prime importance, and the tone and pace of chapters 9–11 do not match the exalted language of chapter 8. Nevertheless, Paul was always heading toward the content of Rom 9—11 given his "Jew first" perspective and the rhetorical flow of the epistle.[3] This connection can also be seen in the details, with Paul returning to key ideas from 1:1–6 such as God's calling and God's preparation for the gospel, and Paul restriking notes from Rom 3—4 such as the advantage of being a Jew, the promises of God, and the righteousness-by-faith versus righteousness-by-works dichotomy.[4]

---

1. Cranfield, *Romans*, 2:445; Dunn, *Romans*, 2:519–20.
2. *Pace* Witherington and Hyatt, *Romans*, 237.
3. Fitzmyer, *Romans*, 539.
4. Dunn, *Romans*, 2:519, 543.

Inner and Inter-Texture

Whereas Rom 8:18–39 is characterized by polished literary techniques, the style of Rom 9—11 is more like methodical rhetoric.[5] These chapters can be viewed as a mini-argument in themselves, made up of an *exordium*, *narratio*, *constitutio*, *confirmatio*, and a series of *refutationes*, each of which is marked by a rhetorical question, before finishing with a rousing doxology in 11:33–36.[6] This internal coherence along with differences in language and style from other parts of Romans lends credence to the idea that chapters 9–11 may have had a life of their own prior to being incorporated into Romans.[7] There is possibly also a narrative substructure, with possible use of early Christian confessional material.[8] There are some indications of a chiastic structure, which N. T. Wright argues peaks at 10:9.[9] This can lend itself to fruitful comparisons and contrasts between various parts of the argument.

The inter-texture dominates Rom 9—11, with these chapters containing the most intensive engagement with Scripture within the Pauline corpus.[10] There is a stream of citations, references, and allusions to Scripture, to which Paul applies a midrashic interpretation that both engages with the literal meaning and considers how passages bear on one another.[11] This heavy use of Scripture leads to the inner and inter-textures being intertwined, so they are best looked at together.

A structure for Rom 9—11 is proposed below. The subdivision is largely uncontroversial, it being similar to the arrangements of most major commentators.[12] Each of these subsections will be explored to understand how the argument works as a whole and how that whole might impinge on the parts before conducting a detailed exegesis of Rom 9:1–29. The notes on the subsections of Rom 9:1–29 are briefer to avoid duplication in the detailed exegesis.

---

5. Longenecker, *Romans*, 772.
6. Bryan, *Preface to Romans*, 160; Witherington and Hyatt, *Romans*, 236.
7. Dunn, *Romans*, 2:520; Longenecker, *Romans*, 765.
8. Longenecker, *Romans*, 774.
9. Wright, *Paul and the Faithfulness of God*, 2:1163.
10. Matera, *Romans*, 214; Witherington and Hyatt, *Romans*, 237; Dunn, *Romans*, 2:520.
11. Longenecker, *Romans*, 811.
12. Aquinas, *Romans*, viii; Dunn, *Romans*, 1:ix; Matera, *Romans*, vii, 218; Barth, *Romans*, xx; Cranfield, *Romans*, 2:451, 470, 503.

The Rhetorical Flow of Romans 9–11			
•	9:1–3	*exordium*	Paul's compassion toward unbelieving Israelites
•	9:4–5	*narratio*	Israelites' many opportunities
•	9:6	*constitutio*	God's word has not failed; not all from Israel are Israel
•	9:7–13	*confirmatio*	Physical descent does not make one a child of God
	○ 9:14–18	*refutatio*	Is God unjust?
	○ 9:19–29	*refutatio*	Why does God blame us?
	○ 9:30–10:13	*refutatio*	Gentiles found righteousness and Israel did not?
	○ 10:14–21	*refutatio*	How can unbelieving Israelites call on Christ?
	○ 11:1–6	*refutatio*	Did God reject his people?
	○ 11:7–10	*refutatio*	What about those not chosen?
	○ 11:11–32	*refutatio*	Did unbelieving Israelites fall beyond recovery?
•	11:33–36	doxology	The glorious plans of God

9:1–3 *Exordium*: Paul's Compassion Toward Unbelieving Israelites

Paul opens Rom 9–11 with a dramatic change of mood and style. Whereas chapter 8 concludes with inspiring rhetoric and triumphant exaltation, chapter 9 begins with Paul laying out the anguish in his heart for those of his kin by flesh who have not welcomed the gospel. Paul aims in these verses to gain the sympathy of his audience and to invite the reader to approach this difficult discussion with empathy for the Israelites.

9:4–5 *Narratio*: Israelites' Many Opportunities

The change in content from Paul's self-reflection in 9:3 to a description of what Israelites have in 9:4–5 suggests a change in rhetorical purpose to a *narratio*. Paul is acknowledging that a case needs to be made as to how the gospel could be consistent with the unbelief of so many of his kin, who otherwise had access to so much from God. It is striking that Paul does not include election in this list, calling into question whether election is a key motif of chapters 9–11. Why did Paul choose these particular epithets?

9:6 *Constitutio*: God's Word Has Not Failed, for Not All from Israel Are Israel

In 9:6, Paul lays out his thesis statement or *constitutio* for Rom 9—11.[13] Paul's response to the unbelief of Israelites is that God's word has not failed because not all descendants from Israel are Israel. This was not an uncommon perspective in late Second Temple Judaism,[14] but it is of interest to see if there is something unique in Paul's argument and how Paul challenges the alternate view that all descendants of Israel are in God's family.[15] An explanation is also required for Paul's preference for "Israel" (used eleven times in 9–11) over "Jew" (used nine times in 1:16–3:29, and otherwise only at 9:24 and 10:12).

9:7–13 *Confirmatio*: Physical Descent Does Not Make One a Child of God

Paul appeals to Israel's own background to establish his premise, pointing out that both Abraham and Isaac had multiple children but in each case God's attention was on just one offspring. Isaac was the child of the promise. Jacob was the one chosen by God to lead and to experience God's love.[16] Israel's origins show that being a physical descendant is not enough. The terms ἐκλογή (elect) and καλέω (call) are used to describe Jacob, and the reference to God's πρόθεσις (plan) reappears. How these work within the specifics of the argument needs careful consideration.

9:14–18 *Refutatio:* Is God Unjust?

Having presented his case, Paul then deals with objections to physical descent being insufficient, the first of which is expressed in the rhetorical question, "Is God unjust?" To refute this, Paul refers to two divine revelations to Moses that show that Israelites were dependent on God's mercy, and that God is free to harden those who defy him. It is not a matter of justice, but mercy. In view of the way in which these verses have been

---

13. Dunn, *Romans*, 2:539.
14. Staples, *Paul and the Resurrection*, 19.
15. See Thornhill, *Chosen People*, 14.
16. Dunn, *Romans*, 2:518.

interpreted historically, it will be important to understand how these ideas function within the context of Paul's argument.

9:19–29 *Refutatio*: Why Does God Blame Us?

If it is purely a matter of God's will, then how could God blame us? Paul turns to pottery metaphors from the prophets to respond to this objection. It will be important to examine the inter-texture of Isaiah and Jeremiah closely before drawing conclusions on when and how the discrimination occurred between the honorable and dishonorable vessels. Paul expands on his explanation with quotations from Hosea and Isaiah, which point to a remnant being saved by God to assure the continuation of God's family. The reappearance of καλέω (call) and the introduction of gentiles into the argument both require explanation.

9:30–10:13 *Refutatio:* Gentiles Found Righteousness and Israel Did Not?

Paul's next rhetorical question addresses the apparent absurdity that gentiles found what they were not looking for while Israelites failed to find what they were earnestly seeking. Paul returns to the core vocabulary of the epistle of righteousness, faith, and law, which suggests that 9:1–29 should be interpreted with a view to how it prepares for 9:30—10:13. Paul touches briefly on the gentiles finding righteousness through faith, but he focuses his attention on the failed attempt by Israelites to gain righteousness through the law. Paul argues that Israelites should not have been caught out because it had long been announced that pursuing righteousness by works is a stumbling stone. This argument is supported by citations from Isa 8:14 and 28:16. In Isa 8, it is the Lord who is the stumbling stone because the unholy will be snared by God's holiness. Isaiah 28:16 refers to a cornerstone, but the effect is the same. The cornerstone shows God's holiness, which sweeps away the unholy. Israelites have the opportunity for honor, but those who pursue righteousness through works end up in dishonor and destruction, a sequence of events that mirrors Rom 9:22–23. Paul's reasoning based on Isaiah is that righteousness by works of the law fails because the law exposes a person's unrighteousness, so it is only the one who has righteousness because of faith who will be spared humiliation.

Witherington appears to excuse the Israelites for choosing to seek righteousness through the law as if that was what they were compelled to try,[17] but that is contrary to Paul's argument. Paul regards unbelieving Israelites to be at fault for neglecting the starting point of faith even before Christ. Dunn is also off the mark in suggesting that 9:33 shows God's intention to work through election and rejection.[18] God will not shrink back from rejecting those who do not believe, however that is not presented as God's predetermined desire but as a consequence of human sin.

In 10:1, Paul again mentions his sympathy toward his fellow countrymen to soften his message. He admires them for their zeal, but it is a misplaced zeal due to their flawed understanding. Instead of following God's path, they are trying to make their own path. Thus, they have effectively rejected God's way and are undertaking an unrighteous pursuit. The law does not lead to righteousness but to Christ, so that everyone who believes can be righteous. This is made clear by two citations, one from Lev 18:5 and the other from Deut 30:12–14. Both citations come from passages that paint dire consequences for those who do not obey God's law in full. Those words may be inspiring, but they are also foreboding, so one needs to cling to righteousness by faith (as Paul explained in Rom 3:21–22 and restated in Rom 10:11 by appeal to Isa 28:16). To make this point, Paul innovatively employs midrash to connect Deut 30:12–14 with the gospel. God's new word is that confession of Jesus as Lord leads to salvation, and belief in his resurrection leads to justification, for both Israelite and gentile (cf. 1:16–17; 4:24–25).[19] Thus, Paul has declared how to identify Israel from among the descendants of Israel. The way in which gentiles are brought to the fore in the argument may shed light on their introduction in 9:24.

10:14–21 *Refutatio*: How Can Unbelieving Israelites Call on Christ?

If Jesus Christ is the answer, what hope is there for those Israelites who have rejected him? The problem is not the lack of preaching. The gospel has been proclaimed but not believed since the days of Isaiah (Isa 52:7; 53:1). The problem is that those who rely on their physical descent from Israel are not alert to the calling of the Lord. Further quotations from Ps 19:4,

---

17. Witherington and Hyatt, *Romans*, 259.
18. Dunn, *Romans*, 2:591.
19. Oakes, "Galatians and Romans," 105.

Deut 32:21, and Isa 65:1–2 drive this point home. God has patiently reached out to the people of Israel, but they remain disobedient and obstinate. The problem lies with those who have not believed, not with the message and its transmission. The rejection of the gospel is not new. It continues a long pattern of hardheartedness among the descendants of Israel.

11:1–6   *Refutatio*: Did God Reject His People?

God has not abandoned Israel but, as already argued in 9:24–29, a remnant has been chosen by grace and not by its own deserving (11:5).[20] Paul cites himself as evidence, possibly echoing his argument in 2 Cor 11:22.[21] Ἐκλογή (election) is used of saved individuals, the remnant, and not of the nation. Paul shows from 1 Kgs 19 that God's maintenance of a remnant was just as true in OT times as it is in Paul's day.

11:7–10   *Refutatio*: What About Those Not Chosen?

Romans 11:7–10 goes over similar ground to the *refutatio* in 10:14–21. What is added here is the hardening of obstinate Israelites (cf. 10:21), which had long been announced (Deut 29:4; Ps 69:22–23). Paul has foreshadowed this argument in his reference to Pharaoh in Rom 9:17–18.

11:11–32 *Refutatio*: Did Unbelieving Israelites Fall Beyond Recovery?

God works through the hardening of unbelieving Israelites to bring salvation to gentiles, with the intention that this would go on to lead Israelites to desire that salvation for themselves. Their hardening is not necessarily permanent (11:23). This is not an innovation by Paul, but the application of Deut 32:21, which Paul cites in Rom 10:19. Gentiles also need to have the same heartfelt response to Israelite unbelief with a view to sparking Israelites to belief. God can graft repentant Israelites back in again (11:23). Their destruction is not a foregone conclusion because God remains patient (cf. 9:22). Gentiles must not presume upon God. They need to maintain their humility and faith. Paul's use of the second-person

---

20. Longenecker and Still, *Thinking Through Paul*, 187.
21. Fitzmyer, *Romans*, 72.

singular pronoun in 11:17–24 drives home his concern that each and every gentile needs to avoid any sense of superiority.[22]

Romans 11:25–26 has been highly controversial down the ages, with it being interpreted from as early as the second century that "all Israel" includes the full number of gentiles, thus detaching it from its ethnic roots, and eventually leading the mostly gentile Christian community to see no place for Judaism in the church.[23] Discomfort following the Holocaust led commentators in the other direction, noting that on every other occasion Paul is referring to ethnic Israel, so it is unlikely that is should be understood differently in 11:26.[24] The detailed exegesis will need to be alert to this controversy. Following Staples, it is possible that the answer lies someway in between.

Romans 11:28 reiterates that God has hardened obstinate Israelites so that the gospel would reach the gentiles, but Paul reintroduces ἐκλογή (election) and alludes to Mal 1:2–3 to remind the reader that God will keep his commitment to the patriarchs. The calling in 10:14–21 remains open to descendants from Israel.[25]

11:33–36 *Doxology:* The Glorious Plans of God

Greco-Roman rhetoric typically concludes with an emotional appeal to join the audience's heart with their mind, which Paul does with this doxology.[26] Drawing on more biblical citations, Paul celebrates God's plans as profound, merciful, and glorious. Unlike classical rhetoric, Paul does not restate key parts of his argument but celebrates the wisdom of God as if the case has already been won.

Sociocultural Texture

The sociocultural texture of Rom 9–11 is not prominent but is very firmly located in the tension between the Christian community and the

---

22. Cranfield, *Romans*, 2:553.
23. Staples, *Paul and the Resurrection*, 12–14.
24. Moo, *Romans*, 736.
25. Sievers notes that not only Luther, but in fact most exegetes and theologians in the past centuries, Catholic as well as Protestant, denied this ongoing commitment of God to the descendants of Israel. Sievers, "God's Gifts and Call," 138.
26. Witherington and Hyatt, *Romans*, 237.

remainder of Judaism. Paul repeatedly expresses his anxiety over his kin's salvation (9:1-3; 10:1; 11:11). His rhetorical questions and diatribe do not necessarily represent actual arguments taking place, but they hint at opponents of the gospel in the background (15:31). Paul counsels gentile Christians to take a conciliatory attitude (11:13).

Ideological Texture

At the ideological level, the text separates out Paul's Jewish and gentile readers at times, with Paul's opponents also hovering in the background. In subsequent centuries, Rom 9:6–29 was often called on to justify various doctrinal positions, as documented by Sanday and Headlam.[27] Christian gnostics relied on 9:14–18 to identify themselves as the elect ones. Origen reacted strongly to this by interpreting Rom 9 in a manner that supported human free will.[28] John Chrysostom and Christian writers in the East generally followed Origen in this regard.[29] The next major development was by Augustine in response to the overemphasis on human freedom by Pelagius, but that reignited rather than settled the controversy, which continues to this day. Longenecker lays out five significant interpretations that continue to be debated:[30]

- a theological understanding that emphasizes humanity's God-given free will, for which Origen, Chrysostom, and Arminianism[31] are known;
- Augustine's theological exposition of God's sovereign grace and predestination of the elect, which was heightened and developed by John Calvin and others in the Protestant reformations;
- a salvation history perspective that finds in Rom 9—11 the redemptive history of Jewish Christianity;

---

27. Sanday and Headlam, *Romans*, 269–75.

28. Origen, *First Principles* (ANF 3:606).

29. Chrysostom, *Hom. Rom. 9:1* (NPNF¹ 11:834); Longenecker, *Romans*, 801.

30. Longenecker, *Romans*, 766. Levering considers these developments in more detail. Levering, *Predestination*.

31. Longenecker ascribes this to Arminius, but that is not strictly the case. Arminius taught that people were only free to continue in unbelief, and ascribed faith fully to God's predestined work, unaffected by something foreseen in the believer. See Arminius, *Works of James Arminius*, 2:226, 394.

- a history-of-religions approach that concludes that the ongoing existence of both Judaism and Christianity is in accord with God's will; and
- an apologetic understanding that treats Rom 9—11 as a theodicy for God's actions in redeeming some people and condemning others.

To these Longenecker adds a sixth, that Paul is arguing for a remnant theology, although Longenecker acknowledges that not all aspects of remnant theology as expressed in Second Temple Jewish literature can be found in the NT, let alone within Rom 9—11.[32] My survey above has connection points with each of these, but differs from each of them as well, finding that Paul's primary purpose is to show that the rejection of the gospel by many Israelites is tragically consistent with Scripture, but all hope is not lost because God's commitment to Israel remains extant. That summary now needs to be tested by a detailed examination of Rom 9:1–29.

Sacred Texture

Romans 9—11 emphasizes God's sovereignty and freedom, but it is a mistake to conclude that God does not allow some human freedom. The bold statements in Rom 9 are only intended to establish principles that are applied in detail in Rom 10—11. God may harden the obstinate, but it is with a view to provoking envy and the suspension of unbelief. There is nothing that anyone can do that might be deserving of God's mercy, and yet God invites everyone to respond to the gospel in faith to receive that mercy. Romans 9—11 leads the saints to humility and joy before their wise and glorious God, and to having the same deep desire for the salvation of all.

ROMANS 9:1–29 IN DETAIL

9:1–3

> [1] I am telling you the truth in Christ. I am not lying. My conscience testifies on my behalf in the Holy Spirit, [2] that I am grieving deeply and have constant anguish in my heart. [3] For I wish

---

32. Longenecker, *Epistle to the Romans*, 767, 803–10.

that I were cursed to be separated from Christ on behalf of my siblings, my kin by flesh.

The inner texture deliberately slows the reader down by beginning without a conjunction and using a sequence of doubled expressions (e.g., "truth . . . lying").[33] Paul wants his readers to take his words to heart. In an expression comparable to a courtroom oath, Paul declares that he is telling the truth ἐν Χριστῷ (in Christ).[34] This is all supported by the testimony of both his conscience and the Holy Spirit.

From an inter-texture perspective, Paul's multiple qualifications may have been included to fulfill the biblical law of evidence.[35] Alternately, Paul's embellished appeal may be with a view to the ideological texture in that Paul wants to preempt anyone challenging the sincerity of his grief for his fellow Israelites (9:2–3).[36] The reason for Paul's grief is unstated, but it soon becomes apparent in the flow of Paul's argument. As Longenecker points out, Paul would have been regarded by some as having renounced Mosaic law and having set himself against his own countrymen (cf. 15:31).[37] Others may have thought that Paul's focus on the gentiles meant that he had given up on his fellow Jews.[38] On the contrary, Paul genuinely believes the gospel is the means of salvation for the Jew first and is deeply concerned for his unbelieving kin.[39]

Paul's expression of grief in 9:2 evokes memories of the noble laments of Scripture,[40] and is intended to foster sympathy from his readers. Paul goes so far as to write that he would be willing to be cursed and to be separated from Christ (9:3) for the sake of his unbelieving countrymen.[41] This is an extreme wish that is practically unfulfillable,[42] although it is probably inspired by Moses's prayer in Exod 32:31–32, since Paul shows he is reflecting on this inter-texture at Rom 9:15.[43] Regardless,

---

33. Dunn, *Romans*, 2:522.
34. Aquinas, *Romans*, 246; Cranfield, *Romans*, 2:452.
35. Staples, *Idea of Israel*, 188, 191; Cranfield, *Romans*, 2:452.
36. Gorman, *Romans*, 218; Moo, *Romans*, 577.
37. Longenecker, *Romans*, 780; Campbell, "Romans III," 30.
38. Cranfield, *Romans*, 2:454.
39. Cranfield, *Romans*, 2:446; Barth, *Church Dogmatics*, 2.2:202.
40. E.g., Lam 2:13; Matt 26:38. See Aquinas, *Romans*, 246–7; Moo, *Romans*, 577; Gorman, *Romans*, 219.
41. Aquinas, *Romans*, 248.
42. Cranfield, *Romans*, 2:445, 454, 458; Matera, *Romans*, 220.
43. Cranfield, *Romans*, 2:454.

Paul's intent is noble. Whereas victors would normally mock and lord it over the vanquished, Paul subverts expectations and evokes sympathy for his kin by desiring that unbelieving Israelites might share in the victory (cf. 10:1). While the text does not invoke Jesus's command to love one's enemies, Rom 9:1–3 embodies its spirit. Paul is not representing the church, as suggested by Karl Barth, and Barth's extensive juxtaposition of the church and Israel through Rom 9—11 is not exegetically sound.[44] The interpretation of Rom 9—11 needs to remain tethered to the cause of Paul's grief and be sympathetic to its intensity.

9:4–5

> [4]They are Israelites, and theirs is the adoption, the glory, the covenants, the giving of the law, the worship, and the promises; [5]and they have the forefathers and from them came the Christ according to the flesh, who is God over all, blessed forever, amen.

Grammatically, 9:4–5 is an artistic arrangement of two relative clauses under the main verb εὔχομαι (pray, wish) at the beginning of 9:3.[45] Despite this literary connection to 9:3, the change in content from Paul's self-reflection in 9:3 to a recital of Israelite opportunities in 9:4–5 flags a change in rhetorical purpose. In a brief *narratio*, Paul lays out the reasons why he must make a defense, because on the face of it, it is inconceivable that Israelites would be separated from Christ, given what is theirs for the taking.[46]

- οἵτινές εἰσιν Ἰσραηλῖται (They are Israelites): Paul's change of terminology from "Jew" to "Israelite" is abrupt, but it is Paul's preferred term through Rom 9—11. This is not merely a reference to ethnicity or national heritage. It draws the reader's attention to the patriarchs, in particular Israel, and the promises and principles that were established at that time.[47] It also reminds those of the tribe of Judah (Jews) that they are part of a greater whole (Israel), which needs to be

---

44. Barth, *Romans*, 330.
45. Cranfield, *Romans*, 2:460.
46. Cranfield, *Romans*, 2:459.
47. Cranfield, *Romans*, 2:460; Moo, *Romans*, 582.

restored in full for those promises to be fulfilled (cf. Rom 11:26).[48] Paul picks out the following characteristics that were relevant to Israelites.

- ὧν ἡ υἱοθεσία (theirs is the adoption): Paul is the only biblical author to use the term "adoption," but the concept of being drawn into God's family is widely attested across the NT, including in Romans (4:16; 7:4).[49] Adoption reinforces the sense that one's standing in God's family is not based on entitlement but on God's grace. Many scholars infer that Paul has in mind the nation of Israel as God's firstborn son (cf. Exod 4:22; Jer 31:9),[50] but Paul consistently uses υἱοθεσία to refer to those redeemed by Christ Jesus and enlivened by the Spirit (Rom 8:15, 23; Gal 4:5). This suggests that Paul is listing opportunities that originate out of Israel rather than things that descendants of Israel benefit from as a matter of course (cf. Rom 3:2).

  - ἡ δόξα (the glory): In Romans, human glory is future (2:7, 10; 5:2; 8:18, 21; 9:23), so Paul is likely referring to the future glory in store for the children of God. While some scholars think Paul is referring to past manifestations of God's glory that were treasured by Judeans (Exod 40:32; 1 Kgs 8:11),[51] Paul's consistent reference to future glory and lack of any intertextual allusion to past glory suggest otherwise.

  - αἱ διαθῆκαι (the covenants): The plural form is surprising, which is probably what led to the singular appearing as a textual variant.[52] As in Gal 3:17, the reference is probably to the covenants with Abraham and Moses, since Paul has already referred to both in Romans,[53] but it also sets up Paul's reference to the new covenant in Rom 11:27.[54]

---

48. Staples, *Idea of Israel*, 23–84.
49. Braumann, "υἱός," *NIDNTT* 1:287–90; Knobloch, "Adoption," *ABD* 1:78.
50. Aquinas, *Romans*, 248; Calvin, *Romans*, 339; Moo, *Romans*, 583.
51. Aquinas, *Romans*, 248; Dunn, *Romans*, 2:526; Cranfield, *Romans*, 2:462.
52. Cranfield, *Romans*, 2:462.
53. Calvin, *Romans*, 340; Cranfield, *Romans*, 2:462.
54. Gorman, *Romans*, 220.

- ἡ νομοθεσία (the giving of the law): Paul likely has in mind the giving of the law rather than the legislation itself,[55] emphasizing both the tragedy of Israel's failure to benefit from God's gracious act and the opportunity to understand it afresh. This is the law that the gospel upholds (Rom 3:31).

- ἡ λατρεία (the worship): This is a word usually reserved for cultic ritual, and commentators often consider that this is what is alluded to here,[56] but Paul likely also has in mind the opportunity for the new form of worship (12:1), which is available to those who live by the Spirit.[57]

- αἱ ἐπαγγελίαι (the promises): The plural indicates that Paul has in mind the many promises of Yahweh to the patriarchs (cf. Rom 4:13–17; 15:8),[58] even if Paul focuses on only one promise to Abraham in Rom 9:7. A promise points to grace and leads to faith, not to entitlement and merit.

- ὧν οἱ πατέρες (they have the forefathers): The new relative pronoun breaks the flow and gives these last two epithets room to breathe. The story of the patriarchs is foundational to Paul's thinking (cf. Rom 4),[59] and the opportunities that are open to Israelites arise from there.

  - ἐξ ὧν ὁ Χριστός (from them came the Christ): Israel's honor of delivering the Christ makes their rejection of Christ all the more tragic.[60] While it is possible that ὁ θεός begins a separate benediction,[61] grammatically and thematically it is more likely to be predicated to Χριστός.[62] Κατὰ σάρκα (according to the flesh) reminds the reader

---

55. Moo, *Romans*, 584; Gorman, *Romans*, 220.
56. E.g., Cranfield, *Romans*, 2:463.
57. Longenecker, *Romans*, 786.
58. Longenecker, *Romans*, 787; Cranfield, *Romans*, 2:464.
59. Moo, *Romans*, 585.
60. Cranfield, *Romans*, 2:464.
61. Dunn, *Romans*, 2:529.
62. Porter and Yoon, *Romans*, 202; Cranfield, *Romans*, 2:468; Witherington and Hyatt, *Romans*, 251; Moo, *Romans*, 587.

of Christ's physical descent from Israel (cf. 1:3), and ὁ ὢν ἐπὶ πάντων θεός (who is God over all) points to his divine standing over Israel (cf. 1:4).[63]

Interestingly, Paul's description of his fellow Israelites in 9:4–5 does not include election. On the one hand, this observation could be considered pedantic. The term "Israel" conveys the sense of being God's elect.[64] The word υἱοθεσία (adoption) suggests a conscious choice by God, as does the establishment of covenants and the giving of the law and the promises. Many scholars use "election" as the all-encompassing term for these Israelite benefits.[65] On the other hand, it is possible that Paul deliberately does not use the word "election" in this context because it would not align with how he goes on to use the term in the rest of Rom 9—11.[66] Paul cites and alludes to Deuteronomy several times in Rom 9—11, but not once does he refer to Deut 7:6 or any other OT passage that describes the nation of Israel as God's chosen people.[67] Paul appears to reserve election terminology to refer to God's commitment to individuals rather than to corporate Israel. This will be explored further in the exegesis of Rom 9:11.

9:6

> [6]Not that the word of God is failing, because not all who are from Israel are Israel.

The main verb, ἐκπίπτω (to fail), marks the beginning of a new paragraph, which extends to 9:13 in a series of subordinate clauses, citations, and developing thoughts. The opening denial ("Not that . . .") breaks the rhetorical flow and warns the reader to avoid the false conclusion that the word of God has failed.[68] The trustworthiness of God's word is a strong sentiment within Judaism (e.g., Ps 119:89; Isa 55:11).[69] Paul must explain

---

63. Aquinas, *Romans*, 249; Calvin, *Romans*, 342; Matera, *Romans*, 220; Gorman, *Romans*, 220.
64. Dunn, *Romans*, 2:526; Jewett, *Romans*, 562.
65. Cranfield, *Romans*, 2:460; Longenecker, *Romans*, 783; Moo, *Romans*, 570.
66. Schrenk, "ἐκλεκτός," *TDNT* 4:189.
67. Pace Moo, *Romans*, 571.
68. Dunn, *Romans*, 2:518; Gorman, *Romans*, 221.
69. Aquinas, *Romans*, 251.

why there is no inconsistency between God's promises to the forefathers and the rejection of the gospel by many of their descendants.

The answer is provided in the following causal subordinate clause. Not all who are from Israel are Israel. Romans 9:7–13 makes it clear that the phrase ἐξ Ἰσραήλ (from Israel) is referring to physical descendants of Israel, and οὗτοι Ἰσραήλ (those who are Israel) is referring to the subset who are the children of God and truly Israel. As Staples points out, by this expression Paul flags that the term "Israel" can be used in multiple ways, and that it will be important to be alert to this while following Paul's argument.[70] Staples goes to some length to show how this distinction between descendants and true Israel flows through the entirety of Rom 9—11.

Paul's primary concern in this *refutatio* is to explain why physical descent from Israel is insufficient to inherit the promises to Israel.[71] By shifting the perspective from Jews to Israelites, Paul brings the patriarchs to the foreground and Jewish hopes for the restoration of all of Israel. Longenecker rightly points out that Paul is introducing remnant theology into his argument,[72] but he goes too far in making that the primary motif of the passage. Paul is not arguing for that doctrine but rather using aspects of it to support his principal argument that the rejection of the gospel by many Israelites does not invalidate the gospel. In Rom 2:28–29, Paul announced that a true Jew is not one who is circumcised outwardly but one who is circumcised inwardly, and in that same vein Paul states in Rom 9:6 that mere physical descent from Israel is insufficient to be Israel.

The *constitutio* does not support suggestions that election is the central motif of Paul's argument, such as proposed by Cranfield and Matera.[73] Election is not highlighted as one of the benefits of being an Israelite (9:4–5), is not present in 9:6, and only comes up in a supporting role at the end of the *confirmatio*. Even less likely is Barth's suggestion that Paul sees true Israel in the church.[74] The church does not replace Israel.[75] If anything, Rom 9—11 concludes with believing gentiles being nourished by true Israel (11:17–21).

---

70. Staples, *Paul and the Resurrection*, 70.

71. This is a nuanced restatement of what Dunn describes as the dominant view that Rom 9–11 concerns the place of Jew and gentile within the purpose of God. See Dunn, *Theology of Paul*, 501.

72. Longenecker, *Romans*, 814.

73. Cranfield, *Romans*, 2:473–74; Matera, *Romans*, 214.

74. Barth, *Church Dogmatics*, 2.2:204, 214.

75. Wasserberg, "Romans 9–11," 182.

9:7-13

⁷Not all children of Abraham are the seed of Abraham, because "seed will be called for you in Isaac." ⁸That is, the children of the flesh are not these children of God, but the children of the promise are reckoned as seed. ⁹For the word of promise is this, "At that time I will return and Sarah will have a son." ¹⁰Not only this but also consider Rebecca, who conceived twins with Isaac our father, ¹¹and before the twins were born and had done anything good or bad, so that God's plan by election would hold true, ¹²not from works but by calling, it was said to her, "The older will serve the younger." ¹³Just as it has been written, "Jacob I loved but Esau I hated."

In Rom 9:7-13, Paul lays out the case for his premise of there being a distinction between being from Israel and being Israel. His argument falls into two parts, 9:7-9 and 9:10-13, with each focused on a particular patriarch's progeny, and each supported by Scripture.

The οὐδέ . . . ἀλλά construction of 9:7 replaces the false notion that all the children of Abraham are the seed of Abraham, with the declaration that only in Isaac would the seed be called (citing Gen 21:12).[76] Paul's explanatory note in 9:8 confirms that it is not a matter of being a physical descendant but of being a child of the promise, and 9:9 supports this argument with citations from Gen 18:10 and 18:14.[77] Σπέρμα (seed) is a key word in the inner texture.[78] Σπέρμα occurs nine times in Romans (1:3; 4:13, 16, 18; 9:7 [twice], 8, 29; 11:1) compared with only six times in the rest of the Pauline corpus. In Rom 1:3, Christ is ἐκ σπέρματος Δαυὶδ (of the seed of David). In chapter 4, the seed of Abraham receive the promised inheritance through righteousness that comes by faith. In 9:7-8 σπέρμα and σάρξ are contrasted, with the latter insufficient for being a child of God, and the former being τέκνα τῆς ἐπαγγελίας (the children of the promise).[79] In Rom 9:29, the σπέρμα are the saved remnant.[80] Σπέρμα represents those who inherit what God promised.

---

76. Dunn, *Romans*, 2:540; Porter and Yoon, *Romans*, 205.

77. Cranfield, *Romans*, 2:476; Moo, *Romans*, 598; Abasciano, *Paul's Use of the Old Testament*, 40.

78. Longenecker, *Romans*, 812.

79. Dunn, *Romans*, 2:540.

80. Longenecker, *Romans*, 812.

Paul has already argued that the promise is received through faith (Rom 4:13–16),[81] and he will go on to argue again for the criticality of faith in 9:30—10:10. Romans 9:7–9 supports that by showing that Israel came from a promised child and was not merely a physical descendant. Witherington, wanting to avoid any sense of predetermined election, argues that 9:7–8 does not imply a personal connection with God, but that case is invalid and unnecessary.[82] The phrases "child of God," "seed of Abraham," and "children of the promise" are used interchangeably and imply a special standing with God (cf. 8:16, 17, 21).[83] The text, however, does not equate Isaac bearing the promise of Gen 21:12 with election to salvation, as suggested by Calvin and Ridderbos.[84] The citation only states that it is from Isaac and his descendants that seed will be called (reflected in the LXX and BHS). Paul has more to say in 9:10–13 and 9:30—10:13 on how one participates in the promise, so extrapolating a doctrine of election based purely on 9:7–9 is premature.[85] It is better only to draw the conclusion that Paul does in 9:7–9, that from the beginning of God's dealings with the patriarchs, being a child of God is a matter of promise, not of physical descent.

Next Paul turns to Jacob/Israel's own origin story (9:10–13). The transitional phrase οὐ μόνον δέ (and not only this) shows that Paul is taking his argument one step further.[86] After emphasizing that both Esau and Jacob descended from Isaac in the same way (9:10), a series of short clauses in 9:11–12 establishes an important principle.

- "Before they were born" sets up the following statement as indisputable.
- "Before . . . they had done anything good or bad" establishes that works were not the basis for what follows.
- "So that the plan of God according to election would hold true." Κατ' ἐκλογὴν πρόθεσις (plan by election) is the same construction as κατὰ πρόθεσιν κλητοῖς (called according to plan) in 8:28 but with the concepts in the expression reversed. This changes the emphasis from calling in 8:28 to God's plan/purpose in 9:11,[87] which reflects

---

81. Ridderbos, *Paul*, 342.
82. Witherington and Hyatt, *Romans*, 253–255.
83. Moo, *Romans*, 597.
84. Calvin, *Romans*, 345; Ridderbos, *Paul*, 343; Moo, *Romans*, 591.
85. E.g., Moo, *Romans*, 597; Barth, *Church Dogmatics*, 2.2:214.
86. Moo, *Romans*, 599.
87. Abasciano, *Paul's Use of the Old Testament*, 49.

Paul's change of focus from comforting believers to understanding how God works.

- "Not from works but by calling" places καλέω (to call) in parallel with ἐκλογή (election). God's purpose is to call. That God's purpose is not in response to human works is a consistent theme throughout Romans.[88]

- Paul concludes with a loose quotation of Gen 25:23, showing God's purpose was focused on Jacob. Paul is subverting the prevalent theological conviction among his fellow Jews, such as in Philo's writings and Rabbinic literature, that God's preference for Israel was based on its good works.[89]

Of particular interest to this study is the appearance of ἐκλογή (election), πρόθεσις (plan), and καλέω (to call) in 9:11–12 (cf. 8:28). In 9:11, Paul affirms that God's plan for election is maintained, echoing the opening statement in 9:6 that God's word does not fail.[90] The way in which "doing anything good or bad" is paired with "election" in 9:11 and "works" is paired with "calling" in 9:12 indicates that election and calling are closely related. The inclusion of πρόθεσις in 9:11 connects these verses with 8:28–30, but election is used in the same expression as "called" rather than being connected with "predestined."

The relationship between calling and election is often described as the divine call giving effect to the divine election.[91] As already discussed in the notes for 8:28, that explanation is not consistent with how the term "called" is used in the Bible more generally. The divine call does not compel nor always result in a positive response. Furthermore, as discussed in part 2, it is questionable that election of someone into God's family precedes their call because that understanding relies on a particular interpretation of Eph 1:4 that may not respect the unique aspects of Paul's expression in that passage. In Rom 9:11–12, rather than calling following election, both terms are used to describe the same divine declaration. God's preference for Jacob over Esau is both a choice and a calling. Paul does not refer to a subsequent calling of Jacob. Paul seems to be using the terms in a different manner to the traditional understanding.

---

88. Dunn, *Romans*, 2:543.

89. Abasciano, *Paul's Use of the Old Testament*, 58; Staples, *Paul and the Resurrection*, 190.

90. Abasciano, *Paul's Use of the Old Testament*, 51.

91. Cranfield, *Romans*, 2:478.

Because of the significance of the concept of election, much is written about how the background of the term might have informed Paul's use of it. The Hebrew word for "choose," *bāchar*, is introduced in Deut 7:6, where it refers to God having chosen the corporate body of Israel. Deuteronomy 14:2 links this with Exod 19:5 (where *bāchar* is not used), suggesting that, from the perspective of Deuteronomy, the idea that the people of Israel are chosen by God has been implicit in Israel's preceding history. Silberman agrees, arguing that the concept is found in the notion of covenant.[92] Because election conveys that the object has been separated out by God for a divine purpose, it also shares much in common with the "holiness" group of words.[93] The concept of election can also be found in general expressions such as "call,"[94] which is particularly relevant to Rom 9—11. While the terminology of election is not prominent in the OT, the concept of election is present in all of God's actions. God is thoughtful and deliberate, not instinctive and capricious. It would be a mistake, however, to turn election into the central doctrine which explains all others. It is an aspect of God's character which is worth emphasizing when it is necessary to remind people that their circumstances are not accidental and that God's plans for them are not incidental. God chooses people or objects for a specific purpose, with the emphasis being that it is by grace and not because of the inherent worthiness of the object. The OT only uses the verb form (to choose), which maintains the focus on the divine action.

It is not until the late Second Temple Greek texts that the noun "the elect" begins to appear and the focus shifts to the chosen objects, with writers beginning to imply or outright claiming that election is merited and a reason for pride. Schrenk and Quell argue that Jews adopted this posture as an aid in enduring persecution and oppression.[95] Silberman notes that this sense of worthiness of the elect is also found in the Rabbinic literature.[96] The Qumran community took this a step further, understanding election as God's hand in their lives to give them an

---

92. Silberman, "Chosen People," *EncJud* 4:669.

93. Schrenk and Quell, "Ἐκλέγομαι," *TDNT* 4:145.

94. Schrenk and Quell, "Ἐκλέγομαι," *TDNT* 4:148.

95. Coenen, "ἐκλέγομαι," *NIDNTT* 1:538; Schrenk and Quell, "Ἐκλέγομαι," *TDNT* 4:170.

96. Silberman, "Chosen People," *EncJud* 4:670.

opportunity to show their worth.⁹⁷ The Essenes required covenanters to fulfill their obligations to maintain their salvation.⁹⁸

While the NT also makes use of noun forms of election (ἐκλεκτός and ἐκλογή), the NT reverts to the perspective of the OT, with the emphasis being back on God's grace toward the chosen and there being no implicit value in those chosen (e.g., 1 Cor 1:27–29 where the verb form ἐκλέγομαι is employed). Coenen claims that ἐκλογή in Rom 9:11; 11:5, 7, 28 refers to the nation Israel,⁹⁹ but this is not the case in 9:11 and 11:28 where it is applied to the patriarchs, nor in 11:5, 7, where the elect remnant and the nation of Israel are juxtaposed. In Rom 9—11, Paul seems to avoid using the term "elect" to refer to the nation of Israel, instead reserving it for individual patriarchs and those who live by faith.¹⁰⁰

While "the elect" is mostly used of the plurality of believers, suggestions that it is a collective noun would seem to undermine how Paul uses the term.¹⁰¹ In Rom 8:33, relief is gained by God's personal interest, not by being in the collective. In 11:4–5, the seven thousand are kept because of each individual's ongoing allegiance to God. It is also notable that Paul can use ἐκλεκτός to refer to a single Christian (Rom 16:13). It would seem better to understand "elect" as singular noun that can also be used as a plural.¹⁰²

In considering how "elect" and "calling" interrelate, it is important to note that "calling" is Paul's preferred term in Rom 9—11.¹⁰³ Paul's use of ἐκλογή and his preference for καλέω in Rom 9—11 is at odds with the views of those commentators who seek to connect these verses with predestination. By focusing on ἐκλογή at the expense of καλέω, Moo and Matera do not do justice to the prominence of καλέω as a key word in the inner texture of chapters 9 and 10, and they give ἐκλογή an importance that is not reflected in Rom 9—11.¹⁰⁴ In this they follow Calvin, who barely

---

97. Kuhn, "Impact of Selected Qumran Texts," 169. *Pace* Broshi, "Predestination in the Bible," 237–238.

98. Qimron, "Dualism in the Essene Communities," 196; Thornhill, *Chosen People*, 17–18.

99. Coenen, "ἐκλέγομαι," *NIDNTT* 1:536–42; Thornhill, "Election and Predestination," 239; Klein, *New Chosen People*, 146.

100. Schrenk and Quell, "Ἐκλέγομαι," *TDNT* 4:179, 189.

101. *Pace* Thornhill, *Chosen People*, 171; Klein, *New Chosen People*, 146.

102. Shogren, "Election: New Testament," *ABD* 2:441–44.

103. Dunn, *Theology of Paul*, 510.

104. Matera, *Romans*, 223; Moo, *Romans*, 601.

mentions calling in his discussion of 9:11–12 and instead stresses God's free election of one and rejection of the other.[105] Aquinas also emphasizes God's free choice and goes on to link 9:11 with the predestination and election of the saints via Eph 1:4 and 1:15.[106] This reliance on Eph 1:4 is unfortunate for two reasons. Firstly, both Rom 9:11–12 and the related expression in 8:28 connect election with calling, not predestination. Secondly, the expression of Eph 1:4 is unique, with election being "in Christ" and pretemporal. Rather than the election of individual saints, Eph 1:4 appears to be describing God's choice of Christ for the saints, similar to my explanation of predestination in Rom 8:29 (cf. Eph 1:5; 1 Pet 1:20). I suggest that Eph 1:4 is an exception to rather than the norm for how Paul uses the word "election." When viewed in the context of Rom 9—11, election is a subset of the broader motif of calling, and the reason that Paul focuses on calling becomes apparent in Rom 10.

Keeping the attention on calling in Rom 9:11–12 leads to the passage having quite a different tenor. As Gorman shows, it shifts the focus to God's mercy and faithfulness.[107] The calling of Jacob before he was born is presented as an unusual circumstance that makes it clear that God's calling is based neither on merit nor on the circumstances of one's birth.[108] Neither is faith a prerequisite for divine calling,[109] contrary to Abasciano.[110] While the juxtaposition of calling and works in 9:12 is comparable to that of faith and works in 4:4–5 and 9:32, it does not follow that faith and calling are intertwined. In 10:6–17, faith follows God's calling.

Viewing election in the same vein as calling in Rom 9:11–12 returns it to its OT sense. The focus is on God's gracious act and interest in the one chosen. Unlike calling, however, no one is found who resists God's choice. This is not surprising, because it is implicit in the verb "to choose" that a free choice is being made of available options.[111] Election is inevitable because the person or object is available and welcomed by God into the intended purpose. The detailed circumstances around that choice may vary. The important point is that it is God's choice, not that

---

105. Calvin, *Romans*, 350.

106. Aquinas, *Romans*, 253, 255.

107. Gorman, *Romans*, 221; Wright, *Paul and the Faithfulness of God*, 2:1183.

108. Aquinas, *Romans*, 253; Longenecker, *Romans*, 816; Ridderbos, *Paul*, 345; Caird, "Expository Problems," 325.

109. Moo, *Romans*, 603.

110. Abasciano, *Paul's Use of the Old Testament*, 52–53.

111. Coenen, "ἐκλέγομαι," *NIDNTT* 1:536.

of the object or person (cf. John 15:16), and that God's choice is always free and not compelled by some attribute of what is chosen, even if God might find some aspects of the chosen object appealing.

In Rom 9:13, Paul employs midrash by using the presence of the names of Jacob and Esau to connect Mal 1:2–3 with his argument.[112] The Greek μισέω, just like the Hebrew śānē', ranges in meaning from ill intent to merely showing less love,[113] and both Malachi and Paul exploit this sematic range. Esau was loved less when he was called to serve Jacob but, by the time of Malachi, the wicked behavior of Esau's descendants had led to them being condemned by God. In contrast, God's faithfulness to Jacob's calling meant Jacob's descendants were still sustained by God despite their past wickedness. As Paul goes on to write in 11:28, Israelites continue to be loved by God on account of God's choice of Jacob, not because they are more worthy. Contrary to Moo and Dunn, there is no sense of double predestination in these verses,[114] only of God's faithfulness on the one hand and deserved condemnation on the other. Jacob's election has an implication for all of Jacob's offspring. This effect is not, however, the opportunity for election to salvation as per the traditional Calvinistic interpretation of Rom 9:6–29,[115] nor is it corporate election as proposed by Thornhill.[116] Jacob's election results in God's ongoing favor toward Israel's descendants with the hope that they might respond to God's call as per Rom 11:14, 23, 26–28 (and Mal 1), and so also be chosen by God.

To understand the reference to Mal 1:2–3, just as with the argument regarding Isaac, it is important to remain attached to the reasoning of the text in the first instance. Having made the point that being a child of God is a matter of promise, not of physical descent, Paul's principal purpose in 9:10–12 is that God's calling/election is not on the basis of an individual's merit or birthright. This contrasts with many Jewish writings from the centuries immediately prior to Paul. Furthermore, the different outcome for Jacob and Esau's descendants was not due to predestination, but due to the asymmetric commitment and promises of God, leading God to continue to show favor to some who did not deserve it while generally

---

112. Longenecker, *Romans*, 815.
113. Cranfield, *Romans*, 2:481.
114. Moo, *Romans*, 607; Dunn, *Romans*, 2:545.
115. Moo, *Romans*, 606; Cranfield, *Romans*, 2:480.
116. Thornhill, *Chosen People*, 164.

condemning the wicked. This is important preparation for Paul's core argument on the calling of Israel in Rom 10.

Understanding Rom 9:7–13 this way returns it to the flow of Paul's argument. Paul's *constitutio* is that not all of Israel's physical descendants are Israel. Romans 9:7–13 proves this point by showing that physical descent was not the primary criterion for the patriarchs. What is of critical importance is receiving the promise and being called and chosen by God, of which Paul has already written much (e.g., Rom 4), and he will have more to say in Rom 10. Before that, he must address the objections of those descendants of Israel who now feel disenfranchised.

9:14–18

> [14]Therefore, what shall we say? Is God being unjust? By no means. [15]For he says to Moses, "I will have mercy on whom I have mercy, and I will have compassion on whom I have compassion." [16]So, it depends not on will or effort but on the mercy of God. [17]For the Scripture says to Pharaoh, "I raised you up so that I might show my power in you and so that my name might be proclaimed in all the earth." [18]So, he shows mercy on whomever he wants, and he hardens whomever he wants.

Romans 9:14 is the first of a series of *refutationes*, each of which commences with a rhetorical question that reflects a potential counterargument of Paul's hypothetical opponents.[117] The first objection is "μὴ ἀδικία παρὰ τῷ θεῷ" (Is God being unjust)? Are descendants of Israel being denied their rightful inheritance?[118] Μὴ γένοιτο (by no means) is Paul's typical response to a false premise.[119] Paul puts forward two arguments in support of his position, each introduced with the particle γάρ (for) and concluding with an inference introduced by ἄρα οὖν (so) (9:15–16 and 9:17–18).[120]

In the first argument (9:15–16), Paul cites Exod 33:19 and then in three genitive participle phrases explains that Israel's standing with God depends not on human will or effort but on the mercy of God.[121] In the

---

117. Longenecker, *Romans*, 816.

118. Abasciano, *Paul's Use of the Old Testament*, 167; Cranfield, *Romans*, 2:473.

119. Cranfield, *Romans*, 2:481.

120. Abasciano, *Paul's Use of the Old Testament*, 193. Origen's suggestion that 9:15–19 continues to represent the argument of Paul's opponents is not well supported. See Dunn, *Romans*, 2:551.

121. Gorman, *Romans*, 221; Abasciano, *Paul's Use of the Old Testament*, 186.

inter-texture, the declaration of God's character follows Israel's worship of the golden calf, after which the Israelites' only hope is God's mercy. Matera understands this, but then makes the mistake of drawing Augustinian election into the spotlight when the term does not appear in this section.[122] Longenecker makes a similar error by identifying God's sovereign election of the nation of Israel from Deut 7:6 as core background to Rom 9:14–18, despite Paul not alluding to that text.[123] Luther ignores the OT context altogether and makes the doctrine of predestination the context for his interpretation of this passage.[124] Augustine is closer to the mark in understanding these verses as describing the proper order of grace and good works.[125] Paul's argument is that Israelites must relate to God on the basis of divine mercy and compassion, and must not approach God on the basis of their effort or determination.[126] If it were a matter of works, then the Israelites would have been destroyed following their idolatry with the golden calf.

Paul's second supporting argument (Rom 9:17–18) moves to the other side of the coin of God condemning and hardening people. Paul cites Exod 9:16 concerning God's declaration to build up Pharaoh so that God's triumph over Pharaoh would be all the more glorious. In the inter-texture, Moses was to confront Pharaoh with these words to make it clear who really was in power and how Pharaoh would be punished for his opposition to God. It is divine will, not human will, that ultimately prevails. Paul then adds an allusion to God's hardening of Pharaoh's heart (Rom 9:18b), which is also a well-known part of the story (e.g., Exod 9:12).[127] God announces the intention to harden Pharaoh's heart in Exod 4:21 and then acts on that in Exod 7:3. These actions by God, however, are not without cause. God first foresees Pharaoh's intention to be obstinate (Exod 3:19), and Pharaoh's initial refusal and cruelty toward the Israelites is presented as all Pharaoh's own work (Exod 5:1–9). God's hardening of Pharaoh's heart is presented in Exodus not as the cause of Pharaoh's sin but as following it.

---

122. Matera, *Romans*, 225.
123. Longenecker, *Romans*, 817.
124. Luther, *Lectures on Romans*, 386.
125. Augustine, "Miscellany," 185.
126. Jewett, *Romans*, 583.
127. Cranfield, *Romans*, 2:488.

Dunn and Matera argue that Pharaoh's initiative is not relevant because Paul did not cite those verses or make that case,[128] but this ignores that the story of Moses and Pharaoh is prominent in the Scriptures and would have been well known to Paul and at least his Jewish audience. Furthermore, Paul goes on to describe God's hardening of Israel in the same vein, in that Israel's hardening by God also followed their obstinate rejection of God's word (10:18—11:10). Pharaoh even has moments of a change of heart (e.g., Exod 9:27–28), which is like the opportunity that is open to hardened Israelites to give up their unbelief (Rom 11:23). In 9:17–18, Paul does not need to layout these comparisons, because at this point in his argument Paul is just establishing the principle that God can harden people.[129] It is only necessary for the interpreter to consider the context of Exodus to avoid making invalid inferences.

God's hardening of Pharaoh is not presented as coming from the past hidden counsel of God, as Calvin supposes.[130] Neither is God's hardening of Pharaoh in response to Pharaoh's sinful nature, as Aquinas suggests,[131] because it follows Pharaoh's specific evil deeds. Perspectives such as those by Calvin and Aquinas lead to Dodd's criticism of Paul's argument as a false step, O'Neill's description of it as thoroughly immoral, and Moo's declaration that it is beyond human logic.[132] These are reactions to a misinterpretation of Paul's argument. In Romans and in Exodus, hardening by God is a response to human obstinance and serves to let people experience the consequences of their sin, but it does not prevent subsequent repentance. Paul is using these references to Moses and Pharaoh as an apt biblical precedent for the more difficult matters of the hardening of the Israelites (11:7) and the mercy shown to the gentiles (11:22, 30). Contrary to Barth, 9:14–18 does concern personal salvation,[133] however, it is only the beginning of Paul's argument, not the conclusion.

---

128. Matera, *Romans*, 226; Dunn, *Romans*, 2:555.
129. Pace Moo, *Romans*, 618.
130. Calvin, *Romans*, 359. Refuted by Cranfield, *Romans*, 2:489.
131. Aquinas, *Romans*, 261.
132. Moo, *Romans*, 610.
133. Pace Barth, *Church Dogmatics*, 2.2:221.

9:19–29

> ¹⁹You might say to me, "How then is anyone found at fault, for who has resisted his will?" ²⁰O questioner, on the contrary, who are you to answer back to God? Does what is molded say to the mold, why did you make me like this? ²¹Does the potter of the clay not have the right to use the same lump of clay to make one vessel for honor and another for dishonor? ²²What if God, although wanting to demonstrate his wrath and to make known his power, very patiently endured vessels of wrath that would be consummated in destruction, ²³so that he might make known the riches of his glory on vessels of mercy, which he prepared in advance for glory? ²⁴These he called, not only from us Jews, but also from the gentiles. ²⁵As it says in Hosea, "I will call those who aren't my people, my people, and those who aren't loved, beloved, ²⁶and it will not be said to them in that place, 'You are not my people.' There they will be called children of the living God." ²⁷Isaiah cries out concerning Israel, "Though the number of the children of Israel were like the sand of the sea, only the remnant will be saved. ²⁸For the Lord will bring his word to bear on the earth completely and decisively." ²⁹Just as it has been foretold in Isaiah, "If the Lord of Hosts did not leave seed to us, we would be like Sodom and we would resemble Gomorrah."

The rhetorical question in Rom 9:19 signifies the commencement of the next *refutatio*. Following the conclusion in 9:18 that one cannot merit God's mercy and God can harden the obstinate, the question that arises is how could anyone be found at fault, because no one has overcome God's will? Paul returns to diatribe to deal with this objection. At Rom 9:20, Paul's principal rebuttal is that it is wrong for people to contradict God (ἀνταποκρίνομαι).[134] Many infer from this statement that Paul is asserting that everyone must accept what God has decided for each person and not complain. That is not, however, what Paul has in mind. To understand Paul's argument, it is necessary to look in detail at the inter-texture of the pottery metaphor.

In Rom 9:20b, Paul cites Isa 29:16 to make the point that a pot cannot question its form. In Rom 9:21, the potter is free to make anything from the same lump of clay, possibly alluding to Jer 18:1–12. While pottery metaphors occur in several places in the Second Temple literature, it is likely that Isa 29 and Jer 18 are the key passages from which Paul is

---

134. Brannan, *Lexham Research Lexicon*, ἀνταποκρίνομαι.

drawing.[135] From the inter-texture, the clay can be all nations, but the focus is on physical Israel,[136] and the two types of pots represent outcomes based on whether Israelites repent (Jer 18:11) or do evil (Jer 18:12). The purpose of the metaphor in Isaiah and Jeremiah is to illustrate the absurdity of humans trying to dictate the path to God's blessing, which is likely what is meant by Paul's opening rebuttal (ἀνταποκρίνομαι). God decides what is required of people, what the right and wrong paths are, not the other way around. This is also the sense of Paul's argument in Rom 9:30–10:4. The OT texts do not present God as arbitrary, but as patient and just and responsive to human behavior and character (Isa 29:19–21).[137] It is not a matter of having to resist God's will, but of conforming to it. In this sense, the potter metaphor is consistent with the common motif throughout biblical and early Jewish literature that disobedient Israelites would be cut off even as Israel is preserved (cf. Rom 11:2–4).[138] As Staples points out, understanding it this way maintains a consistency with the *constitutio* (9:6),[139] showing that Paul's argument is well considered and flows logically. Most commentators on Rom 9:20–21 emphasize God's sovereignty.[140] While that is relevant, since it is God who determines the path to glory, Paul's primary aim is to challenge Israelite error and presumption.

Romans 9:22–23 is a condition without an apodosis, which is not an unusual construction and is translated "What if . . . ?"[141] This makes Paul's words an expansion of the potter metaphor, not merely an explanation.[142] In 9:22, the sense of the participle clause governed by θέλων (to want) is likely concessive rather than causative[143] in that rather than destroying the vessels of wrath, God concedes to endure them while showing the riches of his glory in the vessels of mercy.[144] In each case the vessel is the recipient of either God's wrath or mercy. The repetition of γνωρίζω (to make known) shows that the focus is on the revelation of God's

---

135. Gorman, *Romans*, 223; Cranfield, *Romans*, 2:491.
136. Staples, *Paul and the Resurrection*, 193.
137. Staples, *Paul and the Resurrection*, 197.
138. Staples, *Paul and the Resurrection*, 186.
139. Staples, *Paul and the Resurrection*, 193.
140. E.g., Fitzmyer, *Romans*, 565.
141. Cranfield, *Romans*, 2:492.
142. Cranfield, *Romans*, 2:493.
143. For a discussion of these options, see Cranfield, *Romans*, 2:493.
144. Fitzmyer, *Romans*, 72.

character.¹⁴⁵ Thus, 9:20b–23 declares that God is free to patiently endure disobedient Israelites rather than destroy them immediately, while at the same time preparing glory for the recipients of God's mercy.¹⁴⁶

The timing of the preparations for destruction and glory are not presented symmetrically. The vocabulary changes from καταρτίζω (to complete) to προετοιμάζω (to prepare), from the perfect tense to the aorist, and from the passive to the active voice.¹⁴⁷ The use of an ordinary verb without a προ- prefix in 9:22 seems to imply that the preparation for destruction is concurrent with God's enduring patience,¹⁴⁸ which is consistent with the example of Pharaoh.¹⁴⁹ The selection of the passive voice without an explicit actor has the effect of downplaying God's role and the perfect tense leaves open the final outcome (cf. Rom 11:23).¹⁵⁰ Chrysostom's suggestion that κατηρτισμένα (to prepare) is in the middle voice and refers to the destroyed preparing themselves¹⁵¹ is not likely because it is inconsistent with the passage's emphasis on God's sovereignty,¹⁵² and it is contrary to the inter-texture.

The moment of preparation of the vessels of mercy in Rom 9:23 is more difficult to discern. The prefix προ- in προετοιμάζω possibly connects it to πρόθεσις and the like.¹⁵³ This and the references to "glory" (9:23) and "called" (9:24) suggest that Paul is making a similar point to that in 8:29–30. That is, Paul is alluding to God's predetermined plan to bring vessels of mercy to glory through Christ,¹⁵⁴ and having prepared the path to glory, God called people to receive mercy (9:24). This is supported by the inter-texture, in which God prepares an outcome for types of people rather than for specific individuals.

Rather than being informed by the inter-texture, Aquinas follows Augustine and describes God's decision-making as arbitrary.¹⁵⁵ Aquinas

---

145. Barth, *Church Dogmatics*, 2.2:225.
146. Campbell, "Divergent Images of Paul," 200; Longenecker, *Romans*, 819; Fitzmyer, *Romans*, 572.
147. Cranfield, *Romans*, 2:494.
148. Cranfield, *Romans*, 2:495; Staples, *Paul and the Resurrection*, 196.
149. Jewett, *Romans*, 584.
150. Cranfield, *Romans*, 2:495.
151. Chrysostom, *Hom. Rom.* 9:1 (*NPNF*¹ 11:841).
152. Witherington and Hyatt, *Romans*, 258.
153. BDAG 869.
154. Witherington and Hyatt, *Romans*, 258–59.
155. Aquinas, *Romans*, 264–65.

spends some time drawing on prooftexts for this theological position, but he does not explore in depth those passages to which Paul directs his readers. Likewise, Calvin interprets Isaiah's words in the context of his own doctrine of predestination.[156] Moo fairly interprets the text as having implications for individual salvation, but also does not give due consideration to how the inter-texture describes how that comes about (or not), nor how Paul goes on to develop his thoughts.[157] When Rom 9—11 and its inter-texture is considered as a whole, there is no dilemma as to whether the vessels of wrath are deserving of their outcome.[158] Witherington points out that the Second Temple literature also contains this doctrinal perspective.[159] God is always free to condemn sinful people, even those Israelites who had the opportunity for a more noble outcome. Understood in context, neither Isaiah, Jeremiah, nor Paul are articulating the Augustinian doctrine of predestination.[160] They are stating that despite God pouring great effort into the Israelites, God is not obliged to save the obstinate. God is still free to show mercy or justly condemn. In effect, Paul is refuting a dogma of predestination by birth.[161]

Romans 9:24 probably does not mark a section break but is rather a relative clause dependent on σκεύη ἐλέους (vessels of mercy).[162] This makes 9:24–29 a further elaboration on how the potter metaphor refutes the objection that unbelieving Israelites cannot be blamed.[163] The reappearance of καλέω shows that "calling" rather than "election" is Paul's preferred term. This emphasizes the need for a response rather than waiting for God to act.[164] Paul also reintroduces gentiles into the argument, echoing the epistle's *constitutio* (1:16–17). The parallel consideration of Jews/Israelites and gentiles continues from here until the end of chapter 11. The inclusion of the gentiles gives weight to the argument that Israelites also need to respond to God in the same way (cf. 9:30).

Two OT references follow, the first of which features καλέω (to call), which may have influenced its selection. Most scholars take the Hosea

---

156. Calvin, *Romans*, 368.
157. Moo, *Romans*, 622–23.
158. Pace Longenecker, *Romans*, 820; Moo, *Romans*, 621.
159. Witherington and Hyatt, *Romans*, 258.
160. Dunn, *Romans*, 2:546.
161. Dunn, *Theology of Paul*, 512.
162. Cranfield, *Romans*, 2:498. Pace Moo, *Romans*, 630.
163. Staples, *Paul and the Resurrection*, 203.
164. Wright, *Paul and the Faithfulness*, 2:1026.

and Isaiah citations as referring to gentiles and Israelites respectively, thus supporting the statement of 9:24 completely.[165] The difficulty with this interpretation is that the prophet Hosea appears to be concerned with the return of purified Israelites (Hos 1:10; 2:1, 14; 11:8–11). Nevertheless, the expression "those who are not my people" opens the possibility of the inclusion of gentiles, and Paul chooses to run together Hos 1:10 and 2:23 from the Septuagint to make this point.[166] By later describing believing gentiles as wild olive branches grafted into the tree following the pruning of some natural branches (11:17–18), it is possible that Paul understands the return of the Israelites who were scattered among the nations (Hos 8:8) as being fulfilled by believers from the nations being grafted onto the olive tree.[167] While many scholars criticize Paul for suggesting such an interpretation of Hosea, it was not without precedent in Rabbinic literature.[168] Staples notes that this was also a common interpretation among Christian writers from the second century AD, although since the Holocaust there has been considerable discomfort with interpreting Rom 9—11 this way.[169] Such unease need not be the case because those Israelites broken off from the olive tree are still regarded as natural rather than wild branches who would ideally be reattached, and gentiles are reminded that they are no more deserving and not naturally there (11:11–32). The olive tree remains rooted in God's promises to the patriarchs. Any gentiles graciously grafted on must appreciate those Israelites they have come to join and earnestly desire more Israelites to rejoin.

Paul next quotes from Isa 10:22–23 and 1:9, which is more clearly a reference to God mercifully calling a remnant/seed of Israel from the nation that had been justly condemned.[170] Paul is reinforcing his *constitutio* in 9:6 that only a remnant and not all Israelites would be among those saved,[171] the reason being that many Israelites (like many gentiles) rejected

---

165. Calvin, *Romans*, 272; Matera, *Romans*, 228; Gorman, *Romans*, 223; Dunn, *Romans*, 2:572; Cranfield, *Romans*, 2:499. Aquinas prefers to understand the Hosea citation as referring to the remnant of Israel. Aquinas, *Romans*, 271; Campbell, "Divergent Images of Paul," 199.

166. Aquinas, *Romans*, 271; Starling, *Not My People*, 111.

167. Staples, *Paul and the Resurrection*, 205; Starling, *Not My People*, 164.

168. Staples, *Paul and the Resurrection*, 202, 208.

169. Staples, *Paul and the Resurrection*, 13.

170. Longenecker, *Romans*, 823.

171. Cranfield, *Romans*, 2:501. Levering aptly describes the distinction between all Israelites and the reference to all Israel in Rom 11:26. Levering, *Predestination*, 32.

God's way and pursued their own ends.¹⁷² Longenecker's argument that 9:6 and 9:27–29 bracket an *inclusio* on the ideas of seed and remnant has merit,¹⁷³ but it is not Paul's purpose in 9:6–29 to expound a remnant theology. Longenecker's focus on "remnant" is to the detriment of his detailed exegesis. "Called" rather than "remnant" is the more prominent motif of 9:6–29, with Paul concluding that it was because of God's desire to hold true to his promise that Israelites and gentiles are being called to faith.

It is much easier to make sense of Paul's answer to the question at 9:19 if the classical doctrine of predestination is set aside. Paul's argument is that the gospel is aligned with Scripture. God has a long history of enduring but eventually condemning rebellious Israelites,¹⁷⁴ while seeking a faithful remnant to make up true Israel. Those rebellious Israelites, whom God may harden and prepare for destruction, set their own destiny, although as Paul goes on to write, hope is not lost in this life (11:11, 24). God continues to remain faithful to his promises to the patriarchs and continues to call a remnant from Israel into God's family, along with believing gentiles.

---

172. Aquinas, *Romans*, 273.
173. Longenecker, *Romans*, 812.
174. Barth, *Church Dogmatics*, 2.2:222.

13

Synthesis

What is apparent from the exegesis of Rom 8:18–9:29 is how much Augustine's combined doctrine of predestination and election has detrimentally affected its interpretation. The SRI approach has helped to identify how commentators interact with the various textures and has highlighted where one texture, in particular the ideological texture, may dominate at the expense of others. This is most apparent in Rom 9:1–29, with many commentators beginning with the premise that the passage is principally about election,[1] when the term plays only a supporting role. Karl Barth goes further by importing the doctrine of the church into Rom 9—11, identifying the church as the elect community and Israel in its pure form.[2] In contrast, Paul's focus is on the tragedy of obstinance on the part of many Israelites and on explaining how God is still working to overcome it. The emphasis on the ideological texture is also often to the detriment of the inter-texture, with the passages to which Paul points being downplayed or overwhelmed by other texts to which Paul does not directly refer.

In the post-Holocaust world, attention shifted to the Jewish sociocultural context of those who first proclaimed the Christian faith and to a more positive attitude toward Judaism generally.[3] Within this new

---

1. E.g., Wright, *Paul and the Faithfulness of God*, 2:1187; Matera, *Romans*, 214; Cranfield, *Romans*, 2:450; Moo, *Romans*, 570; Witherington and Hyatt, *Romans*, 246; Luther, *Romans*, 386.

2. Barth, *Church Dogmatics*, 2.2:203. Dunn rejects that Rom 9–11 concerns the church and Israel. See Dunn, *Theology of Paul*, 507.

3. Wright, "Romans," 621; Thornhill, "Election and Predestination," 240.

ideological texture, Rom 9—11 is read as a development of thought from tension to resolution,[4] with Paul ultimately advocating for parallel paths for salvation, one for Jews in the Torah and the other for gentiles in Christ.[5] Wigoder is particularly critical of those who interpret Rom 9—11 in such a way as to leave Judaism scarcely any right to exist.[6] Such sensitivities need to be acknowledged, and passages such as 11:17–21 make it clear that gentiles should hold out hope for all Israelites. Nevertheless, Rom 11:26–32 does not undo all that has gone before in the epistle. Paul regards it as essential for all people, whether Jew or gentile, to confess Jesus Christ as Lord. This is not at odds with living as a Jew with Torah.

The post-Holocaust shift also fed into the now-popular view that election is of corporate Israel or the church.[7] Dunn follows F. C. Baur in understanding election in a national sense,[8] but for Dunn election begins with historical Israel and then shifts to eschatological Israel, with participation based on a positive response to God's call.[9] For Wright, Israel's election in the OT is for the purpose of ushering in the Christ,[10] while under the new covenant election is achieved by becoming one of the messiah's justified people in the inaugurated eschatological age.[11] Both Dunn and Wright continue to conflate predestination with election without explanation. Thornhill also argues for a corporate view of election by understanding election in a manner similar to my definition of predestination.[12] The corporate election viewpoint, however, is not sensitive to the detail of Rom 9—11 because it gives election a prominence that is not warranted, and it is unsympathetic to how Paul uses the term. In Rom 9—11, "election" refers to the person Israel, not the nation Israel. All those who believe in Jesus Christ are referred to as the elect in 8:33 but, as in 11:4–7, it makes most sense to understand the elect as those individuals who make up the body rather than the elect being the body which

---

4. Campbell, "Divergent Images of Paul," 201.

5. Wasserberg, "Romans 9–11," 184; Nanos, "Challenging the Limits," 220.

6. Wigoder, "Christianity," *EncJud* 4:682.

7. E.g., Fitzmyer, *Romans*, 522; Dunn, *Theology of Paul*, 501; Thornhill, "Election and Predestination," 239.

8. Dunn, *Theology of Paul*, 501.

9. Dunn, *Theology of Paul*, 504.

10. Wright, *Paul and the Faithfulness of God*, 815.

11. Wright, *Paul and the Faithfulness of God*, 912.

12. Thornhill, *Chosen People*, 174.

individuals could join. Ironically, Douglas Moo is closer to the mark in this respect in his explanation of the nature of election.[13]

Gorman and Longenecker come closest to not being distracted by Augustine in their commentaries. Gorman's identification of God's mercy as the principal theme of Rom 9 warrants careful consideration. The language of mercy is more prominent than that of election in 9:1–29, and mercy is related to calling in 9:23–24, one of the other prominent terms in the passage. The problem with using mercy as the passage headline is that it is not the focus of the *constitutio* of Rom 9—11 (9:6). Longenecker respects this and makes remnant theology the key concept. This, however, grates with the flow of Paul's argument because Paul is not writing to affirm remnant theology, but only using it occasionally to support his core point, that participation in God's family is not achieved by a person's works, will, or ethnic heritage. As Longenecker acknowledges himself, not all elements of remnant theology appear in Romans.

Nevertheless, it is best to follow the Gorman/Longenecker path by setting aside outside concerns such as Augustine's struggle with Pelagianism and recent concerns regarding modern-day Israel. Looked at afresh in its first-century Jewish context, the argument in Rom 9:1–29 appears to be as follows.

- Israel is not merely made up of the physical descendants of Israel.
- Israelites are descendants who receive the promise (received through faith, 4:13).
- Israelites are called by God (a call that comes in the gospel, 10:6–8).
- God may harden (the obstinate, 11:7) or show mercy (to those who give up unbelief, 11:23).
- God is not obliged to be merciful to all descendants of Israel, any more than a potter is obliged to make only fine pottery from the same lump of clay.
- God is calling a remnant from the residue of condemned Israel, along with the gentiles, to form God's family.

Paul's desire is that his fellow Israelites would be saved (10:1). It brings Paul no joy to point out that physical descent from Israel is insufficient to belong to God's family. He does so to warn against deadly complacency and to point to the life-saving gospel of Jesus Christ. Paul's

---
13. Moo, *Romans*, 606.

mission to the gentiles does not signify that he has given up on his kin. Rather, it too serves to lead Israelites to salvation by provoking them to envy.

Extending the purview to gentiles, the implication for gentiles is that they also need to respond to the call of God in the gospel and receive the promise through faith. Gentiles must avoid becoming presumptuous, a snare that tripped up many Israelites. Instead, gentiles must always lean on God's kindness and grace and play their part in evoking a response of faith among Israelites.

There is no sense in Rom 9—11 of God predetermining before time what would become of people. Firstly, the temporal perspective of the epistle is the biblical timeline. Secondly, nearly all examples in Rom 9—11 show God responding to human sin, with God's calling of Jacob before he was born presented as an exceptional circumstance that establishes the principle that God's calling is not in response to human works or will. The example of Jacob is not used by Paul to establish that every person's eternal destiny is foreordained. The rest of Rom 9—11 regards each person's ultimate outcome as largely an open question that depends on not persisting in unbelief, harkening to God's call in the gospel, and placing one's faith in the resurrected Lord Jesus Christ. There may come a time when obstinance and wickedness leads to God hardening hearts, but even that is reversible. What cannot be changed is that each person's future is completely dependent on God's mercy. That is why the term "election" is at home in Paul's expression. The elect are not people who present their understanding and faith to God as a ticket to eternity. The elect are those who, having humbly heard and responded to the gospel, appeal to God's mercy, fully recognizing that they are owed nothing and yet discover that they are granted everything. God elects believers by showing mercy to them.

Returning to Rom 8:28–30, its interpretation is also strongly affected by the ideological texture. There is a considerable time gap between the NT documents and any references to predestination in subsequent Christian writings. On the rare occasions predestination was discussed, it came to be understood as of the individual but was based on divine foreknowledge of that person's faith. This perspective appears to emerge in the mid-second century AD among apologists seeking to accommodate Greek proponents of human free will and is given theological depth in the school of Alexandria by Clement and Origen. While it is likely that this explanation was informed by Rom 8:29, that verse does not state that God's decisions were influenced by divine foreknowledge of something meritorious in future believers. Early Christian writers appear to be reading that into the text to try and align unfamiliar concepts with their general understanding.

While initially following the early church's teaching, Augustine changed his understanding in the course of his argument against Pelagianism. Augustine still took predestination as being of individuals, but he reasoned that there was nothing about the predestined that warranted God determining a person's eternity, one way or the other. Aquinas and Calvin, relying on Eph 1:4–5, followed Augustine in interpreting Rom 8:28–30 as concerning personal pretemporal predestination, and many commentators have followed suit. The Ephesian passage, however, is not the best starting point, since it was likely written later and has peculiarities that are not present in Romans. The expression in Ephesians is more mystical, suiting the sociocultural context of Ephesus, and the poetry of Eph 1:3–14 is such that a single verse is difficult to properly appreciate once it is removed from its context. Furthermore, the description of election being in Christ is unique, making it unwise to use Eph 1:4–5 as a basis for understanding election more broadly.

First Corinthians 2:7 precedes Romans and shares more in common with it,[14] so is a better starting point for understanding Paul's thoughts on predestination. In 1 Cor 2:7, predestination is of Jesus Christ and him crucified for the glory of the saints, and from that perspective, Rom 8:29 takes on a new life. What Paul adds to his teaching in Rom 8:29 is that the predestination of the ministry of Jesus Christ included a plan to build a family of God around the Son. Paul is not writing of the predetermination of those who would love God, but of God's predetermined plan for lovers of God, a plan that revolves around Jesus Christ. Προγινώσκω (to foreknow) is paired with προορίζω (to predestine) to convey the sense that God understood our need and anticipated how best to establish the family of God.

Ridderbos is close to the sentiment of Rom 8—11 in his explanation of the doctrines of election and predestination. He describes "elect" as a synonym of "saint" with an emphasis on the divine promise.[15] Election rests on God's good pleasure but is not foreordained. Ridderbos correctly identifies Christ as the center of God's purpose,[16] but I differ

---

14. Fitzmyer, *Romans*, 73; Witherington and Hyatt, *Romans*, 24.
15. Ridderbos, *Paul*, 332, 343.
16. Ridderbos, *Paul*, 346.

from the suggestion by Ridderbos that the church is the object of God's predestination. Instead, I regard the predestination as focused on Jesus Christ, albeit giving rise to the opportunity for the church. In my view, predestination is God's plan for his Son to make possible the family of God, and election is God's choice to show mercy on those who respond to the call of God.

Augustine's error is understandable. He was locked in a struggle to maintain the primacy and essentiality of God's grace in the church. Unfortunately, that led him to develop a doctrine of pretemporal predestination and election of individuals to salvation that is, I suggest, a misinterpretation of Eph 1:3–14 and Rom 8:18—9:29. Sixteenth-century Reformers picked up on Augustine's doctrine for much the same reason and continued the confusion. Romans 8—11 supports the core point of both Augustine and the Reformers, that all people are fully dependent on God's mercy and the granting of mercy is not dependent on good works. Romans 8—11, however, does not do so via some form of the Augustinian doctrine of predestination and election. Paul's argument is that all people need to respond to God's call to faith in the resurrected Lord Jesus Christ, and God chooses to show undeserved mercy on those who give up their unbelief. It was always God's plan to build a family around the Son. Now that the plan has been fully revealed, lovers of God can be even more confident that, no matter what their present circumstances might be, God will bring them to glory.

PART 4

Opportunities and Ramifications

The early church leaders moved predestination from being about the ministry of Jesus Christ to the pretemporal identification of those who would have faith in Christ. This shift in focus is understandable given the context in which they approached the relevant texts, and it did not cause a great stir. It made the doctrine of predestination nothing more than divine foreknowledge in order to prevent any interference with biblical discussions of human responsibility and free will. Furthermore, there were still many other ways that the ministry of Jesus Christ was declared to be the deliberate plan of God, so the loss of the term "predestination" to describe this was not felt.

It was when Augustine removed the foreknowledge of faith that trouble arrived. Consequently, all sorts of logical and exegetical problems arose. The vast majority of passages of Scripture that presented people as having free choices had to be reinterpreted by reading into the text theological views that were not present. The perseverance of the saints became a practically useless doctrine because no one could ever know if they would persevere to the end. It was only relevant to the divine mind to which no one has access. Augustine's doctrine was rightly criticized at the time as being morally demotivating because biblical injunctions to godliness were being reinterpreted as directed to the Holy Spirit rather than to the human spirit.

The reason for these problems was that Augustine developed his new understanding during his theological argument with Pelagianism rather than from careful exegesis. Augustine himself acknowledged that he struggled to understand Romans, and chapter 9 in particular, and he displayed no careful exegetical study of Eph 1 in his anti-Pelagian works. This led to Augustine building on the early church's mistaken understanding of predestination by removing any divine-human interaction in the process of a person coming to salvation. Augustine was engaged in the noble cause of defending salvation by grace alone, and his new interpretation of predestination seemed to give him a knock-down argument to that effect. But it was not so. There were serious concerns with it at the time and attempts to repair it over the centuries have been problematic. They all end up with significant exegetical questions remaining and at times box themselves into dubious theological conclusions.

It is only by returning to the first-century Jewish context and conducting a careful exegesis of the key texts that the problems disappear. Predestination can once again be understood as stating that from before the beginning, it was the Father's plan to establish the family of God through the Son. Jesus Christ was not Plan B. He was always Plan A, and there has only ever been one divine plan. Predestination does not impinge on human will and responsibility. Predestination is not God deciding what you will do. It is God deciding what God will do.

Thus, the theology of predestination is Christ-focused and can be supplemented by the biblical motif of the fulfillment of Scripture, which also presupposes God's forethought and planning of the ministry of Jesus Christ. Jesus Christ's claim that he fulfills the law and the prophets (Matt 5:17) and Paul's declaration that all of God's promises find their "Yes" in Christ (2 Cor 1:20) indicate that the unfolding revelation of Scripture was intended from the beginning to lead to Christ.

Predestination can be considered a type of election (Eph 1:4; 1 Pet 1:20) because to predestine anything is to choose an outcome. Nevertheless, it is best not to envelop a doctrine of predestination into an overarching doctrine of election because it risks confusing predestination with the election of believers, the very thing we are seeking to undo. Such an omnibus doctrine of election would also be difficult to confine because every decision and action of God is a choice.

With predestination understood as Christ-focused, references to the election of believers can be read with fresh eyes. Rather than the term evoking confusion and concern, leading to preachers often glossing over it, election can be seen for the encouragement that it is. By understanding that election is the moment God chooses to show you mercy and welcome you into his family, it can only bring one joy. This leads to four key implications in the minds of the NT authors.

1. It is a comfort to believers to know that no matter how much it looks like the world is against them, God is for them (e.g., Matt 24:22; Luke 18:7; John 15:19; Rom 8:33; 1 Thess 1:4; 1 Pet 1:1; 2:4, 9).

2. Election is a reminder to show brothers and sisters in Christ the same care and compassion that God does. They too are chosen by God (e.g., 2 Tim 2:10; Titus 1:1).

3. Election is an impetus to godliness because believers are chosen to live for God (e.g., John 15:16; Col 3:12; 2 Pet 1:10).

4. Election reminds believers they have no reason to boast (e.g., 1 Cor 1:27; Jas 2:5).

What of the election of Israel? In Romans, Paul argues that it is the person Israel who is elect, and his descendants benefit from that. Paul does not describe the nation of Israel as elect. Only those Israelites who did not bow the knee to Baal are described as elect (Rom 11:4). It is the remnant who respond positively to God's call who are chosen, not every single descendant of Israel. The description of the people of Israel as chosen in Deut 7:6 appears to be a separate category because God has chosen them to live out the Deuteronomic covenant and their ongoing participation is conditional on their faithfulness to that covenant (Deut 7:12). This relationship between the broader people of Israel and the faithful remnant in the OT is intriguing and worthy of further study.

What of free will? There has been as much speculation in the secular world as in the theological world on the degree to which humans can choose freely. Quantum mechanics has opened up new opportunities to rebut determinism, but it is still apparent that human decision-making is highly affected by prior causes and the environment. Similarly, Scripture is at ease in limiting the degree of human freedom, such as describing a person's vocation as chosen by God from birth. The saying "pushing my buttons" recognizes that one can be manipulated to some extent by others. How much more could God do so? Nevertheless, Scripture is equally clear that God in his sovereignty carves out some space for human choices, and God holds us accountable for them. This includes how we respond to God's call. That does not mean that God is uninvolved in our lives prior to that call, but it equally does not mean that our response is solely divinely determined.

What of perseverance of the saints? While not affected by predestination, this is still affected by election. Will God allow someone he has chosen to fall away? Several NT authors explore that possibility (e.g., Matt 18:7–9, 15–19; 1 Cor 10:12; Gal 5:4; Heb 2:1–3; 2 Pet 2:15; 1 John 5:16), and yet there are also strong statements to the contrary (John 17:6, 12; 1 John 2:19). A way of understanding this may be that God does everything to ensure that one need not fall away (1 Cor 10:13), but if a believer develops reckless abandon (1 John 5:16–17), God will not prevent his or her rebellion. Understood this way, it brings both comfort to the faithful and a warning to the careless.

There are no doubt many other ramifications of the understanding of predestination and election presented in this book. They will emerge as this study is reviewed and critiqued. While I am confident that I have not represented Scripture perfectly, I am hopeful that my thoughts have taken the debate in a helpful direction, not only for considerations of doctrine but also for pastoral concerns. For the NT authors, predestination is a cause of great joy and comfort, and I hope I have been able to show why it is naturally so. Similarly, election has important implications for the soul, and I hope that by removing an unnecessary controversy, pastors and teachers can once again bring those soothing effects to bear.

Bibliography

Abasciano, Brian J. *Paul's Use of the Old Testament in Romans 9.10–18: An Intertextual and Theological Exegesis*. Library of New Testament Studies 317. London: T. & T. Clark, 2011.

Abbott, T. K. *A Critical and Exegetical Commentary on the Epistles to the Ephesians and to the Colossians*. International Critical Commentary (ICC). Edinburgh: T. & T. Clark, 1897.

Aland, Barbara et al., eds. *The Greek New Testament*. 5th rev. ed. Stuttgart: Deutsche Bibelgesellschaft, 2014.

Allen, Leslie C. "The Old Testament Background of (προ)ορίζω in the New Testament." *New Testament Studies* 17 (1970) 104–8.

Allison, Gregg R. *Historical Theology: An Introduction to Christian Doctrine*. Grand Rapids: Zondervan, 2011.

Aquinas, Thomas. *Commentary on the Letters of Saint Paul to the Galatians and Ephesians*. Vol. 39 of Latin/English Edition of the Works of St. Thomas Aquinas. Edited by J. Mortensen and E. Alarcón. Translated by F. R. Larcher and M. L. Lamb. Lander, WY: The Aquinas Institute for the Study of Sacred Doctrine, 2012.

———. *Commentary on the Letter of Saint Paul to the Romans*. Vol. 37 of Latin/English Edition of the Works of St. Thomas Aquinas. Edited by J. Mortensen and E. Alarcón. Translated by F. R. Larcher. Lander, WY: The Aquinas Institute for the Study of Sacred Doctrine, 2012.

———. *Summa Theologiæ*. Translated by Thomas Gilby. London: Eyre & Spottiswoode, 1967.

Arminius, Jacobus. *The Works of James Arminius*. 3 vols. Translated by James Nichols and William Nichols. London ed. Grand Rapids: Baker, 1986.

Ascough, Richard S. "What Kind of World Did Paul's Communities Live In?" In *The New Cambridge Companion to St. Paul*, edited by Bruce W. Longenecker, 48–66. Cambridge: Cambridge University Press, 2020.

Augustine, Aurelius. "Miscellany of Questions in Response to Simplician." In *Response to Miscellaneous Questions*, edited by Raymond Canning, 159–231. Vol. 1 of *The Works of Saint Augustine: A Translation for the 21st Century*. Hyde Park, NY: New City, 2008.

———. *Retractions*. In vol. 60 of *The Fathers of the Church*. Edited by Roy Joseph Eferrariur. Translated by Mary Inex Bogan. Washington: The Catholic University Press of America, 1968.

Aune, David E. "Introduction." In *The Blackwell Companion to the New Testament*, edited by David E. Aune, 1–14. Chichester: Wiley, 2010.

———. *The New Testament in Its Literary Environment*. 1st ed. Philadelphia: Westminster, 1987.

———. "Romans as a Logos Protreptikos." In *The Romans Debate*, edited by Karl P. Donfried, 278–96. Rev. and expand. ed. Edinburgh: T. & T. Clark, 1991.

Barr, James. *The Semantics of Biblical Language*. New York: Oxford University Press, 1961.

Barth, Karl. *Church Dogmatics*. Edited G. W. Bromiley and T. F. Torrance. Translated by G. W. Bromiley et al. Study ed. London: T. & T. Clark, 2009.

———. *The Epistle to the Ephesians*. Edited by R. David Nelson. Translated by Ross M. Wright. Grand Rapids: Baker Academic, 2017.

———. *The Epistle to the Romans*. 6th ed. Translated by Edwyn C. Hoskyns. London: Oxford University Press, 1933.

Barth, Markus. *Ephesians*. In vols. 34 and 34A of *The Anchor Bible*. New York: Doubleday, 1974.

Bauer, David R., and Robert A. Traina. *Inductive Bible Study: A Comprehensive Guide to the Practice of Hermeneutics*. Grand Rapids: Baker Academic, 2011.

Berkouwer, G. C. *Divine Election*. Grand Rapids: Eerdmans, 1960.

Best, Ernest. *A Critical and Exegetical Commentary on Ephesians*. International Critical Commentary. Edinburgh: T. & T. Clark, 1998.

Betz, Hans Deiter, et al., eds. *Religion Past and Present: Encyclopedia of Theology and Religion*. 14 vols. Leiden: Brill, 2007–13.

Bornkamm, Günther. "The Letter to the Romans as Paul's Last Will and Testament." *Australian Biblical Review* (1963) 2–14.

Brannan, Rick, ed. *Lexham Research Lexicon of the Greek New Testament*. Lexham Research Lexicons. Bellingham, WA: Lexham, 2020.

Bromiley, Geoffrey W., ed. *International Standard Bible Encyclopedia*. 4 vols. Grand Rapids: Eerdmans, 1979–88.

Broshi, Magen. "Predestination in the Bible and the Dead Sea Scrolls." In *The Dead Sea Scrolls and the Qumran Community*, edited by James H. Charlesworth, 235–46. Vol. 2 of *The Bible and the Dead Sea Scrolls*. Waco, TX: Baylor University Press, 2006.

Brown, Colin, ed. *New International Dictionary of New Testament Theology*. 4 vols. Grand Rapids: Zondervan, 1975–85.

Brown, William P. *A Handbook to Old Testament Exegesis*. Louisville: Westminster John Knox, 2017.

Bruce, F. F. "The Romans Debate—Continued." *Bulletin of the John Rylands University Library of Manchester* (1982) 334–59.

Bryan, C. *A Preface to Romans: Notes on the Epistle and Its Literary Cultural Setting*. Oxford: Oxford University Press, 2000.

Busch, Eberhard. *The Great Passion: An Introduction to Karl Barth's Theology*. Edited by Darrell L. Guder and Judith J. Guder. Translated by Geoffrey W. Bromiley. Grand Rapids: Eerdmans, 2004.

Caird, G. B. "Expository Problems: Predestination—Romans ix–xi." *Expository Times* 68 (1957) 324–7.

Calvin, John. *Commentaries on the Epistles of Paul the Apostle to the Galatians and Ephesians*. Translated by William Pringle. Grand Rapids: Eerdmans, 1957.

———. *Commentaries on the Epistle of Paul the Apostle to the Romans*. Translated and edited by John Owen. Grand Rapids: Eerdmans, 1959.

———. *The Institutes of the Christian Religion.* LCC 20 and 21. Philadelphia: Westminster, 1960.

———. *Institutio Christianae Religionis.* Edited by P. Barth and G. Niesel, 1926–52. https://calvin.reformation.nl/.

Campbell, Constantine R. *The Letter to the Ephesians.* Grand Rapids: Eerdmans, 2023.

Campbell, Douglas A. *The Deliverance of God: An Apocalyptic Rereading of Justification in Paul.* Grand Rapids: Eerdmans, 2009.

Campbell, William S. "Divergent Images of Paul and His Mission." In *Reading Israel in Romans: Legitimacy and Plausibility of Divergent Interpretations,* edited by Cristina Grenholm and Daniel Patte, 187–211. Harrisburg, PA: Trinity, 2000.

———. "Romans III as a Key to the Structure and Thought of the Letter." *Novum Testamentum* (1981) 22–40.

Carson, Don. *Divine Sovereignty and Human Responsibility: Biblical Perspectives in Tension.* London: Marshall, Morgan & Scott, 1981.

Childs, Brevard. "The Semantics of Biblical Language." *Journal of Biblical Literature* 80 (1961) 374–77.

Cicero. *De Inventione.* Translated by H. M. Hubbell. Cambridge, MA: Harvard University Press, 1949.

Clark, Mary T. *Augustine.* London: Bloomsbury, 2005.

Clement of Alexandria. *The Stromata, or Miscellanies.* Translated by William Wilson. In *The Ante-Nicene Fathers* 2, edited by Alexander Roberts and James Donaldson, 599–1201. Revised by A. Cleveland Coxe. Grand Rapids: Eerdmans, 1989.

Clement of Rome. *The First Epistle of Clement to the Corinthians.* Translated by Alexander Roberts and James Donaldson. In *The Apostolic Fathers—Justin Martyr-Irenæus,* edited by Alexander Roberts and James Donaldson, revised by A. Cleveland Coxe, 15–54. Vol. 1 of *The Ante-Nicene Fathers.* Grand Rapids: Eerdmans, 1989.

Cohick, Lynn H. *The Letter to the Ephesians.* The New International Commentary on the New Testament. Grand Rapids: Eerdmans, 2020.

Corrigan, Kevin, and L. Michael Harrington. "Pseudo-Dionysius the Areopagite." *Stanford Encyclopedia of Philosophy,* June 5, 2023. Edited by Edward N. Zalta and Uri Nodelman. https://plato.stanford.edu/entries/pseudo-dionysius-areopagite/.

Cranfield, C. E. B. *A Critical and Exegetical Commentary on the Epistle to the Romans.* 2 vols. Edinburgh: T. & T. Clark, 1975.

Danker, Frederick William, et al., eds. *Greek-English Lexicon of the New Testament and Other Early Christian Literature.* 3rd ed. Chicago: University of Chicago Press, 2000.

Davies, Brian. *Thomas Aquinas's* Summa Theologiae: *A Guide and Commentary.* Oxford: Oxford University Press, 2014.

———. *The Thought of Thomas Aquinas.* Oxford: Clarendon, 1992.

de Boer, Erik A. "Augustine on Election: The Birth of an Article of Faith." *Acta Theologica* 32.2 (2012) 54–73.

de Greef, Wulfert. "Calvin's Writings." In *The Cambridge Companion to John Calvin,* edited by Donald K. McKim, 41–57. Cambridge: Cambridge University Press, 2004.

deSilva, David A. *Ephesians.* New Cambridge Bible Commentary. Cambridge: Cambridge University Press, 2022.

———. *Perseverance in Gratitude: A Socio-Rhetorical Commentary on the Epistle "to the Hebrews."* Grand Rapids: Eerdmans, 2000.

Donfried, Karl P., ed. *The Romans Debate*. Rev. and expand. ed. Edinburgh: T. & T. Clark, 1991.

Donfried, Karl P. "A Short Note on Romans 16." *Journal of Biblical Literature* 89 (1970) 441–49.

Dunn, James D. G. "The Formal and Theological Coherence of Romans." In *The Romans Debate*, edited by Karl P. Donfried, 246–50. Rev. and expand. ed. Edinburgh: T. & T. Clark, 1991.

———. *Romans*. 2 vols. Dallas: Word, 1988.

———. *The Theology of Paul the Apostle*. Grand Rapids: Eerdmans, 1998.

Elwell, W. A. "Election and Predestination." In *Dictionary of Paul and His Letters*, edited by Gerald F. Hawthorne and Ralph P. Martin, 225–29. Downers Grove, IL: InterVarsity, 1993.

Embry, Brad, et al., eds. *Early Jewish Literature: An Anthology*. Grand Rapids: Eerdmans, 2018.

Erasumus, and Martin Luther. *The Battle over Free Will*. Edited by Clarence H. Miller. Translated by Clarence H. Miller and Peter Macardle. Indianapolis: Hackett, 2012.

Eskola, Timo. *Theodicy and Predestination in Pauline Soteriology*. Eugene, OR: Wipf & Stock, 1998.

Fahlbusch, Erwin, et al., eds. *Evangelisches Kirchenlexikon*. 4 vols. 3rd ed. Göttingen: Vandenhoeck & Ruprecht, 1985–96.

Fee, Gordon D. *The First Epistle to the Corinthians*. Rev. ed. Grand Rapids: Eerdmans, 2014.

———. *New Testament Exegesis: A Handbook for Students and Pastors*. Rev. ed. Louisville: Westminster John Knox, 1993.

Ferde, Tucker S. "'Sealed' with the Holy Spirit (Eph 1, 13–14) and Circumcision." *Biblica* 93 (2012) 557–79.

Fitzmyer, J. A. *Romans*. New York: Doubleday, 1992.

Fowl, Stephen E. *Ephesians: A Commentary*. New Testament Library. Louisville: Westminster John Knox, 2012.

Freedman, David Noel, ed. *The Anchor Bible Dictionary*. New York: Doubleday, 1992.

Gamble, Richard C. "Calvin's Controversies." In *The Cambridge Companion to John Calvin*, edited by Donald K. McKim, 188–206. Cambridge: Cambridge University Press, 2004.

Ganoczy, Alexandre. "Calvin's Life." In *The Cambridge Companion to John Calvin*, edited by Donald K. McKim, 3–24. Cambridge: Cambridge University Press, 2004.

Gorman, Michael J. *Apostle of the Crucified Lord: A Theological Introduction to Paul and His Letters*. 2nd ed. Grand Rapids: Eerdmans, 2017.

———. *Elements of Biblical Exegesis: A Basic Guide for Students and Ministers*. Rev. and expand. ed. Grand Rapids: Baker, 2009.

———. *Romans: A Theological and Pastoral Commentary*. Grand Rapids: Eerdmans, 2022.

Gowler, David B. "Socio-Rhetorical Interpretation: Textures of a Text and Its Reception." *Journal for the Study of the New Testament* (2010) 191–206.

Graham, Glenn H. *An Exegetical Summary of Ephesians*. 2nd ed. Dallas: SIL International, 2008.

Gunton, Colin. "Salvation." In *The Cambridge Companion to Karl Barth*, edited by John Webster, 143–58. Cambridge: Cambridge University Press, 2000.

Haacker, Klaus. "Der Römerbrief als Friedensmemorandum." *New Testament Studies* 36 (1990) 25–41.

———. *The Theology of Paul's Letter to the Romans*. Cambridge: Cambridge University Press, 2003.

Hastings, James, ed. *Encyclopedia of Religion and Ethics*. 7 vols. Reprint. New York: Scribner's Sons, 1951.

Heil, John Paul. *Ephesians: Empowerment to Walk in Love for the Unity of All in Christ*. Atlanta: Society of Biblical Literature, 2007.

Hesselink, I. John. "Calvin's Theology." In *The Cambridge Companion to John Calvin*, edited by Donald K. McKim, 74–92. Cambridge: Cambridge University Press, 2004.

Hoehner, Harold W. *Ephesians: An Exegetical Commentary*. Grand Rapids: Baker Academic, 2002.

Jacob, Haley Goranson. *Conformed to the Image of His Son: Reconsidering Paul's Theology of Glory in Romans*. Downer's Grove, IL: IVP Academic, 2018.

James III, Frank A. "Confluence and Influence: Peter Martyr Vermigli and Thomas Aquinas on Predestination." In *Church and School in Early Modern Protestantism: Studies in Honor of Richard A. Muller on the Maturation of a Theological Tradition*, edited by Jordan J. Ballor et al., 165–83. Leiden: Brill, 2013.

Jervell, Jacob. "The Letter to Jerusalem." *Studia Theologica* (1971) 61–73.

Jervis, L. Ann. *The Purpose of Romans: A Comparative Letter Structure Investigation*. Sheffield: JSOT Press, 1991.

Jewett, Paul K. *Election and Predestination*. Grand Rapids: Eerdmans, 1985.

Jewett, Robert. "Ecumenical Theology for the Sake of Mission: Romans 1:1–17 + 15:14–16:24." In *Pauline Theology: III: Romans*, edited by D. M. Hays and E. E. Johnson, 89–108. Minneapolis: Fortress, 1995.

———. "Following the Argument of Romans." In *The Romans Debate*, edited by Karl P. Donfried, 265–77. Rev. and expand. ed. Edinburgh: T. & T. Clark, 1991.

———. *Romans: A Commentary*. Minneapolis: Fortress, 2007.

Johnson, Keith L. *The Essential Karl Barth: A Reader and Commentary*. Grand Rapids: Baker Academic, 2019.

Justin. *First Apology of Justin Martyr*. In *The Apostolic Fathers—Justin Martyr-Irenæus*, edited by Alexander Roberts and James Donaldson, revised by A. Cleveland Coxe, 300–56. Vol. 1 of *The Ante-Nicene Fathers*. Reprint. Grand Rapids: Eerdmans, 1989.

Kaminsky, Joel S., and Joel N. Lohr. "Election in the Bible." In *Oxford Bibliographies. Biblical Studies*, edited by Christopher R. Matthews. Oxford: Oxford University Press, 2010. https://www.oxfordbibliographies.com/display/document/obo-9780195393361/obo-9780195393361-0250.xml?rskey=Okf7Ki&result=1&q=election#firstMatch.

Karris, Robert J. "Romans 14:1–15:13 and the Occasion of Romans." *Catholic Biblical Quarterly* (1973) 155–78.

Keesmaat, Sylvia C. "Colossians and Ephesians." In *The New Cambridge Companion to St. Paul*, edited by Bruce W. Longenecker, 135–51. Cambridge: Cambridge University Press, 2020.

Kelly, J. N. D. *Early Christian Doctrines*. 5th rev. ed. London: Adam & Charles Black, 1977.

Kim, Kyu Seop. "God's Household Management: οἰκονομία in Greek Contract Papyri and Ephesians 1:10 and 3:2, 9." 신약연구 19.2 (2020) 387–414. https://doi.org/10.24229/kents.2020.19.2.004.

Kittel, Gerhard, and Gerhard Friedrich, eds. *Theological Dictionary of the New Testament.* Translated by Geoffrey W. Bromiley. 10 vols. Grand Rapids: Eerdmans, 1964–76.

Klein, Gunter. "Paul's Purpose in Writing the Epistle to the Romans." In *The Romans Debate*, edited by Karl P. Donfried, 278–96. Rev. and expand. ed. Edinburgh: T. & T. Clark, 1991.

Klein, William W. *The New Chosen People: A Corporate View of Election.* Rev. and expand. ed. Eugene, OR: Wipf & Stock, 2015.

Kuhn, Heinz-Wolfgang. "The Impact of Selected Qumran Texts on the Understanding of Pauline Theology." In *The Scrolls and Christian Origins*, edited by James H. Charlesworth, 153–85. Vol. 3 of *The Bible and the Dead Sea Scrolls.* Waco, TX: Baylor University Press, 2006.

Kuhn, Karl Georg. "The Epistle to the Ephesians in the Light of the Qumran Texts." In *Paul and Qumran: Studies in New Testament Exegesis*, edited by Jerome Murphy-O'Connor, 115–31. London: Geoffrey Chapman, 1968.

Lamberigts, Mathijs. "Predestination." In *Augustine Through the Ages: An Encyclopedia*, edited by Allan D. Fitzgerald, 677–79. Grand Rapids: Eerdmans, 1999.

Lamerson, S. "Forgiveness." In *Dictionary of Paul and His Letters*, edited by Scot McKnight et al., 318–25. 2nd ed. Downers Grove, IL: InterVarsity Press, 2023.

Lampe, Peter. "The Roman Christians of Romans 16." In *The Romans Debate*, edited by Karl P. Donfried, 216–30. Rev. and expand. ed. Edinburgh: T. & T. Clark, 1991.

———. "Rhetorical Analysis of Pauline Texts—Quo Vadit?" In *Paul and Rhetoric*, edited by J. Paul Sampley and Peter Lampe, 3–24. New York: T. & T. Clark, 2010.

Lane, Anthony N. S. "Augustine and Calvin." In *T. & T. Clark Companion to Augustine and Modern Theology*, edited by C. C. Pecknold and Tarmo Toom, 174–95. London: T. & T. Clark, 2013.

Larkin, William J. *Ephesians: A Handbook on the Greek Text.* Baylor Handbook on the Greek New Testament. Waco, TX: Baylor University Press, 2009.

Lemmer, H. R. "Reciprocity Between Eschatology and Pneuma in Ephesians 1:3–14." *Neotestamentica* 21 (1987) 159–82.

Levering, Matthew. *Predestination: Biblical and Theological Paths.* Oxford: Oxford University Press, 2011.

Lincoln, Andrew T. *Ephesians.* Word Biblical Commentary 42. Dallas: Word, 1990.

———. "The Use of the OT in Ephesians." *Journal for the Study of the New Testament* 14 (1982) 16–57.

Longenecker, Bruce W. "What Do We Find in Paul's Letters?" In *The New Cambridge Companion to St. Paul*, edited by Bruce W. Longenecker, 3–22. Cambridge: Cambridge University Press, 2020.

Longenecker, Bruce W., and Todd D. Still. *Thinking Through Paul: A Survey of His Life, Letters, and Theology.* Grand Rapids: Zondervan, 2014.

Longenecker, Richard N. *The Epistle to the Romans.* Grand Rapids: Eerdmans, 2016.

———. *Introducing Romans: Critical Issues in Paul's Most Famous Letter.* Grand Rapids: Eerdmans, 2011.

López, René A. "A Study of Pauline Passages on Inheriting the Kingdom." *Bibliotheca Sacra* 168 (2011) 443–59.

Luther, Martin. *The Bondage of the Will*. Translated by J. I. Packer and O. R. Johnston. Cambridge: James Clarke & Co., 1957.

———. *Lectures on Romans: Glosses and Scholia*. Luther's Works 25. Translated by Walter G. Tillmans and Jacob A. O. Preus. Edited by Hilton C. Oswald. Saint Louis: Concordia, 1972.

MacDonald, Margaret Y. *Colossians and Ephesians*. Sacra Pagina 17. Collegeville, Minnesota: Liturgical Press, 2000.

MacDonald, William G. "The Biblical Doctrine of Election." In *A Case for Arminianism: The Grace of God, the Will of Man*, edited by Clark H. Pinnock, 207–30. Grand Rapids: Academie, 1989.

Matera, Frank J. *Romans*. Grand Rapids: Baker Academic, 2010.

Mathieson, Ruth Christa. *Matthew's Parable of the Royal Wedding Feast: A Sociorhetorical Interpretation*. Atlanta: Society of Biblical Literature, 2023.

McCormack, Bruce. "Grace and Being." In *The Cambridge Companion to Karl Barth*, edited by John Webster, 92–110. Cambridge: Cambridge University Press, 2000.

McDonald, William J., et al., eds. *New Catholic Encyclopedia*. 15 vols. New York: McGraw-Hill, 1967.

McGeown, Martyn. "Calvin's Institutes: A Comparison Between the 1536 and 1559 Editions." Covenant Protestant Reformed Church. https://cprc.co.uk/articles/calvinsinstitutescomparison/.

Miller, James C. "The Romans Debate: 1991–2001." *CurBS* 9 (2001) 306–49.

Mitton, C. L. "The Relationship Between 1 Peter and Ephesians." *The Journal of Theological Studies* 1 (1950) 67–73.

Moo, Douglas J. *The Epistle to the Romans*. New International Commentary on the New Testament. 2nd ed. Grand Rapids: Eerdmans, 2018.

———. *A Theology of Paul and His Letters: The Gift of the New Realm in Christ*. Vol. 7 of Biblical Theology of the New Testament. Grand Rapids: Zondervan Academic, 2021.

Moritz, Thorsten. "'Summing Up All Things': Religious Pluralism and Universalism in Ephesians." In *One God One Lord in a World of Religious Pluralism*, edited by Andrew D. Clarke and Bruce Winter, 88–111. Cambridge: Tyndale House, 1991.

Nanos, Mark D. "Challenging the Limits that Contribute to Define Paul's Perspective." In *Reading Israel in Romans: Legitimacy and Plausibility of Divergent Interpretations*, edited by Cristina Grenholm and Daniel Patte, 212–24. Harrisburg, PA: Trinity, 2000.

Naphy, William G. "Calvin's Geneva." In *The Cambridge Companion to John Calvin*, edited by Donald K. McKim, 25–40. Cambridge: Cambridge University Press, 2004.

Newman, Carey C. "Election and Predestination in Ephesians 1:4–6a: An Exegetical-Theological Study of the Historical, Christological Realization of God's Purpose." *Review and Expositor* 93 (1996) 237–47.

Nickelsburg, George W. E. *Jewish Literature Between the Bible and the Mishnah: A Historical and Literary Introduction*. 2nd ed. Minneapolis: Fortress, 2005.

Niesel, Wilhelm. *The Theology of Calvin*. Translated by Harold Knight. London: Lutterworth, 1956.

O'Brien, Peter T. *Colossians, Philemon*. Word Biblical Commentary 44. Waco, TX: Word, 1982.

Oakes, Peter. "Galatians and Romans." In *The New Cambridge Companion to St. Paul*, edited by Bruce W. Longenecker, 92–118. Cambridge: Cambridge University Press, 2020.

Packer, J. I., and O. R. Johnston. Introduction to *The Bondage of the Will*, by Martin Luther. Cambridge: James Clarke & Co., 1957.

Pannenberg, Wolfhart. *Human Nature, Election, and History*. Philadelphia: Westminster, 1977.

———. *Systematic Theology*. Translated by Geoffrey W. Bromiley. Grand Rapids: Eerdmans, 1998.

Parker, T. H. L. *Calvin's New Testament Commentaries*. London: SCM, 1971.

Porter, Stanley E., and David I. Yoon. *Romans: A Handbook on the Greek Text*. Waco, TX: Baylor University Press, 2023.

Qimron, Elisha. "Dualism in the Essene Communities." In *The Dead Sea Scrolls and the Qumran Community*, edited by James H. Charlesworth, 195–202. Vol. 3 of *The Bible and the Dead Sea Scrolls*. Waco, TX: Baylor University Press, 2006.

Rambiert-Kwaśniewska, Anna. "Paul's 'Fullness of Time' (Gal 4:4) and 'Fullness of Times' (Eph 1:10)." *Verbum Vitae* 38 (2020) 199–218.

Ramsey, Boniface. "Ambrose." In *The First Christian Theologians: An Introduction to Theology in the Early Church*, edited by G. R. Evans, 225–33. Oxford: Blackwell, 2004.

Reid, W. S. "Election." In *International Standard Bible Encyclopedia*, edited by Geoffrey W. Bromiley, 2:56–57. Grand Rapids: Eerdmans, 1979–88.

Ridderbos, Herman. *Paul: An Outline of His Theology*. Translated by John Richard De Witt. Grand Rapids: Eerdmans, 1975.

Rist, John M. *Augustine: Ancient Thought Baptized*. Cambridge: Cambridge University Press, 1994.

Robbins, Charles J. "The Composition of Eph 1:3–14." *Journal of Biblical Literature* 105 (1986) 677–87.

Robbins, Vernon K. *Exploring the Texture of Texts: A Guide to Socio-Rhetorical Interpretation*. Valley Forge, PA: Trinity, 1996.

———. *The Invention of Christian Discourse*. Vol. 1. Blandford Forum, Dorset: Deo, 2009.

———. "Socio-Rhetorical Interpretation." In *The Blackwell Companion to The New Testament*, edited by David E. Aune, 192–219. Chichester: Wiley-Blackwell, 2010.

Roberts, Alexander, and James Donaldson, eds. *The Ante-Nicene Fathers*. 10 vols. Revised by A. Cleveland Coxe. Grand Rapids: Eerdmans, 1989.

Robinson, J. Armitage. *Epistle to the Ephesians: A Revised Text and Translation with Exposition and Notes*. 2nd ed. London: MacMillan, 1904.

Rowland, Christopher. "The Eschatology of the New Testament Church." In *The Oxford Handbook of Eschatology*, edited by Jerry L. Walls, 56–72. Oxford: Oxford University Press, 2008.

Sanday, William, and Arthur C. Headlam. *A Critical and Exegetical Commentary on the Epistle to the Romans*. International Critical Commentary. Edinburgh: T. & T. Clark, 1895.

Sanders, E. P. *Paul and Palestinian Judaism: A Comparison of Patterns of Religion*. Philadelphia: Fortress, 1977.

Schaff, Philip, ed. *The Nicene and Post-Nicene Fathers*, First Series. 14 vols. Reprinted. Grand Rapids: Eerdmans, 1989.

———. *The Nicene and Post-Nicene Fathers*, Second Series. 14 vols. Grand Rapids: Eerdmans, 1957.

Schleiermacher, Friedrich. *The Christian Faith*. Edited by H. R. Mackintosh and J. S. Stewart. English translation of the 2nd German ed. Edinburgh: T. & T. Clark, 1928.

Seal, David. "The Role of the Letter and the Lector in Early Christian Liturgy: A Few Examples from Ephesians 1." *Calvin Theological Journal* 55.1 (2020) 101–14.

Sievers, Joseph. "God's Gifts and Call Are Irrevocable." In *Reading Israel in Romans: Legitimacy and Plausibility of Divergent Interpretations*, edited by Cristina Grenholm and Daniel Patte, 127–73. Harrisburg, PA: Trinity, 2000.

Skolnik, Fred, and Michael Berenbaum, eds. *Encyclopedia Judaica*. 2nd ed. 22 vols. Detroit: Macmillan Reference USA, 2007.

Staples, Jason A. *The Idea of Israel in Second Temple Judaism: A New Theory of People, Exile, and Israelite Identity*. Cambridge: Cambridge University Press, 2021.

———. *Paul and the Resurrection of Israel: Jews, Former Gentiles, Israelites*. Cambridge: Cambridge University Press, 2024.

Starling, David I. *Not My People: Gentiles as Exiles in Pauline Hermeneutics*. Berlin: De Gruyter, 2011.

Stuhlmacher, Peter. "The Purpose of Romans." In *The Romans Debate*, edited by Karl P. Donfried, 231–44. Rev. and expand. ed. Edinburgh: T. & T. Clark, 1991.

Talbert, Charles H. *Ephesians and Colossians*. Grand Rapids: Baker Academic, 2007.

Tanner, Kathryn. "Creation and Providence." In *The Cambridge Companion to Karl Barth*, edited by John Webster, 111–26. Cambridge: Cambridge University Press, 2000.

Thielman, Frank. *Ephesians*. Baker Exegetical Commentary on the New Testament. Grand Rapids: Baker Academic, 2010.

Thornhill, A. Chadwick. *The Chosen People: Election, Paul and Second Temple Judaism*. Downers Grove, IL: InterVarsity, 2015.

———. "Election and Predestination." In *Dictionary of Paul and His Letters*, edited by Scot McKnight et al., 238–41. 2nd ed. Downers Grove, IL: InterVarsity, 2023.

Timmins, Will N. "Why Paul Wrote Romans: Putting the Pieces Together." *Themelios* 43.3 (2018) 387–404.

Trinidad, John T. "The Mystery Hidden in God: A Study of Eph. 1, 3–14." *Biblica* 31 (1950) 1–26.

Wasserberg, Günter. "Romans 9–11 and Jewish-Christian Dialogue: Prospects and Provisios." In *Reading Israel in Romans: Legitimacy and Plausibility of Divergent Interpretations*, edited by Cristina Grenholm and Daniel Patte, 174–86. Harrisburg, PA: Trinity, 2000.

Watson, Duane F. "The Role of Style in the Pauline Epistles: From Ornamentation to Argumentative Strategies." In *Paul and Rhetoric*, edited by J. Paul Sampley and Peter Lampe, 119–42. New York: T. & T. Clark, 2010.

———. "The Three Species of Rhetoric and the Study of the Pauline Epistles." In *Paul and Rhetoric*, edited by J. Paul Sampley and Peter Lampe, 25–47. New York: T. & T. Clark, 2010.

Watson, Francis. *Paul, Judaism and the Gentiles: A Sociological Approach*. Cambridge: Cambridge University Press, 1986.

———. "The Two Roman Congregations." In *The Romans Debate*, edited by Karl P. Donfried, 203–15. Rev. and expand. ed. Edinburgh: T. & T. Clark, 1991.

Wedderburn, A. J. M. "Purpose and Occasion of Romans Again." *Expository Times* (1979) 137–41.
Wetzel, James. "Predestination, Pelagianism, and Foreknowledge." In *The Cambridge Companion to Augustine*, edited by Eleonore Stump and Norman Kretzmann, 49–58. Cambridge: Cambridge University Press, 2001.
Whiteley, D. E. H. *The Theology of St Paul*. Philadelphia: Fortress, 1966.
Wiefel, Wolfgang. "The Jewish Community in Ancient Rome and the Origins of Roman Christianity." In *The Romans Debate*, edited by Karl P. Donfried, 85–101. Rev. and expand. ed. Edinburgh: T. & T. Clark, 1991.
Witherington III, Ben. *1 and 2 Thessalonians: A Socio-Rhetorical Commentary*. Grand Rapids: Eerdmans, 2006.
———. *The Acts of the Apostles: A Socio-Rhetorical Commentary*. Grand Rapids: Eerdmans, 1998.
———. *The Letters to Philemon, the Colossians, and the Ephesians: A Socio-Rhetorical Commentary on the Captivity Epistles*. Grand Rapids: Eerdmans, 2007.
———. *The Problem with Evangelical Theology*. Rev. ed. Waco, TX: Baylor University Press, 2016.
Witherington III, Ben, and Darlene Hyatt. *Paul's Letter to the Romans: A Socio-Rhetorical Commentary*. Grand Rapids: Eerdmans, 2004.
Wright, N. T. *Into the Heart of Romans*. London: SPCK, 2023.
———. *Paul and the Faithfulness of God*. 2 vols. London: SPCK, 2013.
———. "Romans." In *The New Interpreter's Bible* 10:393–770. Nashville: Abingdon, 2002.
Wuellner, Wilhelm. "Paul's Rhetoric of Argumentation in Romans: An Alternative to the Donfried-Karris Debate over Romans." *Catholic Biblical Quarterly* 38 (1976) 330–51.
Yates, Roy. "Principalities and Powers in Ephesians." *New Blackfriars* 58 (1977) 516–21.
Yinger, K. L. "Interpretation: New Perspective." In *Dictionary of Paul and His Letters*, edited by Scot McKnight et al., 516–21. 2nd ed. Downers Grove, IL: InterVarsity, 2023.
Young, Richard A. *Intermediate New Testament Greek: A Linguistic and Exegetical Approach*. Nashville: Broadman & Holman, 1994.

www.ingramcontent.com/pod-product-compliance
Lightning Source LLC
Chambersburg PA
CBHW071448150426
43191CB00008B/1274